# CONFEDERATE HEROINES

120 SOUTHERN WOMEN CONVICTED
BY UNION MILITARY JUSTICE

# CONFEDERATE
## *Heroines*

THOMAS P. LOWRY

LOUISIANA STATE UNIVERSITY PRESS
BATON ROUGE

Published by Louisiana State University Press

Copyright © 2006 by Louisiana State University Press

All rights reserved

Manufactured in the United States of America

FIRST PRINTING

DESIGNER: Michelle A. Garrod

TYPEFACE: Quadraat

PRINTER AND BINDER: Edwards Brothers, Inc.

LIBRARY OF CONGRESS CATALOGING-IN-PUBLICATION DATA

Lowry, Thomas P. (Thomas Power), 1932–

  Confederate heroines : 120 southern women convicted by Union military justice / Thomas P. Lowry.

  p. cm.

  Includes bibliographical references and index.

  ISBN-13: 978-0-8071-2990-6 (cloth : alk. paper)

  ISBN-10: 0-8071-2990-9 (cloth : alk. paper)

    1. United States—History—Civil War, 1861–1865—Participation, Female. 2. United States—History—Civil War, 1861–1865—Prisoners and prisons. 3. Women prisoners of war—United States—History—19th century—Anecdotes. 4. United States—History—Civil War, 1861–1865—Women. 5. Women—Confederate States of America—History. 6. Women—Confederate States of America—Social conditions. 7. Military courts—United States—History—19th century.

  I. Title.

  E628.L69 2006

  973.7'72—dc22

                                               2006001284

# CONTENTS

Illustrations follow page 76

# PREFACE

The Civil War greatly expanded the number and kinds of roles available to women, if only temporarily. Without meaning to, the men who marched off to war, and the men who stayed at home to oil the vast war machine, set the stage for self-empowerment by the women of both the North and the South.

The antebellum societies of the Union and the future Confederacy were very different. The nascent wave of female political and economic power in the North was far advanced in comparison with that of the South. Although the North was still largely rural, a host of factors—expanding industrialization, the growth of urban life, the rise of a mercantile middle class, and the relative egalitarianism of influential religious and philosophical movements (such as transcendentalism)—marked it as a fertile field for the blossoming of feminism. One early manifestation of women's power was the 1848 convention at Seneca Falls, New York. There, Elizabeth Cady Stanton, Lucretia Mott, and their colleagues issued a call for women's rights to vote and to obtain a divorce. In a similar vein, women's advocate Dorothea Dix was active in the 1840s in the reform of prisons and insane asylums. Even if women did not troop into the voting booths until 1920, when the Nineteenth Amendment was passed, nearly the entire nineteenth century saw agitation for women's rights in the North. Long centuries of disenfranchisement did not dissipate without a protracted struggle, but a struggle there was.

Not so in the South, with its ideal of a patriarchal and hierarchical society in which male slaveholders were the dominant class and social force.

The wives of poor southern whites are largely absent from the historical record. The journals, diaries, and legal documents that might enable us to have a glimpse into their lives are relatively scarce. Considerably more rare are records of female slaves, who were legally prohibited from acquiring literacy. The majority of such women were field slaves, whose existence is documented mainly in slave inventories and the artifacts now uncovered by archaeologists. House slaves likewise left no written records of their own; the primary documents detailing their lives are largely the reminiscences of their owners.

In contrast, the mothers, wives, and daughters of the gentry, those who dwelt in the big white house on the hill, were able diarists and productive correspondents. Their lives were also documented by visitors, who themselves were prolific writers. Yet the evidence suggests that elite women were kept under, not atop, a pedestal. They, too, were women in chains, whose golden fetters were forged in the fiery furnace of tradition and expectation. They were given everything—and nothing. Thomas Jefferson, the quintessential Virginia gentleman, felt that women's role was to stay home to "soothe and calm the minds of their husbands returning ruffled from political debate." He saw no reason to give women the vote, as they had plenty to do at home. As he added, "No laborious person was ever yet hysterical."[1] There were exceptions to the absence of southern women in public life, a prime example being the Mount Vernon Ladies' Association, which in 1859 saved (and still preserves) George Washington's home. But this was only after male politicians had refused to save it.

On the eve of the Civil War, all of this was about to change. Southern women were, without the slightest forewarning, about to be given greater freedom by the nation's internal struggle. It was not a freedom that they knew they needed. It was not a freedom that they even wanted, because it came at a terrible price. During the years of the Civil War, however, many southern women unwittingly redefined themselves as independent and forceful. For example, in 1860 the notion of a Ladies' Gunboat Society would have been beyond the imagination of even the most clairvoyant woman. Yet only two years later, southern women, disillusioned by their new government's inability to protect the river cities of the South, were raising funds to construct war vessels.[2]

The war had bent the most basic framework of southern society, a society in which a vast black majority was kept in check by the planter aristocracy, whose authority was extended, night and day, by "patrollers," armed men who arrested slaves suspected of escape or of unlawful assembly. To defend this way of life, the men had gone off to war, leaving their wives behind to control the slaves, both field and domestic, by moral authority, the inertia of tradition, and the doubtful help of old men, young boys, and a handful of overseers. No longer could southern women be mere decorative figureheads. Instead, they were forced to shoulder new and unwelcome responsibilities.

This change is well attested in the published records, but new and previously unknown evidence has come to light, evidence of over a hundred southern women who directly confronted the northern authorities. These women so threatened the Union war effort that they were tried in courts of law conducted by the U.S. Army, in what were called "military commissions." Tried—and convicted.

To be tried by a military court was to be taken seriously. Whether women were charged with spying, smuggling, carrying on illegal correspondence, or cutting Union telegraph lines, their actions were manifestations of empowerment. These women's stories, told here for the first time, can be seen as evidence of the tectonic, if temporary, shifts in the dynamic between men and women.

# ACKNOWLEDGMENTS

During the Civil War, over a hundred southern women were tried and convicted by Union military courts. How were they rescued from obscurity? The answer is—patience. The author and his wife, Beverly Ann Lowry, read the records of every Union court-martial, military commission, and court of inquiry for the Civil War, a total of more than eighty thousand trial transcripts. Nearly a million handwritten pages. Beverly Ann Lowry suggested the topic of this book, found most of the court-martial records in the National Archives, created the computer database that located these women, transcribed my manuscript, and edited the first draft. She is also my favorite Kentucky colonel. In many ways, this is her book.

DeAnne Blanton made many suggestions for the introduction. John Bradbury read the Missouri chapter and added new dimensions to it. Dorothy Kelly did the same for Tennessee and unraveled the intricacies of cotton cards with the help of her ninety-two-year-old aunt. Betsy Estilow was of vital help with Maryland. John and Ruth Ann Coski reviewed the entire manuscript and added much to it. Others to whom I am deeply grateful include Freda Chabot, Robert E. Denney, William B. Feis, Robert K. Krick, Jim McGhee, Michael P. Musick, Nancy Adgent Morgan, Dennis Northcutt, Craig L. Symonds, and Lou Wehmer.

William C. Davis, an editor's editor, gave me my start in 1993 and remains a guiding light over the turbulent seas of Civil War writing.

For any evidence of expository clarity or narrative flow I give thanks to my high school English teacher, Mrs. Evelyn Sharon of Piedmont, California.

The field of history is filled with colleagues generous with their time and expertise. For all of those not formally acknowledged here, I offer my apologies and my continued thanks. Any errors and omissions, of course, are mine alone.

The P. Willey Charitable Foundation provided partial funding for this study.

# INTRODUCTION

The eighteen-year-old southern girl sat in her cell in a Union prison. Suddenly a Federal officer loomed in the doorway, and a scene something like the following must have played out between them. The officer stood still a moment and then spoke. "It is my sad duty to inform you that ten days from now, you will be hanged by the neck until dead. The details are in this letter from Colonel Darr. I will leave it with you." He stepped forward; she silently lifted her hand and took the paper. He turned and was gone. The cell door slammed and she was alone again.[1] (While we do not have his exact words, everything else about this moment is found in the Federal records.)

This terrifying moment in the short life of Sarah Jane Smith illuminates the high stakes and deadly consequences for women who opposed the Federal forces and did what they could for the cause of southern independence. They fought for their new nation in lonely solitude, fought without the comradely support enjoyed by the men in butternut and gray, fought without the blessing of official status, fought without rifles or pistols, fought with the only weapons available to them: courage, nimble minds, and a hopeful reliance upon the elevated social status accorded to womanhood in the Victorian age. Sarah Jane's case is one of over a hundred that have come to light in recent years. These gripping tales of Confederate women tried in Union military courts are part of a revival of interest in women's lives during the American Civil War.

In the first forty years after the war, hundreds of women (and thousands of men), both North and South, published their wartime experiences. Diaries, collected letters, and memoirs flowed from the nation's presses; they were extremely popular and widely sold. These early documents clearly attest to the enthusiasm and patriotism of Confederate women. At the third battle of Winchester, when some of General John D. Imboden's Confederate cavalrymen were fleeing, the respectable women of the town joined hands across the street and dared the Rebel cavalrymen to go further. The wife of Confederate general John B. Gordon seized the bridle of a cowardly cavalryman and told him to return to the battle or she would take his horse and gun and go in his place.[2] Cyrus Drum of the 38th North Carolina (Confederate) deserted and went home, but his wife sent him back to his regiment. General Robert E. Lee suspended Drum's death sentence, writing, "I spare him in consideration of the noble and patriotic conduct of his excellent wife . . . she is one of the heroines of this struggle."[3] Several unnamed Confederate women seem to have been very effective spies. They persuaded F. T. Coleman, acting master of the USS *Mound City*, to give them a guided tour of the vessel; he answered their many questions about the range and powder charges of the great guns. For this bit of masculine foolishness, Coleman was hauled before a U.S. Navy court of inquiry.[4]

In early 1861, Ada Bacot wrote in her diary, "My love for South Carolina is that of an affectionate daughter for her mother, the purest love in the world. I would feel as much mortified if South Carolina should disgrace herself as I would if my mother should."[5] Such sentiments were seen a thousand times, in deed as well as word.

By 1917, the flood of Civil War outpourings had slowed to a trickle. Most of the war's survivors were sick or dead, and the nation's attention was focused on a new war—the war to end all wars. The Civil War was old. A memory. Passé. A dead issue. From 1918 to 1961, new events occupied America's center stage: the great influenza epidemic, the Jazz Age, prohibition, the stock market boom and crash, the Great Depression, World War II, the postwar economic expansion, and the Korean War. Even in the midst of these distractions, however, a few authors penned what have become Civil War classics. Margaret Leech's *Reveille in Washington* documented the momentous changes in Washington, D.C., during the conflict. Bell Wiley's *Life of Johnny Reb* and *Life of Billy Yank* focused on the tribulations of the common soldier. Katharine Jones's *Heroines of Dixie* honored southern women.[6]

By 1950, a slender bridge of ancient widows was all that joined us to the Civil War, which had largely been swept under the rug of the nation's memory. Then, in 1961, there was a great resurgence of interest in the war. The reason was simple: the Civil War centennial. Committees were formed; money flowed; opportunities for historians blossomed. A gradually swelling flood of articles, movies, books, and commemorative events caught the public's fancy. Great works of historical and literary merit— including the works of Douglas Southall Freeman, Allan Nevins, Bruce Catton, and Shelby Foote—found a wider audience. A new generation of historians took up the torch: James I. Robertson Jr., William C. Davis, Robert K. Krick, Richard McMurry, Gary Gallagher, James M. McPherson. Hundreds of historians made their contributions to Civil War scholarship. Yet there was a missing dimension. The authors of the 1960s, 1970s, and 1980s wrote of character and morals, of tactics and strategy, of command and control; there was little about the female half of the Civil War population. Nearly the only cognizance of women in this scholarly feast was Mary Elizabeth Massey's awkwardly titled *Bonnet Brigades*, published in 1966.[7]

Nearly twenty years passed before Massey's voice was joined by others. But recent scholarship amply illustrates the scope and diversity of this flowering of interest in women in the Civil War. Richard Hall's *Patriots in Disguise* presents a wide spectrum of nurses, spies, reformers, and women in uniform. Juanita Leisch's *Who Wore What?* gives an accurate picture of clothing and fashion in the 1860s. Drew Gilpin Faust's *Mothers of Invention* chronicles the lives of five hundred elite southern women at a time when the protections of both whiteness and being a lady began to dissolve. Anne Leclercq's *An Antebellum Household* presents the diary of a young Philadelphia girl, uneasy about slavery, who married a prosperous planter in South Carolina's Low Country. Nancy Garrison's *With Courage and Delicacy* chronicles the lives of elite northern women who cared for the wounded during McClellan's failed Peninsula campaign. Elizabeth Leonard's *All the Daring of the Soldier* describes many female spies and soldiers. Laura F. Edwards's *Scarlett Doesn't Live Here Anymore* presents a strongly feminist interpretation of Civil War society. Jacqueline Tobin and Raymond Dobard's *Hidden in Plain View* reveals the secret underground railroad signals that were sewn into slave-made quilt patterns. Louise Barnett's *Ungentlemanly Acts* explores an incest trial at an isolated western fort just after the war. Robert Denney's *Distaff Civil War* presents a great panorama of female experience, woven from the diaries of a dozen very different women. Michelle Krowl's dissertation, "Dixie's Other Daughters," studies the changes in the lives of African American Virginia women. DeAnne Blanton and Lauren Cook's *They Fought Like Demons* is an extensive study of women soldiers in men's uniforms. Rita Mae Brown's *High Hearts*, a stirring novel, portrays a young aristocrat who follows her husband into the First Virginia Cavalry.[8]

Since the Civil War centennial, a generation of visual artists has also been inspired by the war, and their paintings and prints are miracles of mood and draftsmanship. Typical scenes are of commanders in solemn consultation or soldiers flinging themselves at their opponents in a confusion of smoke and blood. Where women appear in an artwork, its composition is notably different. Two germane examples, both from the brush of Mort Künstler, are "Changing of the Pickets" and "Remember Me." In both, the scene is lit by candlelight falling on evening snow. The men in these paintings are dynamic, tense, poised on the verge of great and dangerous deeds. The women are passive, apprehensive, solicitous. Their role is to wait, to be patient, to be controlled by events.

But my study of more than a hundred women who defied northern authority during the Civil War, and who were tried and convicted for doing so, shows that many southern women were anything but passive. Through espionage, sabotage, smuggling, public demonstrations of Confederate sympathy, and the exercise of what were no doubt seen as womanly wiles, they undermined Federal authority; brought arms, medicine, and mail to the Confederacy; fostered Union desertions; cut telegraph wires; spread disease among Union troops; and generally assisted the crusade for southern independence.

Two southern women are absent from this book because their deeds are familiar to every student of the Civil War. Rose O'Neal Greenhow ran a very effective espionage ring out of Washington, D.C.—even from her prison cell. Belle Boyd, who operated mainly in the Shenandoah Valley, was famed for her ability to charm men while making fools of them. Greenhow and Boyd richly deserve their reputations as creative and resourceful spies, but here they will be put aside in favor of women whose equally daring and dangerous missions have been heretofore unexamined.

These women were tried by military commissions. In areas under martial law, the commanding general had the power of appointing boards of officers, usually three in number, to try civilians accused of crimes against either the occupying authority or other civilians. In such courts, the defendant was presumed innocent until proved guilty and had the right to counsel. The trials were not closed, nor were they held in secret. The defendant was afforded the opportunity to introduce and cross-examine witnesses, as well as to submit a written defense statement. Before being carried out, the sentence had to be approved by the general who appointed the court. (See Appendix A.)

In some of these trials, the offenses seemed anything but heroic. They included liquor sales, prostitution, and smuggling. Yet the women who engaged in such activities were considered harmful to the Union war effort by the Union authorities themselves. Anything that diverted Union resources or undermined northern morale was of use to the Confederacy. The very necessity of a trial diverted officers for court duty and soldiers for recording transcripts and guarding prisoners. One woman helped more than 60 percent of a Union cavalry company to desert. Another woman smuggled enough medicine to treat half the Confederacy, while a third woman smuggled fifty thousand percussion caps to the southern army. Even if profit was the motive, the activity was of clear benefit to the men and boys in butternut and gray.

The locations of the defendants' activities were not random. The border states of Tennessee, Missouri, and Maryland were the most productive of these women. There are no cases from Vermont, Maine, or Minnesota, and nearly none from Florida. But where North and South intersected, where violent differences of opinion affected not just states but tiny neighborhoods, that was where passions flared, conflicts exploded, and a southern woman could become a Confederate heroine.

CONFEDERATE HEROINES

# MISSOURI

SARAH JANE SMITH, sentenced to hang, was arrested in a state that was conceived in conflict and born in controversy. In 1820, in order to preserve the sectional balance in the U.S. Senate between slave states and free states, Missouri was admitted to the Union with slavery and Maine was admitted without it. This so-called "Missouri Compromise" also forbade slavery in the rest of the Louisiana Purchase north of latitude 36° 30′. With this as settled law, the people of Missouri had every reason to believe that the possession of slaves was guaranteed to them.

But in 1854, a storm burst over Missouri when Congress passed the Kansas-Nebraska Act, which provided that those territories could decide for themselves whether they would be slave or free. Most of the Missouri-Kansas boundary was only a dotted line, certainly no barrier to escaping slaves. Further, antislavery abolitionists were encouraged to settle in Kansas. This artificially induced influx of antislavery Kansas settlers was seen as a direct threat to Missouri's slaveholding rights. Proslavery men moved to Kansas to counter the threat to the part of Missouri's economy that was based on slaves. (In today's dollars, a healthy slave was worth about $40,000.) Under the doctrine of popular sovereignty, the voters of Kansas were to decide whether their state would be slave or free.

Soon the two factions in Kansas were murdering each other, and raiding parties passed back and forth over the border. The eastern press portrayed Missourians as bloodthirsty ruffians and white savages, although the great majority of Missouri residents were against secession; they simply wanted the freedom to preserve slavery. Worsening this combustible mix was the large influx of Germans into St. Louis, refugees from the failed democratic German revolution of 1848, most of whom opposed slavery. These conflicting factions soon produced the "Bleeding Kansas" so prominent in history books.

Matters quickly worsened. In 1855, several thousand armed Missourians entered Kansas, and their votes created a proslavery territory. Three years later, a second election changed Kansas to a free territory. Tensions remained high, since there were now two legislatures, each claiming political legitimacy. In such troubled times, vicious and fanatical men came to the fore. With the formal declaration of war in 1861, the Kansas raiders cloaked themselves in Federal authority, while the Missouri irregular troops claimed the mantle of the Confederate cause. The more violent Kansas men were labeled "jayhawkers," while the term "bushwhacker" denoted the Missouri irregulars. Whatever their label, their ethics and tactics were similar: sudden raids, murder, pillage, and arson, followed by disappearance into the woods and thickets.

The formally organized Missouri troops proliferated in a puzzling array of over a dozen categories. The Missouri State Guard became a Confederate military force, while Union units included the Missouri Volunteers, the Missouri State Militia, and the Enrolled Missouri Militia. To further confuse matters, the state had two governors, one Union (provisional) and one Confederate (in exile, usually in Arkansas).[1]

The Federal military authorities tried to assert control in Missouri by declaring martial law and punishing communities that harbored Confederate fighters. One of the most infamous Union moves was General Order No. 11, issued on August 25, 1863. All citizens of Jackson, Cass, and Bates counties were to leave their homes within fifteen days unless they lived within a mile of five designated Federal posts. Those who could prove their loyalty could stay at those posts; those who could not were to leave Missouri entirely. After the fifteen-day grace period, Union troops burned all crops and buildings, leaving the Confederates little sustenance for themselves or their horses. Missourians did not soon forget this moment: nearly a hundred years later, Harry Truman's mother refused to sleep in the Lincoln bedroom. Each punitive act was followed by retaliation and escalation. Within a few months, each side had suffered wrongs that called out for retribution.[2]

Unlike the relative simplicity of Gettysburg—blue on one side, gray on the other—in Missouri a person was just as likely to be murdered by a neighbor as by a stranger. It is in this confused tangle of vengeance, stealth, and distrust that we find Sarah Jane Smith and her entanglement with Union general Henry Halleck's General Orders No. 32, issued in December 1861, which prescribed death for anyone who destroyed railroads or telegraph wires.[3]

Sarah Jane was a native of Washington County, Arkansas, just south of the Missouri state line. Her mother had died when she was thirteen, and her father had been in General Sterling Price's Confederate army since she was sixteen. In May 1864, at Cassville, Missouri, she met up with several of her cousins, young Confederate guerrillas, and lived with them in the woods outside of Springfield, Missouri. They cut down about four miles of Union military telegraph lines, both wires and poles, before they were detected and captured. After three weeks in prison at Springfield, her cousins were retained there but she was sent northeast to Rolla, Missouri, and released. But instead of staying there, as she was told to do, she walked back toward Springfield. She was rearrested at Lebanon, Missouri, returned to Rolla, and released again. She soon made contact with two Union soldiers and a lawyer, S. G. Williams, whom she described as "about 45 years of age, with black hair." By certain signals, Sarah Jane and the three men discovered that they all belonged to the same "secret society" (probably the Order of American Knights), which was sworn to uphold the Confederacy. The lawyer promised Sarah Jane that if she returned to cutting telegraph wires, he would give her five dollars.[4]

On September 8, 1864, Sarah Jane was captured six miles south of Rolla, on the Springfield road, by First Lieutenant Albert Muntzel of the Fifth Missouri State Militia Cavalry (Union). She had just put down her axe. "I cut the wires," she said, "but I was never paid my $5.00." Sarah Jane was transported to St. Louis, tried on November 7, and sentenced to death.

Sarah Jane was unable to read or write. An unknown hand recorded her defense statement, which read: "I am eighteen years of age. My father and mother are in Arkansas. I have no friends or relatives in [Missouri]. I left home without any money. I came to Springfield with a family of refugees from Arkansas. I didn't know it was wrong to cut the wires at the time I did it. They didn't pay me the money they promised me. I never saw them again." This statement is at variance with the testimony of others, who described her cousins in Missouri, the death of her mother five years earlier, and her father's service in General Price's army.

During the Civil War, all court-martial sentences were reviewed by the commanding general of that area. On November 10, 1864, the Department of Missouri's acting provost marshal general, Colonel Joseph Darr Jr., received this word from General William Rosecrans: "Findings and sentence confirmed. The sentence will be carried into effect the 20th day of November, 1864, at St. Louis, Missouri." That same day, Colonel Darr sent this letter to Sarah Jane: "Madame: It becomes my duty to inform you of the following action which has been taken in your case." He repeated Rosecrans's order for hanging. It seemed as though Sarah Jane's short life was over; but on November 12, the execution date was changed to November 25.

Unseen forces were at work. Perhaps the Union authorities sought to avoid the stigma of hanging a woman, in particular a young woman; perhaps the same Union authorities had noted some imbalance in Sarah Jane. Whatever the reason, two doctors were sent to examine her; both reported on November 15. George Rex, surgeon of U.S. Volunteers, who was in charge of the U.S. Military Prison Hospital at St. Louis, wrote, "This will certify that Mrs. Sarah Jane Smith . . . is subject to periodic paroxysms of unconsciousness simulating epilepsy, and although viciously inclined, does not seem to be possessed of a degree of mental capacity to have realized the character of the offenses committed by her and in my opinion she is not a perfectly responsible creature."[5]

A second surgeon, whose signature is illegible, reported, "I have carefully examined the within-named S. J. Smith. I fully concur with the opinion expressed by Surgeon Rex. I do not believe that this woman possesses sufficient mental capacity to fully appreciate the crimes which she has committed, nor do I regard her as an entirely responsible person." Two days later, a new order "by command of Major General Rosecrans" commuted Sarah Jane's sentence to "imprisonment at the Alton [Illinois] military prison, to the end of the war." The prison register notes her arrival on November 15, 1864.[6]

The war was drawing to a close when Lieutenant James T. Cooper, Assistant Inspector of Military Prisons, wrote on March 31, 1865, "Since [Sarah Jane's] confinement here, she has labored under a severe and protracted illness and there is every indication that her disease is permanent and will result in her early or at best premature death. She desires to take the Oath of Allegiance to the government of the United States forces during the continuance of the rebellion. Her condition is such that her removal from the prison (in my opinion) would be an act of humanity and result to no evil to the country." Three days later, Dr. M. B. Cochran, an army surgeon, was asked to examine Sarah Jane. His report was brief but poignant: "She is subject to epilepsy which is very severe. In my opinion, her mind is so impaired that she could do no probable injury to the government and that her release is necessary to prevent her from becoming a troublesome charge." Special Orders No. 76, dated April 13, 1865, released her from prison.

Missouri women served the Confederate cause in numerous other ways as well. After the battle of Palmyra, in northeast Missouri, Mary E. Cook and Priscilla Autrey, "two beautiful Southern girls," dug graves with their own hands for the Confederate fallen. Thus recalled Salem H. Ford, formerly second lieutenant with the 12th Missouri Cavalry (Confederate), who also remembered the scouting and intelligence gathering done by southern women. Kate McBoulard of Granby, Missouri, hid him from Federal patrols, and a beautiful but nameless teenager, "dressed in a long, flowing black riding habit" and mounted on a fine black mule, brought an entire wagonload of provisions to Ford's outnumbered men.[7]

Even in urban St. Louis, Confederate women proved very difficult for the Union authorities. Lieutenant Colonel F. A. Dick, the city's provost marshal, sounded a note of desperation: "I find that a large number of women have been actively concerned both in secret correspondence and in collecting and distributing Rebel letters. I have for some time been thinking of arresting them, but the embarrassment is in knowing what to do with them. Many of them are wives and daughters of officers in Rebel service. These women are wealthy and wield a great influence."[8]

Confederate women could be outspoken as well as daring. On March 31, 1864, Mary Davis was charged with feeding supper to and "entertaining" some of the members of "Shumate's band," which was one of dozens of irregular Confederate partisan groups that roamed the woods of Missouri. When Lieutenant W. C. Lefever, of the Fourth Missouri State Militia Cavalry (Union) approached her house around 10:00 P.M., four men fired at the Union men and then ran into the woods. The Federals wounded and captured one bushwhacker, a man named Wilcox, but the other three escaped—two of the Shumate boys and a man named Clark.[9]

Lefever's men questioned the women in the house—Mary, Cecilia, and Maria Davis—who all denied any knowledge of who had been on their porch. After the Union men found two revolvers, however, Mary Davis became more outspoken. "I'm a Rebel and a Southern sympathizer and I don't care who knows it! If those men come back, I'll feed them again. It's no man's business what a woman's politics are!" Her brash defiance, in the face of armed men, placed her in even greater danger. She was tried at Jefferson City, found guilty of "violating the laws and customs of war," and sentenced to take the oath of allegiance and post a $1,000 bond. General Rosecrans approved the sentence. If she failed in either the oath or the fine, she was to be deported from the state of Missouri, away from her family and friends.

Cecilia and Maria Davis were tried for the same offenses. Lieutenant Lefever had little to say about them. "I heard no disloyal language from Cecilia. Her sister Mary spoke for them." As for Maria: "I know she had gone to school with some of the bushwhackers. That's all." Based on this slender testimony, the two girls were convicted. Each was sentenced to take the oath and post a $500 bond. Yet General Rosecrans did not approve the proceedings, noting that "the testimony does not warrant the sentence. Facts, it appears from the record, have been inferred and acted upon without a proper regard as to the manner in which justice is to be reached. . . . Hearsay evidence has been admitted extensively in this case, which is evidently against the dictates of equity." After further remarks, Rosecrans released Cecilia and Maria. The fate of these two girls had ultimately rested upon the opinion of a single Union officer with nearly absolute power.[10]

## A BUSHWHACKER NAMED TIM

Three women played a part in the dramatic story of Timothy Reves, the only Confederate soldier in Arkansas who was refused a parole in the general surrender and amnesty of May 1865. Reves (also spelled Reeves or Reaves) was a Baptist preacher in the strongly secessionist southeast corner of Missouri. As Union captain William T. Leeper, Third Missouri State Militia—a controversial fellow who was cashiered for incompetence in 1863—accurately described the region's civilian population, "Many men and women who are at home do us more damage than the regular soldier. They feed, harbor and conceal the guerillas." Union soldiers shot suspected bushwhackers on sight, especially since many of them wore Union coats, both for warmth and as a disguise. At Christmas 1863, Reves—officially Captain Tim Reves, 15th Missouri Cavalry (Confederate)—was holding a large conclave near Pulliam Spring, just south of Doniphan, Missouri. The gathering contained men both from his command and other units, together with their wives and children and a number of Union prisoners. As dinner cooked, no less than five preachers exhorted the crowd to attend to their Christian duties. Foremost among them was the Reverend Captain Reves, who preached to his Yankee prisoners "the whole afternoon."[11]

As the preaching proceeded and dinner cooked, Major James S. Wilson of the Third Missouri State Militia Cavalry (Union), who had been tracking Reves for days, surrounded the camp meeting. Just as Christmas dinner was served, the Yankees attacked. In addition to the 30 Confederate soldiers killed and the 112 captured, 60 civilians, many of them unarmed women and children, were killed or wounded. This outrage so inflamed southern sympathizers that the influx of new volunteers into Reves's unit outweighed the Rebel loss. With his new recruits, Reves raised such havoc, burning Union farms and killing Union men, that Wilson returned a few months later and burned the entire town of Doniphan to the ground.[12]

This set the stage for the final encounter of Wilson and Reves. Wilson was captured in late September 1864 at the battle of Pilot Knob. A few days later, Reves took Wilson and six of his men to a little clearing and shot them dead. When the Union relieving force found the bodies, identification was difficult, as hogs had eaten their faces. In retaliation, by order of Major General William Rosecrans, Union soldiers shot six Confederate prisoners and vowed to execute the next Confederate major captured, whether he was associated with Tim Reves or not. He was not. The unlucky man was Major Enoch O. Wolf of Ford's Battalion, Confederate Arkansas Cavalry, whose only known sin was being on the wrong side at the wrong place at the wrong time.

This background forms the setting for the trial of Kate Beattie. In mid-1864, W. W. Caisson of Memphis posted the following query in the *St. Louis Republican:* "Information wanted: Fifty dollars reward will be given for information as to the whereabouts of Mrs. Kate Beattie, wife of Captain Tuck Beattie of Lexington, Missouri. . . . She is about five feet, four inches tall, has light blue eyes, hair closely shingled, and a scar upon the right cheek. She is rather eccentric, intelligent and prepossessing in manners." No reason was given why Caisson was willing to pay the equivalent of three months' soldier's wages for information about her.[13]

Even as Beattie was apparently traveling to St. Louis, events were moving swiftly for Major Wolf. On November 8, without prior notice, a blacksmith riveted a ball and chain to his ankle; as the hot iron cooled, he was handed a notice that he was to be shot in three days. Shortly after that, at his request, he was baptized in a bathtub in the basement of St. Louis's Gratiot Street Prison. As he conversed with the minister, Wolf mentioned that he was a Mason. The divine, shocked by this news, rushed from the prison, and within hours Abraham Lincoln had received telegrams from three prominent St. Louis Masons, all urging clemency. There was no immediate response.

On the night before his execution, Major Wolf was told, "You have a visitor; your wife is here to see you." While indeed he did have a wife, this moment contained a surprise. His cell door swung open and there stood Kate Beattie, "dressed like a butterfly." She rushed forward, sobbing, "My dear husband!" Embracing him tightly, she whispered, "Pretend I am your wife. Their compassion will spare you." Wolf, every inch the gentleman, told his jailors that he could not tell a lie to save his own life. "That is not my wife. I have never seen this woman before."

Beattie was arrested, taken to the female section of the Gratiot Street Prison, and put in solitary confinement on bread and water. Her hands were locked in iron cuffs. A ten-pound iron ball with a ten-foot chain of inch-and-a-half links was fastened so tightly to her ankle that her stockings were soon soaked in blood. Movement, even in her tiny cell, was close to impossible. After sixty days in her dark and airless dungeon, she was brought to trial, charged with smuggling gold lace and gray cloth, spying, and trying to help Major Wolf escape. Her defense counsel was the firm of Garrash and Fairchild.

Witnesses for the prosecution painted a picture of mid-Victorian St. Louis. As one merchant testified, "I am Myron Tichnor, Jr, proprietor of St. Louis' largest clothing store, corner of Fourth Street and Washington Avenue. The accused entered our store, calling herself 'Mistress Beattiee.' She insisted on that spelling, and was wearing a very long and curly wig. She wanted to buy a military hat with a wide gold lace brim, and also asked where she could find a priest or a bishop." After several other questions, the prosecution asked, "Do you think her long string of beads might suggest that she was a spy?" Mr. Tichnor, a sartorial professional, replied, "It would not indicate to me that she was a spy." Another merchant, from whom she had bought nothing, could recall only one thing about her: "She was a very pretty little woman with very pretty curls." His testimony seemed almost as irrelevant as that of P. A. Pignaro, a wig maker, who was called upon to inform the court about the degree of curliness in her wig. A surprise witness was Major Wolf himself, who told the court, "I was out of my mind at the time of my stay in prison. I can recall almost nothing." With this disappointingly brief testimony, the court, which had heard little incriminating evidence, turned now to the defense witnesses, most of whom were Union officials at the Gratiot Street Prison.

Dr. G. F. Dudley described Beattie's solitary cell, her total lack of access to communication with the outside world, and her near-total lack of access to pen and paper. He also testified, "Her treatment improved somewhat when Provost Marshall Darr was replaced by Colonel Baker. When she was sick with intermittent fever [malaria], Colonel Darr did agree to remove her wrist irons." Sergeant Michael Welsh, in charge of the female section of the prison, confirmed that Beattie's stockings were saturated with blood from the chafing of the ankle ring of her ball and chain. No one commented on the physical pain of her lacerations. Captain Robert C. Allen, 40th Missouri, the prison commander, told the court that Beattie was the only woman in the prison with either a ball and chain or handcuffs, and he confirmed that Colonel Darr had ordered them. All the prison officers agreed that Beattie was "very well behaved" while in their custody.

It was customary in military courts to allow the defendant to submit a written defense. In hers, Beattie began with a general statement that the burden of proof was on the court: "I need not prove myself innocent; the prosecution must show that I am guilty." After a brief digression on the subject of being "pursued by the prejudices and malignanty [sic] of two officers," she came to the heart of the matter: "Yes, it is true that I was able to see Major Wolf by the use of deception when he was selected to be shot. The community still staggered under pity for the six young men put to death—the dreadful law of retaliation, but Major Wolf did not even belong to the same command as Captain Reves. In a moment of frenzied sympathy, I resolved to, if possible, effect his escape, a man an utter stranger to me. A woman is guided by her feelings; she is not supposed to be guided by the inflexibility of will, and force of judgment, which rules men."

Beattie was acquitted of smuggling and spying but convicted of trying to help Major Wolf escape, and she was duly sentenced to spend one more month in prison. The court ascribed this lenient sentence to her previous harsh mode of imprisonment. Her dramatic entrance into St. Louis might have inspired Colonel Darr's December 2, 1864, memo to hotelkeepers, urging them to report any "suspicious characters registered at or lurking about their establishments." Darr added ominously, "Women unattended by male escorts will be closely observed." The Beattie case was reviewed by General Grenville Dodge (later the chief engineer of the Union Pacific Railroad), who wrote, "Finding and sentence confirmed. The sentence is remitted but on account of the known disloyalty of the prisoner, she will be sent south into the rebel lines, not to return during the war on penalty of imprisonment."

And what of Major Wolf? On November 10, 1864, Lincoln telegraphed, "Suspend execution of Major Wolf until further orders and meanwhile report to me on the case." General Rosecrans's long reply the next day revealed his desperation at the endless violence in Missouri and his hopes that shooting hostages might bring an end to bloodshed. On January 19, 1865, Lincoln sent another telegram: "If Mrs. Beattie, alias Mrs. Wolff [sic] shall be sentenced to death, notify me and postpone execution till further orders." Her future was assured, at least until further orders, which never came. Major Wolf was transferred to Johnson's Island and released when peace was signed. He became the sheriff of Fulton County, Arkansas, and died at age eighty-three. Tim Reves returned to being a Baptist preacher in Ripley County and died in 1885.[14]

During the Civil War years, Reves excited the emotions of many southern women; some of them even wrote him fan letters. One such woman was Nannie T. Douthitt, a native of Pocahontas, Arkansas, whose letter from Ironton, Missouri, earned her a Union court-martial. As she wrote: "Go on Maj. Reaves and may success, glory and honor crown your every exertions in promoting the interests of the South adding one link to the gaining of our independence." According to the charges filed against her, Douthitt made "use also of many other wicked and disloyal expressions intending thereby to give aid and comfort to the rebel enemies of the United States to inflame their passions and furnish them intelligence in aid of said rebellion." Among her "wicked and disloyal expressions" was a wish that a certain Ben Roach be burned at the stake and a denunciation of "Free Negro abolitionists." After a few similar sentiments, Douthitt concluded, "May the proud banner that waves over the South soon wave in peace and prosperity."[15]

When this letter was intercepted by the Union authorities (correspondence with the South was a criminal offense), Douthitt was charged with giving aid to the enemy. She pled guilty but entered a defense statement claiming that she had only sent family news, nothing political and certainly no matters of military intelligence. She probably did not help her case when she added, with considerable courage, that if she did have military information, she certainly would have sent it. When asked what she knew of "Major Reaves," she stated, "I last saw him in mid-June, raising a battalion in Arkansas." The twenty-one-year-old woman was sentenced to the dangerous and disease-ridden Alton Prison until the end of the war, a fate approved by General Rosecrans.

Private Drury Poston served in Company A, 15th Missouri Cavalry (Confederate), Tim Reves's regiment. In June 1864, Pauline White wrote to him from Greenville, Missouri, placing her letter in an envelope directed to "Private Poston, care of Mrs. Captain Reeves, Doniphan, Missouri." It read:

> Dear Friend, I have not received any news from you since you left. Eva received a letter from Lieutenant Hughes, which announced the death of your comrade (and my brother) DeKalb White. He died the 21st of January in prison at St. Louis. Lieutenant Hughes and about 40 other Confederate officers were sent to Camp Chase, Ohio. [Several officers] all send their compliments to you and to Captain Reeves and to all the rest of the boys. God bless you all is the prayer of one sinner. . . . Long live the Rebels, peace and comfort rest upon their heads. Forget me not, for, alas, we may never meet again.[16]

The court asked White, who was charged with disloyalty, if she had ever taken the oath of allegiance. She had. She was asked, "Did you not know that you were violating it when you wrote that letter and sent it to a Rebel soldier?" Her reply might have caused some vexation to the men who judged her; it certainly did her defense no good. "I never considered the Oath binding," she proclaimed. She was found guilty of violating the oath of allegiance and giving information to the Confederacy about prisoners held by the Union. She was sentenced not only to imprisonment until the end of the war, but also to spend that time at hard labor. What would constitute hard labor for a young woman? The record is silent on that point.

## CUPID AND MARS

Love, sex, and marriage were issues in the trials of several Union soldiers, three of whom were from Arkansas. In the first trial, Private James Kirby of the Second Arkansas Cavalry was accused of marrying a fourteen-year-old Missouri girl, Sarah Jane Ross, in a fraudulent ceremony, "for the purpose of having carnal knowledge of her person." (In Victorian euphemism, "person" denoted not only the body in general but also the organs of procreation in specific.) Tried with Kirby was a sergeant who had married the couple and a captain who had tried to intercede in the ceremony.[17]

In Kirby's trial, a star prosecution witness was the bride's mother, Charlotte Black. When asked her occupation, she replied, "I live off the government." And her views about the marriage? "I heard they was married and not legally. If Sarah was falsely persuaded, I don't know of it. They've been living together for three weeks as man and wife. I told them, 'You best get lawfully married or you can't live with me any more.'" Sarah herself told the court: "Mr. Kirby told me the sergeant had the right to marry us, but three weeks later, my friend Milly Butler told me it wasn't legal, but I was not falsely persuaded. He told me he'd marry me legal now, but I don't want to be with him."

Captain Samuel P. Dickinson, Kirby's commander, appeared on his behalf and stated, "When I heard of the marriage, I saw it as my duty to look into the matter. When I spoke with Sarah's mother, she said, 'I know they are not legally married, but I don't give a damn anyway.' Sarah herself told me, when I asked about reconciling with Kirby, that she would see him in hell first. She said nothing of being entrapped, and her reputation is that of a lewd woman." Twenty-seven-year-old private James Hoyle testified, "Kirby told me, 'I married her and I'm agoing to take her home with me.' The girl told me that since neither party was named in the ceremony, and since they had not been 'pronounced,' that she was sure the marriage was not valid. I believe that Sarah is not a decent woman."

Kirby's defense—"There is no evidence of a marriage except the girl's testimony"—seems to have persuaded the court. They acquitted him, accepting with little question the assertions of Sarah's immorality and promiscuity. However, the wheels of justice were still turning.

Sergeant Charles Richmond, also of the Second Arkansas Cavalry, was tried on the charge that "he did usurp the function of a minister of the gospel, and perform a ceremony of marriage . . . with the criminal intention to aid the same James Kirby . . . to obtain, contrary to law, carnal knowledge of her person." The testimony of nine witnesses enables us to piece together the story. Kirby and Ross had gone to Parson Sheppard's house to get married, but the parson was not at home. They were sitting on a bed in the parson's house, hugging, when Sergeant Richmond appeared. Some bystanders asked the sergeant to marry the couple, but he refused, saying it would not be legal, and went off to get his supper. An hour later, a girl rode over to his place and pleaded for Richmond to return. When he did, "the boys" urged him to proceed, which he did after reminding the group that he had no authority to perform marriages. Even the parson's seventeen-year-old daughter, Martha, agreed that the marriage was "a joke." Captain Dickinson made an appearance in Richmond's trial as well, testifying, "Sarah told me that she didn't give a damn about the marriage and told me that if she was called as a witness she would swear the courthouse full of lies. While I was talking to her, she said she planned to marry again soon, and turned and winked at a soldier from the Sixth Missouri." Richmond, too, was acquitted.[18]

Next came Captain Dickinson's trial. He was charged with threatening a witness—in this case, Sarah's mother, Charlotte Black. Dickinson had visited the Black household to urge Black to withdraw the charges against Kirby and Richmond. It seems that Black's husband had been murdered recently and that she was under some suspicion in his death. Black then pressed charges against Dickinson, claiming that he had threatened to charge her with being an accessory to her husband's murder if she did not withdraw her charges.[19]

Dickinson, as well as the two soldiers who accompanied him on his visit, asserted that no threats had been made and that the captain had been calm and polite during his visit. Charlotte Black and her daughter disagreed. In his written defense, the captain argued, "Tampering with witnesses is a crime in Missouri. What would I have stood to gain by doing so? Nothing. Both mother and daughter agree that they always knew the marriage to be invalid. Miss Ross' repeated use of profane language in the presence of strangers calls her character into question. The girl may be young in years, but not in moral degradation." Captain Dickinson, like the other two defendants, was found not guilty.

There was at least one other Union minister of dubious ecclesiastical credentials: Sergeant John W. Gibson of the 11th Missouri Cavalry. He was charged with "conduct prejudicial to good order and military discipline."

In late December 1863, at Springfield, in the words of the court proceed-ings, "he did falsely and fraudulently assume and claim to be a minister of the Gospel and married Private Thomas Petty [of the same regiment] and one Nancy Elizabeth Ferguson, saying, 'You will rise to your feet; join your right hands; Thomas Petty, do you take this lady you hold by the right hand to be your lawfully wedded wife, forsaking all others and cleaving only unto her?' which was answered 'I do.' 'Nancy Elizabeth Ferguson, do you take the man you hold by the right hand to be your lawfully wedded husband?' which was answered, 'I will.' 'I then pronounce you man and wife.'"[20]

Sergeant Gibson pleaded guilty but gave this defense:

> On the night that that act was performed I left the city for camp early having been drinking some. I went to the Red Top House there I saw a number of the 11th Cav. among them Thomas Petty of Co. "C" and Mr. Forth of Co. "G." They came to me and wanted me to perform some ceremony so that Petty could sleep with a woman that night so that the guards would not trouble him. I did not ask her name. I told them I did not like to do it. Petty told me it was understood between them, meaning the woman and him self. I again told them I did not like to do it, but through persuasion, I said I would. I informed them I did not know what to say. Mr. Ford then told me what to say.

Encouraged by Ford's coaching, Gibson launched into a discussion of his newfound ecclesiastical role:

> I done so as near as I could supposing it was all right and that I should [think] no more about it, the whole matter being fixed beforehand by themselves for simply sleeping that night. The house had a bad reputa-tion for a long time. Had I any idea of it being anything more than it was represented to me I would not under any circumstances have any-thing to do with it. I think the court will be pleased to look at the matter in the light here represented. I throw myself entirely on the mercy of the court and submit to their decision.

There is no sign of testimony by Ferguson. The court accepted Gibson's plea of guilty and fined him two months' pay, a decision endorsed by Gen-eral Rosecrans.

All the women in these fraudulent marriage cases, whether intentionally or not, contributed to the Confederate cause. Dozens of officers were taken from their usual duties to sit on these four courts-martial. Nearly a dozen witnesses were called from their other contributions to the Federal war effort. Private Kirby was in confinement for weeks, performing no military service, and four other men were busy for days defending themselves.

Sarah Jane Smith—the cutter of telegraph wires—was eighteen years old when sentenced to hang. Emily E. Weaver, a native of Batesville, Arkansas, was only seventeen when she was sentenced to die, charged with "lurking" throughout Missouri and gathering information on Union troops at St. Louis and Pilot Knob. She had been traveling in consort with a Mr. Tilley (their relationship is unclear), and she had stopped for three weeks with the Lingon family in Carondelet, just south of St. Louis. When called as witnesses, the Lingons did their best to shield Emily (and themselves) from prosecution. Mary Jane Lingon was asked, "Would you not ordinarily consider it a very extraordinary thing for a young lady, a total stranger, to come to your house and visit two or three weeks?" She replied, "Well, it depends." She was queried about Tilley, who had visited her home frequently. Her surprisingly casual reply: "I don't know his line of business and I don't know whether or not he is engaged to my daughter." Laura Lingon, who had known Weaver for three weeks at the Lingon home and several more weeks as her traveling companion on a trip to Rolla and back, claimed to know nothing of her political sympathies. Nor did she know why Weaver had stayed with her family for three weeks. She certainly "had not noticed any Federal troops at Rolla." This is strange, since Rolla was a major Union military depot.[21]

Tilley was unable to account for his travels, other than a vague story that he was going to Illinois on business and was escorting Weaver on her way to see her father in Memphis. Federal detective Frank Riley then testified that he had found letters to and from supporters of the Confederacy hidden in three different locations in the Lingon house and gave his opinion that all the Lingons were "very disloyal."

Weaver herself had a few things to say. Although her brother, Seldon Weaver, was in the First Arkansas Mounted Rifles (Confederate), she claimed that her father was "very pro-Union." When asked why she had gone to Rolla, she answered, "Well, I was going to Memphis, and my cousin was going to St. Louis. When we came through the country, bush-whackers who said they were Reeve's men and wore blue overcoats took our horses." She felt much more talkative with her prison cellmate while awaiting trial, telling the woman:

> The Federals don't know what I've been doing. I've been a spy for two years, helping Confederate guerillas. I fear for Tilley. The charges against him are good and he will hang. I don't fear the Federal officers. My case is in Lieutenant Dodge's hands, but I have him fully under my control. I've never met a Federal officer I couldn't wind around my finger. They think my father is pro-Union, but he is really for the South! [He is the] strongest kind of the bitterest man I ever heard talk—he won't go home on that account until the war is ended.

Sadly for Weaver, her cellmate was Mary Ann Pittman, a Union detective, who had saved not only the letters that Emily gave her to smuggle out of prison, but also a pair of gloves with "Colonel E. H. Weaver, Batesville, Arkansas," marked on them. Barely recognizable fragments of the gloves, dried and faded, are still on file in the National Archives.[22]

On cross-examination, Pittman revealed that she had originally been a Confederate spy for Nathan Bedford Forrest and Leonidas Polk. She had a commission signed by Jefferson Davis and had commanded a company at Shiloh, Tennessee. "Later, I realized the South was wrong and I changed my allegiance," she stated. In brief, this testimony was from a woman who had sworn loyalty to both sides. Still, her testimony seems to have been persuasive. The court found Weaver guilty of both charges and sentenced her "to be hanged by the neck until dead." But General Rosecrans disapproved the findings, noting, "The evidence of the guilt of the accused is not sufficiently conclusive." She was ultimately set free.

Saline County, on the banks of the Missouri River, was the site of five recorded encounters between Federal authority and women sympathetic to

the South. Three of the trials involved members of a single family, the Jack-
sons. In the first trial, Mary Jackson was accused of feeding bushwhackers,
including her own husband. The chief prosecution witness was Lieutenant
William D. Blair of the Fourth Missouri State Militia Cavalry (Union), who
testified:

> I was on a scout near Saline City, hunting Bill Jackson, a known bush-
> whacker. As I passed Mrs. Jackson's house, I saw a colored woman
> standing in the doorway. She beckoned me to stop, which I did. She
> told me that William Jackson and his gang had just been fed in the
> woods by the Jackson women. I found 3 fresh horse tracks which con-
> firmed the story, but a search showed that the men were gone.
>
> I returned to the house, where Mrs. Jackson told me that her hus-
> band and his band had ordered dinner, and that she had preferred to
> feed them in the woods, which she did, sending her two daughters
> with dinner.[23]

Private John Lincoln recalled Mary Jackson saying, "If I had known it was
Bill Jackson [her husband] at the dooryard fence, I would not have went
to the door." James Bailey, a neighbor, recalled that "Mrs. Jackson told the
men they could not have their dinner and must go away, but Bill Jackson
told her, 'I'll be damned if I don't get my dinner, even if I have to take it by
force.' They was armed."

Mary Jackson's written defense was that she was forced to feed her husband and his men:

> This she acknowledges she did by compulsion, & has proved by wit-
> ness who was present that she ordered him off from her premises but
> was forced by them to prepare their dinner and send it to them. This
> she did, not willingly, but by constraint. As to harboring them, she as
> an individual denyes ever having dun any such thing. From the fact that
> she as an individual has ever been opposed to that sistim of warfare.
> She also feels that she has dun nothing for them, but what they forced
> her to do. She wishes also, to appeal to the Court and ask you what els
> she could have dun than what she did.

She ended by asking for leniency and offering to take the oath of allegiance. She was found guilty and banished from the state of Missouri. General John Schofield approved the findings of the court but suspended the sentence "until further orders." No further orders have been found.

Fourteen-year-old Sue Jackson was accused of feeding bushwhackers and saying that she was not ashamed of doing so. It was further alleged that she said she would fight if she had access to firearms. The same Lieutenant Blair testified to these points. In her written rebuttal, Sue presented a different view: "As to harboring bushwackers she denyes ever having dun any such thing. She acknowledges she carried vituals to Jackson & gang yet owing to the imperitive command of Jackson it had to be dun, and she happened to be the one appointed to do it. As saying she could fight for Jackson she positively denyes it. (Having ben insulted by the souldiers) she said she could fight; meaning onely that she could fight those who insulted her."

Sue was in a difficult situation; she was being forced to repudiate her own father. "As to saying Jackson & gang were her friends she has no recollection of having said any sutch thing. The above is her own honest statements and she hops the court will allow them to have their due weight. She is willing to abide the decission of the court, hopeing they will be as mild as posable, remembering she is but a child (only 14 years old), she is also willing to take the Oath if required and will live accordingly." Sue was convicted and ordered to be banished from the state of Missouri. Again, General Schofield suspended the sentence.

The other Jackson daughter, Bettie, was charged with saying that she planned to feed bushwhackers at every opportunity and that she intended "to drive away the old black woman that showed the scout of the Federal soldiers where William Jackson and his gang were." Lieutenant Blair testified again, recalling that Bettie had said of the black woman, "No one will stay around me who would inform on my friends." She had added, "My sister and I both fed Bill Jackson and his gang."

Bettie's defense statement to the court provides a startling glimpse into a female mind of the 1860s. "With refference to uttering disloyal sentiments, her being a lady and unaccustomed to being held responsible for anything she might say, she does not really know what was loyal or disloyal." She further denied calling Bill Jackson her friend, and "as to what she said to the black woman, it was simply this: No one should stay about me and report anything that would bring me into trouble." She also offered to take the oath of allegiance. Like her mother, Bettie Jackson was banished from Missouri; her sentence was also suspended by General Schofield. After their release, did the Jackson women stop feeding the head of their family? In an era where a father's word was law and domestic violence frequently went unreported or even unremarked, it seems unlikely.

In another case, Eliza J. Haynie and her daughter Rachel were charged with disloyalty, harboring guerrillas, aiding the enemy, and receiving stolen property, all near Miami, in Saline County. It was alleged that the women fed Campbell's band of guerrillas, kept mail for them, and hid stolen goods for them—including over a hundred dollars' worth of hardware and dry goods stolen from one Henry D. Smith and hidden at the Haynie residence. The Haynies' troubles began when Captain Wilson Parker, Fourth Missouri State Militia Cavalry (Union), was following the trail of a band of Confederate bushwhackers and came to a campsite where he and his men found a very bloody U.S. Army blanket and two fully equipped horses. As the Federals searched the area, they were fired upon by two men. The militia scouting party rode two hundred yards further to the Haynie household, where they found mother, daughter, and six other young women sewing. As Captain Parker later testified, "My 12 men searched the house and found $50 worth of ladies shoes, and two saddlebags full of Confederate mail, mostly from Parson's Brigade. I sold to the daughter of Mrs. Haynie a fine pair of Morocco shoes for $15 and retained the rest of evidence for the provost marshal. We also found some candy hidden in the garden; we gave that to the youngest girl." A clerk from the provost marshal's office further testified that Henry D. Smith and Johanna Keppler had identified the goods seized from the Haynie household as having been stolen from them by bushwhackers. Eliza Haynie was convicted and sent to Alton Military Prison until the end of the war, in spite of her denial of every charge against her.[24]

Rachel's counsel submitted a written defense, contending, "The prosecution has failed to prove anything. Captain Parker claims he heard a confession, but all courts hold that witnesses can misunderstand words, and that extra-judicial confession, standing alone, will not sustain a conviction. Further, there is no evidence that the defendant knew that there was Rebel mail in those saddlebags." These opinions upon the laws of evidence apparently held no sway with the military court, which ordered Rachel incarcerated in a military prison until the end of the war, a sentence that General Rosecrans commuted to six months at Alton Prison.

Far from the pastoral scenes of rural Missouri, five cases from the metropolis of St. Louis further illustrate the Union judicial treatment of southern women. Zaidee Bagwell was the author of a letter of epic length and burning Confederate patriotism, which, unfortunately for her, was intercepted by the Union forces who controlled St. Louis. In this February 3, 1863, missive, addressed to W. F. Luckett (probably William F. Luckett, Ordnance Sergeant, Second Missouri Infantry [Confederate]), she poured out her heart on the subjects of blacks, prisons, and her mother's concealed portrait of Jefferson Davis. Zaidee, who signed herself "Your true and devoted Rebel," expressed the following opinions:

I suppose by this time you have received my other letter and I'm going to try this [illegal] carrier. Enclosed you will find your Ma's letter and this carrier is so closely watched that I fear he will be captured, but we all hope for the best. Miss Lucy, "our intelligent contraband," watches everything so closely that we do nothing but lie. You just ought to see how the Union people are shaking. The very blackest have very little faith in their glorious Union Government, and I do assure you that we Rebels never felt so sure of a Southern Confederacy as we do now; and we do so pray for the time to come when our brave soldiers and bushwhackers will be released from their prisons and free once more.

There is now 800 prisoners in the Gratiot Street Prison and so many of them have smallpox. There is a thousand in the Alton Prison and they are almost destitute of clothing. Ma and I have been permitted to visit the Alton Prison on next Thursday. I have been sewing and mending old clothes for them all this week. Dick Bromford promised to write a little to you, but I have not seen it as yet. I received a long letter from your Ma and Miss Loutri said I might love you if I was a real good Rebel, and if that is all she asks of me I think you are my property. I will admit that I have talked to Fred, but after Pa shot that soldier, we could not do as we pleased.

He [the Union soldier] lived six days after he was shot, and the night he died four great black-hearted villains came bolting into Ma's room and damned us to everything they could, and not a soul in the house but her and I. Nor was there a person in town or a friend anywhere that would come near us. We moved everything over to Mrs. Johnston's and slept on the floor in our clothes and shoes for six weeks and every night was warned to leave the house that it was going to be burned. We could not live so and all we could do was to take some of the highest officers in our house to board, but Ma never got me to set with the contemptible hounds, if I was compelled to speak with them. No one knows what we have to contend with.

We were getting along splendidly when you was at our house last to what we were when we moved. May the Lord speed General Price and his noble army into Missouri so that we poor persecuted "she-devils" as that elegant paper the *Republican* chooses to term us may have the satisfaction of trampling a few of the Negro-loving ladies under our feet. Your particular friend, Emma Smith, has a gentleman waiting on her. He is an American citizen of African descent and she attends church with him.

To let you know how fast the Negroes are getting along, I send you a marriage of one that was in the list of marriages [not found in the records] and that is just a specimen of the Negro equality that is practiced here among the Negro-loving people. I hope to see the last one of them driven into Africa, where they can all live together and enjoy themselves in each other's society.

I am very sorry to hear that your brother was killed and my prayer is that none of you may share his fate and I don't think you will. I heard yesterday that Al Grimes was a cousin of yours and I know I think a great deal more of him now. Everybody I see asks me if I have not got a very particular friend in Price's army, and now if you have no objection I think hereafter I will tell them I have a [illegible].

Belle and Grandmama have been down and spent a week with us and we had a very gay time. Emma is living here and is just as quarrelsome as ever. We hardly ever speak to each other. Ma is just as good as she can be and often wishes to see you. We have all dreamed of you so often within the last two weeks that she is very uneasy but I think dreams are just the reverse. Mollie and Amanda send love to you. Amanda was here yesterday and I had a letter from Mollie.

Bart has been in the work house for the last month and I hope he may never get out alive. You did not tell me if you was an officer and what company you belong to. We heard you was a lieutenant in a battery, but did not know for certain. It does not make any difference to us whether you are an officer or not. I know we are all just as proud of you as if you were a brigadier general, for what is there in an officer?

I have not been to a party for two years and had a real good time like we used to have. I went to a dance last night to our neighbor's and wore a calico dress. Don't you think I am getting rather old maidish? The snow is almost a foot deep and such sleighing you never saw. You just ought to be here to see it and I would rather think you would try it yourself. We have not had any cold weather at all scarcely and I don't think we will have much now, it is so late in the season.

Dr. came down last night. He is living at College Mound and he says that there was a prisoner shot in that place on the second of February for hollowing for Jeff Davis. We dare not breathe his name aloud here, but I wish you could see the portrait Ma has of him. Mr. CYJ gave it to her and it cost $15.00. It is splendid. He is in the NM ticket office, under the planter's house. Benjamin has been discharged from the road and everybody thinks Ive Gamble will be very soon and I hope so.

Ma just received a letter from our other carrier and I suppose he is now with you all, for the letter has been written ten days. I have such a dreadful cold I can scarcely speak above a whisper, but I will not die, because there is too many pretty southern girls down there. You must come home soon, for such I consider our house and Ma says she does want to see her son Frank so much. Now I know you will come. Why don't you bring the mail once and come and see us.

Write me where Shod Davis is at. We heard he had been wounded.

Give my love to all the Rebels, Ed Barton, Willie Halleck and Shod and more to yourself. Write by the first carrier to me and a long letter. We all send much love to you and to Mr. Flannagan and hope you will give the Feds your best Minnie ball and shoot a few extra balls in revenge for us. You may look for several kisses in this letter and you will find them.

I caught a beau and I am going to petticoat him pretty soon. A poor cowardly thing like him ought to be petticoated if you would excuse the expression, for I seldom make use of such to you, do I? Write soon to your true and devoted Rebel.[25]

Under military law, communicating with the enemy and giving encouragement to the rebellion were equally forbidden. Zaidee was sentenced to be confined to her home until the end of the war, to take the oath of allegiance, and to post a $1,000 bond. Her father, clearly a man of wealth and influence, arranged for mitigation. Zaidee Bagwell's revised sentence was that she leave the country until the end of the war and post a $5,000 bond and that she would give no further encouragement to the Confederacy.

Zaidee's stepmother, Augusta, was equally outspoken, if more concise, in a February 4, 1863, letter to J. M. Flanagan, adjutant of the Second Missouri Infantry (Confederate). In addition to news of friends and family, she expressed her patriotic fervor and detailed her use of flattery to influence Union officers:

It has not been but a short time since I wrote you but not wishing to let an opportunity pass without penning you a few lines, I hasten to tell you of a few more of our trials. You have no idea how rejoiced I was to hear, or have you write me, that expected to come to Missouri soon. May God speed your progress, for if ever a people was subjugated, it is our poor Missourians. Those "Bastilles" that the Lords of our land term prisons, are *groaning* with the *agonies* of our poor friends and relatives and not one comfort will they allow us to administer unless you bow to their majesties. . . . I have learned that to flatter is the key to their consciences and what we term Golden Salve [bribery] goes a good way towards proving your loyalty to Abe Lincoln's Government. I have always contended that right—"was might" and now I feel convinced. God is continually on our side for He shows His omnipotent power in all our victories. I hope and pray that the impending battle at Vicksburg may wind up this already too bloody strife and Mr. Lincoln will compromise with President Davis, but not without our glorious Confederacy. Then I will be supremely happy, but I can never forgive them. I have suffered too intensely from their hands to forget and forgive. I hope to see the day when some of those Yankee vandals that infest our country brought to an account for the falsehoods and scandal they have perpetrated on our innocent people. I profess sometimes to have friends, that is the [Union] officers. Never asked a citizen or a common hireling that is lower than a Col[onel] any favor, but often I have had to apply to them for protection and I never failed to get it, and the more I talked secesh the better they seemed to like me. I never denied my sympathies yet all I ever asked was to be treated as a lady should and have justice meted out. One, a General, replied to me once (when I told him all we asked was justice) was he would leave life. I looked him right in the eye and told him I did not thank him nor none of his army for our lives, that was not what I asked for.[26]

The Bagwells paid dearly for expressing their devotion to the Confederate cause. They also seemed to have considerable political connections, given that Mr. Bagwell killed a Union soldier and escaped prosecution.

"I lost my husband," Amanda Cranville told Union authorities at St. Louis, calculating correctly that they would misinterpret her words. But when a Union detective opened the false bottom of her trunk and found a pistol, three boxes of cartridges, eight boxes of percussion caps, two hats, and fifteen yards of silk cloth, she had no ready answer. After her arrest, persistent interrogation established that she had come to St. Louis from Alabama to see a Judge Krum about a divorce. It seems that she had "lost" her husband when he left her and went to Canada in 1861. The story of the trunk with the false bottom also contained a surprise. Cranville had had it custom-built in St. Louis—by a man who reported its construction to the provost marshal. The Union detective assigned to her case waited until the trunk was packed and delivered to her stateroom on the steamer *Graham*. Minutes before embarkation, he began his search. "She said I could have the pistol, the trunk, or anything she had if I would not expose her," he testified at her trial. She hotly denied having made such an offer, especially the part about offering "anything." (The testimony makes clear her deep resentment of the suggestion that she offered sexual favors.) Her counsel wanted the detective to reveal how he knew of the trunk's false bottom. His reply: "It's not my business to tell you how I know these things." The court upheld the Federal agent's refusal to give information on this point.[27]

In spite of her precarious legal situation, Cranville yielded points to her interrogators only with great reluctance. When asked if she was a "southern sympathizer," she replied, "I don't understand the question." But when asked, "Do you wish the South to gain independence?" her answer was a resounding "Yes." She concluded by refusing to take the oath of allegiance because, she declared, "It would be forswearing the country I was born in."

The military commission that tried Cranville for smuggling was headed by Colonel Thomas P. Herrick of the Seventh Kansas Cavalry. Given the intense animosity between Missourians and Kansans, it must have grated on the St. Louis resident to be judged by a Kansan. The commission sentenced her to be imprisoned until the end of the war, but General Grenville Dodge mitigated the penalty to "banishment southward." Whatever her true motivation for coming North, Cranville had succeeded in consuming the time of a general, a colonel, a detective, and two captains. Further, she nearly succeeded in conveying to the Confederacy a pistol and a significant supply of ammunition.

Amanda Cranville was certainly not only the bird of passage on the wide waters of the Mississippi River. In November 1863, under Special Orders No. 155, issued by the Department of the Missouri, Lieutenant James McKelvey of the Seventh Minnesota supervised the travels south of Annie B. Martin, Martha Cameron, Nellie Mitchell, and Sallie Lockett. All four had been banished for the duration of the war. However, Annie Martin did not stay in the South. When her party reached Vicksburg, she demanded to be put ashore. From there, she traveled into Alabama with her sister,

Therressa [sic] Blonnerhassett. Annie then went on into western Tennessee, which she claimed was "neutral territory," and collected letters to be mailed at Cairo, Illinois.[28]

At Annie's trial for violation of her order of banishment, the court was somewhat doubtful about her Tennessee travels, since there was no official neutral territory during the Civil War. Members of the commission were even less understanding about her return to the North when only ten months earlier she had been ordered south with a free ticket and an escort. She was quite dismissive of their concerns: "I received no order not to come into the Union lines. Lieutenant McKelvey gave us verbal orders not to return, and I was told that verbal orders were of no account." When asked about her current political sympathies, she was much clearer: "I am a southern woman in feeling and I desire the success of the southern Confederacy . . . because I do not think the southern states received their guaranteed rights." Perhaps her forthright disdain for Federal authority rubbed her captors the wrong way. General Rosecrans approved her sentence, which was confinement in Alton Military Prison until the end of the war.

Martha Cassell got into trouble with the Union authorities for a seemingly innocuous offense: possession of a letter that had been sent to her from Paris, Illinois. The correspondent was her brother, L. Rogers, who was definitely out of favor with the Federal authorities at St. Louis.

Rogers (otherwise known as F. M. Kaylor) had been arrested as a "notorious Rebel" and placed in the Gratiot Street Prison. He escaped from there and made his way to eastern Illinois, where he recruited and drilled a few dozen southern sympathizers as a "copperhead militia." Such a force could not be concealed for long. In early 1865, there was an armed conflict between his group and a hundred furloughed Union soldiers. In spite of their training, most of the greatly outnumbered copperheads broke and ran at the first volley. Three horses and no men were killed. In Rogers's letter to Cassell, he recounted the event. Self-incrimination in a letter was a perilous thing, made worse by his closing remarks: "I want to see a Civil War and wide destruction sweep the north. I want a chance to avenge the insults and indignities heaped upon the people of Missouri." Dangerous as it was to write such a letter, its possession was even more dangerous, as

Martha Cassell discovered. She was arrested, imprisoned for four months, tried, convicted, and sent to the Missouri State Penitentiary until the end of the war.[29]

Two months after Cassell's trial, Judge John D. S. Dryden of the Missouri Supreme Court wrote to Edward Bates, Lincoln's attorney general, stating his belief that her correspondence with her brother was "a grave indiscretion, without criminal intent." Dryden continued, "She is a young lady of unspotted reputation, intelligent and refined, quiet and modest in her behavior, of a sensitive and generous nature, possessing an exceedingly frail constitution—already the subject of hemorrhage of the lungs." Bates, one of Missouri's most prominent public figures before the war, wrote to Lincoln, describing Dryden and William Carson (another of Cassell's supporters) as "my old and honored friends." He continued, "I have examined the papers which I now present to you and do fully concur . . . in believing that a free pardon would be just, humane, and altogether right. If it were a civil case, within the common routine of my official duty, I would at once make the requisition for the pardon, but being a case of military cognizance, I prefer this method of advising the pardon." Bates's letter was dated October 24, 1864. Lincoln pardoned Martha Cassell on October 25. By then, she had occupied the time of many commissioned officers, detectives, and jailors, as well as a state supreme court justice, the U.S. attorney general and the president himself. While not a major blow for the Confederacy, it was certainly a spoonful of grit in the gears of the Federal war machine.

In late February 1864, Lexington, Missouri, nestled on the banks of the Missouri River, was the site of a fatal shootout that landed Ann Fickle in deep trouble. She was charged with murder and with connivance in the escape of a criminal. The trouble centered around a citizen of Lafayette County, Otho Hinton, a bushwhacker being held in the Union army guardhouse. Three of Hinton's friends, "noted guerillas and land pirates" named Blunt, Waller, and Burns, were plotting, with Fickle's aid, to free Hinton. They enlisted a Union soldier, Private William Sabens, First Missouri State Militia Cavalry, in their plot. Ann Fickle went "into the country" to see Blunt and returned with thirty dollars in gold and a metal-cutting file. Sabens was supposed to give the gold to Hinton so that he might bribe the guard. The file, of course, was to cut Hinton's chains.[30]

Near the guardhouse was a house simply designated as "Mrs. Reed's place." If bribery did not work, an alternate escape plan for Hinton was for him to tell the guard that he "needed to go to Mrs. Reed's." On the way there, Blunt and Waller would cut the guard's throat and escape with Hinton. Fickle opposed cutting the guard's throat because it "would make a fuss." The final escape action is unclear, but it was sudden and violent. Hinton, Blunt, and Burns were running down the street when they were halted by three Union officers. Burns aimed his pistol at the officers from a distance of twelve feet and pulled the trigger. His gun misfired. Theirs did not. Burns fell dead. Up the street, a Union soldier, William J. Asher, ordered the men to halt. Blunt shot him dead and escaped with Hinton and Waller into the woods.

Fickle was subsequently arrested and brought to trial, where she was convicted of concealing guerrillas, conspiring to release a prisoner, and bribing a U.S. soldier. She was, however, acquitted of murder. General William Rosecrans disagreed with the latter decision. The court reconsidered the matter, found her guilty of second-degree murder, and sentenced her to ten years in the state penitentiary at Jefferson City. General Rosecrans approved the sentence.

Fanny Houx, like Ann Fickle, was a resident of Lafayette County, which was clearly an area of considerable southern sentiment (it bore the nickname "Quantrill country"). She was tried on charges of feeding guerrillas, and her counsel was Allen P. Richardson, formerly colonel of the Cole County Home Guard (Union). The hidden agendas of both the defense and the prosecution, as well as questions of perjury, hover over this trial like flies over carrion.[31]

The chief prosecution witness was "Jackson, a colored man." He told the court that he used to live eight miles south of Lexington, on the Houx farm, but was now a refugee. He said that he had known Fanny Houx for twelve years and that she was the wife of William Houx. In late June 1864, Jackson was plowing at the Houx place about an hour after sunrise. He put the mule to graze and went to ask Fanny Houx if his breakfast was ready.

She said it was not and told him to keep a close watch for Federal troops. Jackson replied that he didn't care if the Federals came or not. She was displeased with this answer and promised trouble for Jackson when the bushwhackers arrived. As Jackson vividly recalled:

> She turned her eyes in the direction of the apple orchard and says yonder they come now. I says let them come. I don't care. The bushwhackers then come up twelve in number, around the house and well— by the time the second one lit she the accused commenced telling what I said—one stepped up and said God damn your black soul what do you mean talking that away. I said nothing to him. The second one says who is that talking that talk. The other says that old nigger setting there the lady (the accused) says so—he stepped up and drew his pistol and struck me on the head, and says the first thing you know you will taken out and have your brains blowed out—he almost knocked me blind for a few minutes by this time they found out I wouldn't watch [for approaching Federals]. She the accused sent her oldest son upon the hill to watch. She the accused then stepped back to the head of the stair steps and said to the bushwhackers come up to breakfast gentleman come up to breakfast. The first and second that hit and struck me with the pistol were the first ones that went up to breakfast. I had not left my chair where I was when they struck me with the pistol. So soon as the same two got their breakfast they went on to the woods and got hickorys. I was still setting at the same place where I first was when they first come up. They come up with a long hoop pole about five or six feet long and hollowed to me. "Come out here God damn you" says come out here I want to show you how to talk—I was putting on my little boys shirt, a little boy about three years old—I raised up my head. He said it is you I am talking to. I sot still for about half a minute or such . . . he says God damn you haven't you comin. I didn't move very fast. He broke to me, put his hand on his pistol and said God damn you I can make you come. He came and catched hold of me in the shirt collar jerked me around and kicked me—and knocked me over the head with his pistol until he got me about the middle way of the yard and told me to stop there. God damn you and pull off that shirt. I pulled

my shirt off—he knocked me with his pistol over the head all the time I was getting shirt off. He took the hickory in both hands, he just tip toes to it and come down on me the same as if he was beating an ox. He said to the others standing around, Boys you've got nothing to do but cut hickorys and fetch them to me as fast as I can wear them out. They went to cutting hickorys as he said. They cut about five.

After the bushwhacker wore out five hickories and a board beating Jackson, he told Jackson to put his shirt on and "go to the Feds," adding that if Jackson did so, he would kill him. Jackson added further details: "A man named Tom Crawber told the men to stop the beating and send [me] back to plowing. Mrs. Houx said she'd go on cooking for bushwhackers as long as she could raise her hand." He also recalled that each of the bushwhackers carried four pistols.

Fanny Houx's counsel then took up his cross-examination, making many unsuccessful attempts to catch Jackson in inconsistencies or contradictions. Often Jackson was asked the same question in a different form half a dozen different times. Having little success with this approach, Colonel Richardson suggested that Jackson's testimony stemmed from a quarrel between Jackson and Jackson's wife, in which Fanny Houx took the wife's side. Jackson denied that this incident influenced his testimony. The defense then introduced its star witness, the sheriff of Lafayette County, Jacob A. Price, who said, "I've known the slave Jackson for 18 years and I would not believe him even under oath—but he's a good boy to work!" On cross-examination, Sheriff Price was asked if he was related to Fanny Houx. "Yes, she is my sister," he replied.

In her written defense, Fanny Houx emphasized her vulnerability as the only white adult on the farm, since her husband was away in the Confederate army. She told the court that it was very difficult to refuse the demands of bushwhackers and attributed all of Jackson's testimony to malice on his part. The commission found her guilty and sent her to Alton Prison until the end of the war, a decision endorsed by General Rosecrans.

When a defendant pleaded guilty, there was usually no testimony and therefore a slender record. Such was the case with Millie N. Goggin, accused of "uttering disloyal sentiments" at Tipton, Missouri. In the presence of Provost Marshal Lieutenant Franklin Swap, Fourth Missouri State Militia (Union), she said that she was a Rebel, that she had helped the rebellion, and that it would be a pleasure to be sent south. At her trial, she offered no defense of her firm stand; she withdrew not one bit of her expressed loyalty to the South. She might have been surprised when, instead of being transported south with a free ticket, she was sent to Alton Prison until the war was over. Her last hope for mitigation died when General Rosecrans approved her imprisonment.[32]

Callaway County, the very heart of secession sentiment in Missouri, was where the widowed Nancy Kemp was accused of "disloyal practices," feeding bushwhackers, warning them of Federal forces, and concealing weapons. Her defense counsel was the firm of Peacock and Cornwell. They noted that the chief prosecution witness, twenty-nine-year-old Henry Kemp, was "colored." Their written defense of their client began, "Here is a Negro, a slave formerly of the defendant, belonging to a race steeped in ignorance and having no moral checks, whose race is noted for two prominent propensities, one stealing and the other lying, and this scion of such a race and such a condition, in opposition to the laws of the State of Missouri, in opposition to all . . . precedent except in the present war, under a color of law unconstitutional in principle." The general trend of their argument is hard to miss. What were the events in which Henry Kemp's testimony was so crucial?[33]

First Lieutenant James McIntire, 67th Enrolled Missouri Militia (Union), was the first witness. He stated, "We were on a scout, having heard that there were guns at the Widow Kemp's place. She denied that there were any, but her black man showed us where they were hidden, in the barn under a corn pile. I think there were two double-barreled shotguns and three rifles. The black man said he was present when they were hidden." Henry Kemp testified next:

> Mrs. Kemp's son hid the guns there and she knew it. We'd been out shooting prairie chickens and she told us to hide the guns. I also know that her daughter, Elizabeth Collins, makes clothes for the Rebels—brown jeans pants and linsey striped shirts. Ammon Kemp and Wesley Kemp are both in the Rebel army, Wood's Cavalry. A few

weeks ago, Company E ate breakfast at Mrs. Kemp's and she behaved very well toward them. There was a bushwhacker camp about 200 yards from the house. She'd sent me out to warn them if the Feds were coming. I don't know exactly how much she fed guerrillas, but it was right smartly though—she told them to come to the house if they needed anything.

Nancy Kemp then cross-examined her former slave:

> "Did I not tell you to hide the guns so the bushwhackers don't get them?"
> "No, ma'am."
> "How do you know I hid the guns from the Feds?"
> "I just know."
> "In other words, you don't really know. Now, how do you know that the 14 men who came to my house were Rebels?"
> "They were all armed and they said they was Rebels. I was in the kitchen with the black woman who was cooking. The Rebels and Mrs. Collins was in the dining room in the white part of the house."

Kemp's daughter added her testimony, denying that her mother had ever fed a bushwhacker and insisting that her mother knew nothing of where any guns were hidden.

The defense again cited the inadmissibility of Henry Kemp's testimony on the grounds that he was black and urged the court to give credence to Elizabeth Collins, "a respectable white married lady," over the word of a former slave. They also suggested that Henry Kemp should be charged as a criminal accomplice, since he helped hide the guns. The judge advocate disagreed, especially with the latter point. As he stated, "A man who is the slave of another, acting under the coercion of another, is a mere instrument, acting under duress and not an accomplice at all." In the end, the court ignored the testimony of the two white women and the arguments of their lawyers in favor of the words of a former slave. Nancy Kemp was sent to the Missouri State Penitentiary until the end of the war, a decision endorsed by General Grenville Dodge, who was then recovering from gunshot wounds of the thigh, hand, and skull.

A consistent (though largely unspoken) thread in these "feeding bush-whacker" trials is this: what is a woman, alone on an isolated farm, to do when a band of desperate men, armed to the teeth, come to her door and demand something? Whether her sympathies are Union or Confederate, she had to comply.

Franklin County, just west of St. Louis, harbored a bushwhacker named Coldwell. In late August 1864, Rebecca Romanoska went to his house to warn him of approaching Federal troops. For this, she was arrested and tried for "criminal conduct." She pleaded guilty but introduced witnesses for mitigation of her sentence. Not all of their testimony clarified matters, however. As T. B. Shelton testified, "I've known Rebecca eight years, since she was a little girl. I always heard her talk loyal. Her husband is in the U.S. Army, but I don't know which regiment." Philla Ann Mitchele's testimony would today most likely be dismissed as hearsay: "I have heard one of the Inlow family say that Rebecca would swear anything." Rebecca herself told the court that she wanted nothing to do with warning Coldwell, but that "young Inlow was a friend of Coldwell and said I must do it." (Sadly, the trial record does little to clarify this web of neighborhood relationships.) She was sentenced to six months in the Fort Wyman prison at Rolla, then the terminus of the railroad coming southwest from St. Louis and a city swarming with bluecoats.[34]

At the little town of Whitesville, in Andrew County, Hannah Martin was charged with "disloyal conduct," specifically that she had spat upon the Union flag. The flag in question was hung partway across the entrance of the local Baptist church. As Minerva Wilson recalled, "I saw her spit toward the flag, but not on it. After church, I heard her say she hoped a streak of lightning would tear the flag all to pieces. Coming in, she passed by the flag very carefully, so that it did not touch her. I have heard her speak in favor of the South." Ellen Hager added her testimony: "She was sitting behind me in church and I heard her say she hoped lightning would strike the flag. On the way out of church she sprang to one side to avoid the flag, then spat on it. She had two brothers in the rebel army with Price, but they are home now. I've never had any personal difficulty with her." Martha Grey confirmed the spitting story, adding, "She jumped to one side to avoid the flag, as if she had been bitten. During the service, the lady with her told her to be quiet." Two more prosecution witnesses told the same story.[35]

Two women spoke for the defense. Martha, Hannah Martin's sister, swore she had seen or heard nothing regarding the flag, an observation echoed by Gilla Combest. Hannah Martin then spoke in her own defense: "I only suggested that the flag should be taken in, as it was going to rain." The court found her guilty and sentenced her to be banished to the Confederacy until the war was over. However, because of her "youth and inexperience," they recommended mitigation to taking the oath of allegiance and posting a bond. General Schofield concurred with mitigation, but noted her "want of good sense and good manners." Her final sentence: take the oath of allegiance and post a $1,000 bond.

Eleven miles east of Rolla, Mary Ann Wilson was arrested for making uniforms for Confederate soldiers. Several men of the Fifth Missouri State Militia Cavalry (Union) were looking for bushwhackers who had stolen horses from "the [Maramec] Iron Works." (The area is now Maramec Spring Park.) The men rode down a hollow about half a mile from the nearest road and there, "in a secret place in the woods," was Mary Ann, repairing a very old, badly worn U.S. infantry officer's coat with lieutenant's shoulder straps. Beside her were two pairs of worn-out Union trousers. One of the militiamen recalled, "She told me a Southern soldier had left them with her about two months before." Whatever her plans for the clothing, her timing was unfortunate: she was arrested on April 4, 1865, five days before the surrender of the Army of Northern Virginia. She pleaded not guilty, but she was convicted and sentenced to military prison until the end of the war. Records show that she was released in June.[36]

These Missouri women and their trials dramatically illustrate the deep schisms and bitter feelings that wracked the state during the Civil War (and afterward) and the risks these brave and steadfast women took for their goal of southern independence.

# 2

# MARYLAND

THE OFFICIAL MARYLAND state song opens with these stirring words: "The despot's heel is on thy shore," the despot in this case being the Federal government. Written as a poem in 1861 by a former resident of the state—then living in Louisiana and upset about the Union allegiance of his home state—it was popular with Marylanders who favored secession. In the Civil War era, Maryland was a state with divided loyalties, and keeping it in the Union was a major concern of the Federal government. Even today, some Marylanders still think of themselves as southerners.

Maryland, then as now, has a most peculiar geographic shape, pinched nearly out of existence at one point between West Virginia and Pennsylvania and widening at the eastern and western extremes. The western part of the state is steep and mountainous, while the Eastern Shore is flat as a table and rich in deep, fertile soil. The eastern flatlands were ideal for large-scale agricultural operations, for which slave labor was well suited. Western Marylanders, with their steep hillsides and small fields, had little use for slaves. Or for secession.

The city of Baltimore, on the Chesapeake Bay, dominated the cultural and financial life of the state. Baltimore was a major port for commerce with the South, and Baltimore bankers were deeply involved in loans and mortgages contracted by the large slaveowning planters of the Deep South. Thus, social and commercial interests ensured that the Confederacy would find many friends in eastern Maryland. This Confederate connection caused intense and immediate concern to the new Lincoln administration. Virginia, just south of the capital, had joined the Confederacy, and

Rebel cannon had closed shipping up the Potomac River. If Maryland went Confederate, Washington, D.C., would have been completely cut off from the rest of the world, and Lincoln and his government would have been prisoners. Or dead.

When President Lincoln called for 75,000 troops following the attack on Fort Sumter, the first to respond was the Sixth Massachusetts. In Baltimore, going from one railroad depot to another, the regiment was set upon by a group of men hurling bricks and firing pistols. When the dust settled, four soldiers and twelve citizens lay dead. The mayor and police chief of Baltimore destroyed the bridges on the railroads leading south from Philadelphia and Harrisburg; other Marylanders loyal to the South cut the telegraph line to Washington, D.C. Lincoln and his capital were isolated for days. There was simply no way to reach the outside world.

After almost a week, rail and telegraph service was restored throughout Maryland, but these events had convinced Lincoln that nothing should stand in the way of holding Maryland in the Union. There was much anti-Federal political maneuvering among the Maryland politicians, which came to a crescendo in September 1861, when it looked as though the Maryland state legislature, meeting in Frederick, would endorse secession. To avert this outcome, Lincoln had thirty-one members of the legislature, plus the mayor of Baltimore, thrown into prison. Even today, legal scholars argue over the merits of Lincoln's action. To southern sympathizers in Maryland, it was tyranny, pure and simple. And many women among them saw Colonel Harry Gilmor as a potential savior of their state.[1]

Today, John Singleton Mosby is perhaps the best-known Confederate partisan ranger, but in Civil War days, Gilmor was a household word, especially in Baltimore, his hometown. A brief stay in a Union prison (for "disloyalty") in the summer of 1861 had sharpened his deep resentment of northerners, and when he was released he placed convictions above the benefits of staying at home in the bosom of his wealthy family. He headed south and cast his lot with the southern cause.[2]

Gilmor fought in the Shenandoah Valley, with long excursions into eastern Maryland. His exploits as a heroic Confederate officer were remarkable. His "William Tell" demonstrations, in which he would shoot an apple off the head of a comrade with a .44-caliber Colt revolver, astonished bystanders. In battle at Bolivar Heights, he commanded a cannon and was injured when the recoil ran a wheel over his foot. In September 1862, during General Robert E. Lee's Maryland campaign, Gilmor decided to take a brief unauthorized leave to visit his family in Baltimore, where he was captured and held prisoner for six months before being exchanged. Other adventures in the service of the southern cause lay ahead. In October 1863, he commanded forty men sent to destroy a railroad bridge on Back Creek, Virginia. On the way to the attack point, he stopped at Carter Hall and was persuaded by a "Rebel maiden" to "linger behind in her delightful company." The rest of his command, led by a private, continued onward and were captured by Federal forces.[3]

In February 1864, Gilmor commanded a group that robbed a railroad train near Duffield's Depot, Virginia. After derailing the train, his men killed one Union soldier and relieved the passengers of "watches, diamonds, rings, and breast pins." In addition, they robbed the passengers of "not less than $30,000" in cash (nearly $1 million in today's money). But they were unable to open the iron safe, the principle object of the raid. Four days later, Gilmor's men robbed a caravan of Jewish merchants, taking "six thousand in gold, two wrist watches, a great coat, fur collar, Hebrew book, in addition to a number of silver coins and medals." The Confederate government sent investigators in response to this incident. Gilmor denied any involvement in the affair, but one of his own men claimed that Gilmor had "acknowledged . . . that he had arranged the affair of robbing the Jew" and that Gilmor had given his quartermaster $160 in gold, "taken from a Jew." Robert E. Lee, disgusted by these acts, denounced them as "plunder," with "no military object." Gilmor was arrested by his own government and court-martialed. In April 1864, he was found not guilty. Instead, because of his record as an energetic officer, excellent horseman, and crack shot, he was given command of the Second Maryland Cavalry Battalion. It was with this force that he encountered the first of our Maryland Confederate sympathizers.[4]

The railroad from Baltimore to Philadelphia ran northeast along the western shore of Chesapeake Bay. About twelve miles outside of Baltimore, it crossed the Gunpowder River. There, near the northern bank of the river, lay the little hamlet of Magnolia Station. On July 12, 1864, as the early train from Baltimore pulled into the station, Gilmor's men fired a volley into the train and brought it to a halt. The engineer fled into the woods. Because none of the partisans could drive a train, they abandoned their original plan of riding north and destroying railroad facilities. Instead, they set to work at forced barter, exchanging their filthy clothes for good ones worn by the male passengers. The chief prize was Union major general William Franklin, who was taken prisoner. The partisans drove the passengers off the train, set fire to it and to the depot, and awaited the arrival of the 10:00 A.M. train, which came to a halt when confronted by tracks blocked with flaming wreckage. Soon, Rebels on horseback were peering in the windows of the newly arrived train.

Among the passengers was a group of Baltimoreans traveling together: James Lee, Harry Lee, Emily Harper, Bessie Perrine, Perrine's small child, and a nurse who was taking care of the child. The other passengers were startled to see Perrine greeting many of the partisans by name, including Lieutenants Carroll and Billings and Hoffman Gilmor. As the partisans surged into the train, Perrine, who had been paying close attention to the passengers who were not part of her group, told the robbers that she would show them the trunks that belonged to Federal officers. She also made sure they wouldn't open her own trunk.[5]

Soon, the Rebels were breaking open trunks under Perrine's tutelage. The first piece of luggage they examined belonged to Delevan Bloodgood, a Union surgeon. From it, they extracted his uniform, including his cocked hat, his sword, and his epaulets. Then Perrine helped them open a sack belonging to a U.S. Marine Corps captain. She busied herself for hours among the Rebels, exclaiming happily and pointing out more trunks to rob. After a while, the frantic pace slowed and she retired under the trees to join a group of Confederate officers for a "collation."

During the excitement, she gave one of Gilmor's men an affection-ate kiss. As a Union navy man, Assistant Engineer Clark Fisher, later re-membered, "I was surprised to see a lady of respectability kissing in so affectionate a manner these vagabonds and thieves. She replied, 'Those young gentlemen are of some of the best families in Baltimore!'" Another passenger heard a Rebel say to Perrine, "I will call upon you at home tomorrow."

Chief Engineer James Thompson, of the U.S. Navy, had removed his uniform coat as the train screeched to a halt and had presented himself as a civilian. The Rebels took his watch and his "pocket book." Thompson recalled seeing Perrine laugh when the Rebels stopped the train with rifle fire. Surgeon N. P. Rice saw Perrine kissing the Confederate flag and assisting Emily Harper in robbing the passengers' trunks.

All this testimony figured prominently in Perrine's trial before a board consisting of three generals and six colonels, in which she was tried for "violating the laws and customs of war." Other witnesses also made a strong case against her. C. E. Clark of Burlington, Vermont, told the court: "I sprang up and said, 'Is not that a shame [to break open people's trunks].' Mrs. Perrine jumped up and said that it was not a shame, that it was right to do it." Ansel Perry of Baltimore observed that most of the passengers were very frightened, whereas Perrine seemed in high spirits and very happy to see the Rebels.

Finally, it was time for the defense. Emily Meyer, nurse for Perrine's child, testified that Perrine had been very excited until her baby was handed out the train window. She also recalled that they had brought some brandy "to give to the baby if it should get sick," and that Perrine had given the brandy to the robbers. Emily Harper told the court that she had seen no improper behavior on the part of Perrine, and adduced her blood relationship with Major Gilmor as the reason why the Rebels had not opened her own trunks.

The next defense witness was Perrine's dentist. He told the court that she had been very nervous for years, at times laughing and crying hysterically, and that she had been too anxious for a much-needed root canal operation. He termed her "nervous, but not insane." The Reverend Dr. H. B. Coskey, vicar general of Baltimore, had known Perrine all her life. In fact, he had baptized her. "She was of a nervous temperament," he testified. Dr. Coskey recalled that when Perrine's mother died, she had entered the family vault and had moved the other bodies to reach the corpse of her mother.

In a completely unexpected development, a Union officer spoke in Perrine's defense. He was L. S. Cropper, master of the U.S. *Wyoming*, who testified:

> On the 11th July, 1864 . . . the train of cars in which I was, was captured, by the Confederate troops, under Harry Gilmore. The cars burnt and I with a large number of passengers left to make our way (after being permitted by Gilmore) to our several destinations . . . without means of transportation . . . or baggage; among those left in that dilemma were a large number of ladies, with their children, the aged, and sick, with some wounded soldiers . . . destitute of food or shelter. . . . The conductor and other employees of the R. Road proved utterly inefficient. . . . After . . . waiting to see what might "turn up" . . . I addressed myself to the work of endeavoring to secure transportation for all, aided by a Jew gentleman. . . . This lady [Perrine], an entire stranger, was among the first . . . to place herself under my care . . . she was with me and under my eye from the moment of the subsidence of confusion attending capture until I took my leave of them . . . and I most unequivocally aver, that during all that time, her deportment was, such as to challenge my admiration of her as dignified and proper, and in all respects befitting a cultivated and accomplished, true woman.

When the parade of witnesses ended, her counsel entered a lengthy defense, all variations on a theme, summed up in these words: "Is the conviction of this poor woman calculated to add to the dignity, honor or glory of this great republic?" The judge advocate then weighed in with his interpretation of these events:

> The case at the bar is one of more than ordinary delicacy and difficulty. I say delicacy and difficulty, gentlemen, not because justice ever distinguished between sexes, or is less than justice as the arbiter of the rights of woman, but because I know the human heart and the human sympathies are not, and cannot be wholly blind to the surroundings and circumstances which environ a question submitted to the judgment of man. To your profession we look for the type of chivalry. To you we naturally turn for the highest exhibition of gallantry: and

that these qualities are appealed to in the present case I cannot doubt. Mars would have shrunk from arraigning and passing sentence upon Venus for an invasion of his kingdom or for giving aid and comfort to the gods with whom he was at war. This is natural. A woman in trouble appeals at once to your sympathies, and you do not ask how or why she is a suppliant. But this, gentleman, is all based upon the idea that in her are found the embodiment of all goodness and excellence: that in her dwell all virtue, purity, and truth. Rob her of these, find her exhibiting antagonistic qualities, separate her from the loveliness with which you have clothed her, see her displaying malice, hatred, cruelty, and a facility to adapt herself to the society of bandits and robbers—see her not only sympathizing with but glorying in the sum of all crime—a party to arson, to larceny and highway robbery—your ideas of heavenly graces, your poetically created creature little lower than the angels, your person too good for earth, becomes a human being like yourself and subject to like passions, governed by the same laws, entitled to the same protection, the same even-handed justice, tempered with the same mercy—this gentlemen and nothing more.

After ten pages of this contrapuntal eloquence, the writer concluded in a single word: "Treason." Perrine's trial board, perhaps one of the highest-ranking assemblages since the court-martial of Major General Fitz John Porter, found her guilty and ordered her imprisoned for three years.

This heavy sentence certainly satisfied the frenzied cry for justice. As the July 23, 1864, *Newport (R.I.) Daily News* told its readers, "The behavior of many of the Baltimore women who were on the captured trains at Magnolia Station was disgraceful and scandalous in the extreme." The article further asserted that the child, which was Perrine's excuse for traveling onward without being arrested, had been "borrowed for the occasion!" and that one northern woman was robbed of over $3,000 in jewels by Gilmor's men.

Three months after she was sentenced, Perrine applied for clemency. Judge Advocate General Joseph Holt said that her sentence should be "fully enforced." In early June 1865, she obtained an interview with President Andrew Johnson, who issued her a full pardon two months later.

Another enthusiastic admirer of Harry Gilmor was Sarah Hutchins of Park Street, Baltimore. In the autumn of 1864 she raised a subscription fund among her friends, and with the donations purchased a splendid sword, suitably engraved, to present to him. She carefully wrapped the sword and enclosed with it a letter to "Dear Harry": "I hope you will receive this with our love. The bearer will inform you concerning it. You can judge him by his deeds. He is true. We have been very unhappy about your wounds but hear you are better. All are well [here] and hopeful. The [bearer] will return. Send a letter by him. This is a token of our appreciation for your noble deeds and daring bravery. Accept it with the heartfelt anxiety and regard of your—Sarah."[6]

The next problem for Hutchins was how to send this sword to Gilmor, who was thought to be somewhere near Duffield's Station, Virginia, the site of one of his earlier train robberies and a spot many miles away in Confederate territory. She instructed her gardener, Joseph Baker, a "colored man," to take the sword and several letters from the Washington Street depot in Baltimore to Duffield's Station, Virginia, and give the items to a Mrs. Jones. For his efforts, he was to receive ten dollars. Baker went to the provost marshal's office, where, using a false name, he obtained a travel permit. As he departed Park Street, with the sword, the letter, and his permit, Hutchins admonished him: "If you are caught, tear up the letters."

As soon as he arrived at the train station with his awkward parcel, Baker was arrested by Union detective Lucius Babcock. He was taken to the office of Lieutenant Colonel John Wooley, provost marshal of the Eighth Army Corps. Wooley heard the story, examined the sword and letters, and had Hutchins arrested and jailed. Nevertheless, her jail time was less arduous than that of women with no social connections. On November 10, 1864, Dr. J. F. Powell wrote to the commanding general: "Mrs. Hutchins, a prisoner in the city jail is suffering from the change in her mode of living and the excitement caused by her arrest. . . . I believe she would be benefited by permitting her friends to furnish her one meal a day." Around Thanksgiving 1864, she faced three charges: having intercourse with the enemies of the United States, violation of the laws of war, and treason.

The trial came to a halt almost as soon as it started, based on the objections of the defense counsel, who wished to exclude the first prosecution witness, Joseph Baker: "In this state of Maryland it is known and settled law that a colored person is not a competent witness in any case against a white person." The judge advocate replied that military courts had decided that "colored persons were universally admitted as competent witnesses." The objection was overruled. Joseph Baker, Lucius Babcock, and John Wolley were allowed to tell their stories.

Hutchins had no defense witnesses. Her attorney filed a 2,000-word written defense based mainly on philosophical abstractions and legal concepts, since the testimony itself offered him little material with which to work. Honor, virtue, and the sanctity of womanhood were thrust forward, and Gilmor's sword was buried in a torrent of Victorian eloquence. Finally, Hutchins threw herself on the mercy of the court: "It is my duty to claim the benefits of all exceptions which the law, in its merciful provisions, affords to the accused. It is my duty to myself, to my children, to my husband, to my widowed mother, and to my suffering aunt, regretting this one act of imprudence and folly."

Moved neither by her contrition nor by the legal logic of her lawyer, the court sent Hutchins to Fitchburg Female Prison for five years and ordered that she serve additional time unless she paid a $5,000 fine. Major General Lew Wallace, future author of *Ben Hur*, approved the sentence. (Wallace, unlike most of his colleagues, was in good health.) But this was not the end of Hutchins's story. Her friends immediately began circulating petitions demanding her release. The Union League of Baltimore quickly circulated counterpetitions and sent a four-page resolution to General Wallace, insisting that she be kept in prison. The southern ladies prevailed. On December 20, 1864, Assistant Secretary of War Charles A. Dana wrote to the warden at Fitchburg, "She is to be released upon making acknowledgement of her wrong and giving her parole of good behavior." She signed the parole papers and on New Year's Eve walked out of prison.

Civil War prisons were, as a rule, grim, oppressive, and unhealthy. Andersonville, Elmira, Point Lookout, Johnson's Island, and Fort McHenry all had well-deserved evil reputations. The civilians locked up at Alton, Illinois, and in St. Louis's Gratiot Street Prison endured dank, disease-ridden conditions. The women sent to Fitchburg, Massachusetts, were, at first glance, more fortunate. Previously known as the Worcester County House of Correction, a four-story brick and granite structure, it had opened only the year before the Civil War began. It was under the management of Alpheus P. Kimball, who believed in a clean and healthful living environment. The matron, Martha L. Nichols, tried to make the female section more cheerful with potted plants and singing birds. Outside the windows were beautifully landscaped gardens.[7] It is not surprising, perhaps, that the southern women sent to Fitchburg remained unmollified by this feeble attempt at interior decoration. They expressed their contempt for their captors by breaking the furniture and cursing the guards.

Like Hutchins, Margarette Barasha also had an opportunity to hear Fitchburg's singing birds. She was tried in Baltimore in November 1864, charged with helping a Union soldier to desert. The soldier in this case was substitute John Foley, just off the boat from Ireland, who was Barasha's brother. He told the court, "I left New York City and then to Philadelphia and then went to Wilmington, Delaware, where I entered the army and received my $400 bounty." He sent $300 to his sister, Margarette. After he was issued a uniform, he was sent to Fort McHenry, where he deserted. His letter to his sister included a request that she bring him civilian clothes in order to aid his escape.[8]

His sister and her husband, Bartholomew Barasha, arrived from New York, saw Foley into his civilian clothes, and proceeded to the Philadelphia depot in Baltimore, where all three of them were arrested by Detective John Starr. Margarette told him that Foley had never been in the army. Her counsel, John Wills, was unable to produce either a defense witness or a defense argument. She did have a slight benefit from her stay in jail—dental care. On December 17, 1864, Dr. Powell, the jail surgeon, wrote that she was "suffering from toothache and should be permitted to proceed to a dentist (under guard) and get the tooth extracted."

Margarette Barasha was sentenced to two years at Fitchburg. A note from M. Edwin, the day turnkey at Fitchburg, confirmed her arrival there on December 29. She spent six months in prison before being pardoned by President Johnson. A heavy price for helping her brother. And perhaps doubly burdensome—would this apparent Irish immigrant have been admitted into the circle of Baltimore matrons already at Fitchburg? Bartholomew Barasha was also convicted. He was sentenced to two years' hard labor at New York's Albany State Prison. Surprisingly, Foley was acquitted.

Mary S. Terry was not only sent to Fitchburg, but also was described by Major General Lew Wallace as "masculine" and "unsexed." Her attorney, in contrast, described her as "a very high-toned lady." To further complicate Terry's case, the prosecutor in her first trial, a Union colonel, was sent to prison himself for a series of frauds. Although Terry was tried in April 1864, much of the three-pound transcript is devoted to the issues of her previous trial of 1863.[9]

In early October 1863, Terry (then calling herself Mary Otey), traveling with a Miss Selden, was arrested in Maryland for possessing almost $2,000 in contraband goods. Colonel William Fish, of the First Connecticut Cavalry, was then provost marshal of the Middle Department. He seized about $200 worth of Otey's goods, which were never recovered. She went to court to regain possession of her things. Baltimore police marshal William Van Nostrand testified that she had the correct permits for the goods in her trunks, and John F. McTilton, surveyor of the port of Baltimore, confirmed that he had issued her a permit. The jury agreed, and her goods (except those which had fallen into the hands of Colonel Fish) were restored to her.

How was it that Terry needed to go to court in order to reclaim goods for which she had the proper permits? The answer seems to lie with Colonel Fish, whose talents, unfortunately, included mischief and theft. In March 1864 he was court-martialed for a variety of abuses of his police powers, including undue familiarity with the operators of three of Baltimore's best-known whorehouses: Emma Morton, Annette Travers, and Nancy Thomas. He not only protected the madams and their whores from the military police, but also attended balls at their establishments in his military uniform.[10]

Colonel Fish also had the power to seize goods deemed contraband. In one instance, he discovered $12,000 in Confederate cotton bonds. Fish sent his clerk, at government expense, to Europe to sell the bonds. On the clerk's return, Fish pocketed the money. He also seized many silk dresses (including dresses of Terry's) that he kept for his own use. His trial board, which included the much-wounded Colonel Joshua Lawrence Chamberlain, convicted him, and he was sent off to prison at Albany, New York.

In April 1863, moreover, Mary Otey was the recipient of the following order: "You are hereby ordered, on account of having violated your parole, and attempting to smuggle contraband goods, to proceed to Point of Rocks, where you will be passed through the Federal lines, not to return under penalty of being treated as a spy. By order of Major General [Robert] Schenck." However, there was considerable disagreement as to whether the person who prepared this order was authorized to invoke Schenck's name in its issuance.

With these 1863 events as background, the complex events of 1864 may be clarified. Terry was charged with "lurking as a spy" around army facilities in Somerset County, Maryland, traveling back and forth from the Confederacy to Union territory without any authority for doing so, and attempting to send goods "of great value" to Virginia. The fourth and final charge was that of returning to Maryland after having been ordered to stay away. Numerous witnesses shed a fragmented light upon her 1864 travails. William H. Ryan, a Baltimore dry-goods merchant, who had known Terry for twelve years, was familiar with her personal history. He testified that she was born in Princeton, New Jersey, the daughter of a Dr. Stockton and a cousin of the well-known Commodore Robert Stockton. She was first married to a Mr. Terry, editor of the *Lynchburg Virginian*. Three years after he was killed in a street fight, she married Dexter Otey, an officer of Farmer's Bank in New York City. He proved to be an unfaithful husband, and she returned to Lynchburg, seeking a divorce. While this action was pending, Otey was killed in a barroom brawl. Ryan was certain that Mary Terry's only goal in visiting Maryland's Eastern Shore was to find a suitable location for her proposed school for young ladies. He concluded by telling the court, "She is as much of a lady as there is in the state of New Jersey or Virginia."[11]

William B. Horsey, 46, a resident of Seaford, Delaware, held in arrest as a witness, then told his story about Ryan and the defendant. Ryan had asked him to escort Terry and her two large trunks on the train trip to Seaford. Horsey suspected that her trunks held contraband and on arrival at

Seaford sent his twenty-one-year-old son, Edward, to her hotel room to gather evidence. She questioned the young man for thirty minutes, trying to see if he was a detective. When she felt assured of his reliability, she confessed to him that the destination for her trunks was Lynchburg and that she had no intention of opening a school. Edward declined her request to help smuggle the trunks south and reported her to a special agent, William Swiggert.

At the trial, Terry cross-examined young Horsey. "Did you become intimate with me right off?" "Not that I know of." "Did you make any strong profession of friendship to me?" "Not that I know of." "What business had you in my room?" "There was a colored servant who thought you were going to run the contraband business." "You get your information from a Negro, do you?" "Yes." A shadow fell over Edward Horsey's testimony when the Reverend Dr. McKelvey claimed (apparently without basis) that Horsey had made "improper advances" to Terry.

Special Agent Swiggett followed Horsey on the witness stand. He had gone to her hotel and had demanded to see the contents of her trunks. She opened them, and he saw enough to convince him that the items far exceeded her personal needs. "I told her I should have to hold them but she told me not to make a hasty decision and that they were not contraband. She said she wanted to see me . . . go into her room. She said she could not sleep any that night and wanted company and wanted me to be her companion and said she wanted to see me in her room," he testified. Swiggett also claimed that she had offered him sixty dollars if he would not arrest her.

Corporal Benjamin Paradiee, 32, of Smith's Independent Maryland Cavalry (Union), had spoken with Terry about her trunks. "She stated to me that her intention was not to go any further than Princess Ann herself, but these goods she intended for her children; As well as I recollect the place, it was Leesburg or Lynchburg, Virginia." The trial board might have had some doubts when they reviewed the material destined for "two small children": 43 yards of bleached muslin, 25 yards of white linen, 25 yards of black silk, 38 yards of fancy delaine (a high-grade worsted wool), 18 yards of drab silk, 24 yards of poplin, 84 yards of calico, 12 yards of cambric muslin, 28 yards of paper muslin, 14 pairs of shoes, 17 ladies' collars, 8 ladies' bonnets, and 135 other items. When confronted with this list, she told the court that she was only bringing her children "a few necessities."

The court noted, after reviewing the inventory of her two trunks, a total absence of educational materials. This seemed strange in view of her expressed intent of starting a school at Princess Anne. Nonetheless, her formal defense statement, prepared by her counsel, asserted that the only object of her travels was to begin a school at Princess Anne, so as not to be a burden on her friends and family.

Members of the military commission were not swayed by this argument, nor did they seem to doubt Swiggett's claim that she had tried to seduce him. They acquitted her of spying and lurking, but convicted her of traveling between the Confederacy and the United States and violating her banishment order. She was sentenced to "take the Oath of Allegiance and give a strict parole of honor, and be sent north of the southerly state line of New Jersey." If she refused these conditions, she was to go to the "female prison at Fitchburg."

This decision came to General Lew Wallace, and it provoked outpouring of sarcasm rarely seen in military records. As Wallace wrote:

> In this case of Mary S. Terry, alias Mary S. Otey, the commission finds the accused "guilty" of coming within the lines of the armies of the United States without proper authority, therefore, but without criminal intent; "guilty" of the attempt to send goods from within the states of Delaware and Maryland to persons within the state of Virginia and parts thereof occupied by the armies of the so-called Confederate States, at war with the United States; "guilty" of intercourse by travel between the states in insurrection and the United States; "guilty" of coming within the lines of the United States contrary to the order of the general commanding the Middle Department, all of which demonstrate the accused to be an intelligent, bold, defiant, energetic, masculine Rebel, bent on mischief, and able to accomplish any measure of it according to opportunity.
>
> The record shows that the commission maturely deliberated upon the testimony, but did it deliberate as carefully upon the sentence? "And the commission do therefore sentence her, the said Mary S. Terry, alias

Mary S. Otey, to take the Oath of Allegiance and give strict parole of honor, and be sent north of the southerly line of New Jersey," . . . et cetera, et cetera. *Parole of honor!!!* "Honor"—found guilty as above-specified, who can give faith to the honor of such an unsexed merchant, traveling through the lines of armies and driving a contraband traffic in the face of orders, for the benefit of an ungodly rebellion.

To take the Oath of Allegiance! The commanding general is aware that one of the most difficult problems of the war, one to which probably quite as much thought has been given as to any other connected with the administration of border departments, has been to find a punishment proper for, and at the same time adequate to, the crimes of female rebels and felons. He begs the Commission to be assured that he appreciates their labors in this great solution not less than the solution itself. The conception is startlingly original. Its simplicity will be the wonder of Commissions past and the admiration of those to come. The astonishing feature of the invention is that the loyal people of the United States have all along misunderstood the Oath of Allegiance. To them, it has been a solemn obligation, precious in estimation, to be sacredly observed, honorable in the taking, and elevating to the taker. Suddenly, but at the end of three years of the war, it is ascertained to be a dishonor, fit for convicted traitors, a punishment alternative to degrading imprisonment, an infamizing act, therefore a proper element in an infamizing sentence for infamous crimes.

The commanding general cannot believe the Commission [is] serious in the infliction of such a judgment. What would be said of the criminal judge who should sentence a convicted thief to go to church on the next Sunday, or—if it pleased him, the convict, better—to go to prison? The finding is therefore disapproved, and returned to the commission, with the suggestion that if they really believe this woman guilty it would be more consistent for them to punish her according to the offense.

The presumably chastened commission reconsidered their verdict and issued the decision: "To be confined in the Female Prison at Salem, Massachusetts, or at such other place as the commanding general may direct, for the term of one year from the 21st day of March, 1864, the date of her arrest, then to be released upon giving her parole of honor not to go south . . . during the war."

Once again, however, Terry's story was not over. Lieutenant Morris Skinner of the 131st Ohio was assigned to escort her to Salem, which he did, only to find that there was no female prison there. Back they went to Baltimore, where she was resentenced, this time to Fitchburg. Escorted a second time by the same lieutenant, she finally arrived at her prison on July 6, 1864. Skinner filed a detailed expense account for the trip; the total was $18.55.

While General Wallace might well have had cause for alarm that Terry might corner the fabric market in Lynchburg, a far greater and much more immediate threat to the success of the Union war effort was literally in the hands of Sallie Pollock. The time was early 1864. Lincoln had found a general. In the eastern theater, McClellan, Burnside, and Hooker had all failed. The new commander was Ulysses S. Grant, whose history of success along the Mississippi River could hardly have escaped the notice of Robert E. Lee. What would Grant do in Virginia, where so many other Yankee commanders had come to grief?

Fortunately for the Confederacy, Robert E. Lee often knew of Grant's plans within a few days of their formulation. Lee worked three military miracles in a single month, shattering Union attacks in Virginia at the Wilderness, Spotsylvania, and Cold Harbor. Lee's defensive placements were unerringly accurate, his counterstrokes equally so. This was due in large part to his extensive spy network, which began in Washington, D.C., and ran all through Virginia. Good espionage agents and couriers remained invisible during the war and rarely wrote their memoirs afterwards; although much remains unknown, the slender surviving evidence points strongly to a first-class network of highly efficient secret agents.

Grant became commander-in-chief in early March 1864. Under strict security, he quickly formulated his grand strategy for the coming spring campaign. Less than two weeks later, Confederate agents in Baltimore prepared a report describing Grant's plan. In a document signed "Pro Bono Publico" and dated March 24, 1864, the anonymous espionage agent(s) wrote:

The Army of the Potomac will be under the immediate command of Major Gen'l Grant—when the grand movement is made—they will move upon Richmond in three columns, one from North Carolina under Butler—one from East Tennessee commanded by Hooker—the Potomac Army will advance by way of Gordonsville. This information is reliable to a fault, the Army of the Potomac will number one hundred thousand men—the Army of North Carolina will number seventy five thousand—the Army of Tennessee will number eighty thousand—all details will be forwarded soon.

Two copies of this report were prepared by the Confederate agent(s), one addressed to Jefferson Davis and the other to Robert E. Lee. (Although Hooker's men were sent to join William T. Sherman rather than Grant and Meade, as a preliminary picture of a grand strategic scheme this report was remarkably accurate.)[12]

Sallie Pollock, 17, carried this vital information—which never got to Davis or Lee, because she was discovered and arrested by Union authorities in the course of her journey. She was charged with violating the laws of war, and specifically with carrying mail to the Confederate lines near Cumberland, Maryland. The story of her capture shows that while the Confederacy had an excellent intelligence operation, Union counterintelligence also displayed some skill.

In her many previous trips across the Potomac River, Sallie had been stopped twice and had either concealed her southbound letters or had sweet-talked her way out of any serious search. Her previous escapes and youthful optimism might have diminished her sense of caution. James Morgan, the assistant postmaster at Cumberland, told the court: "I've known her for two years. She receives about six letters a day, many more than other young ladies. Also, she told me she had received many letters from the south."

Love may have been a contributing factor in Sallie's downfall. One of the letters found in her possession was addressed to her from Baltimore, signed "Your affectionate cousin, J. Clift Galbraith." In his letter to "Coz. Sallie," Galbraith raised a caution about romance: "Glad to hear you have been enjoying yourself so much with the assistance of Mr. Hough—hope you have not fallen as deeply in love with him as the river runs where you forded it. Depth of affection might suggest deep rivers and deep rivers sometimes drown people." Hough, it appears, had led Sallie into deep waters indeed. U.S. Secret Service agent Ira Cole had been approached by Federal detective Michael Graham about a possible Rebel, a Mr. Hough. Cole and Graham both met with Hough and presented themselves as Confederate sympathizers. In a few minutes, Hough, a paroled Confederate cavalryman, was convinced by the tale told by the two Federal detectives, and he offered details about Sallie's courier service. The next day Graham quietly followed Sallie on her "visiting" rounds, which were far busier than most seventeen-year olds'. Cole asked Hough to arrange a meeting with Sallie, and Hough did so, assuring Sallie that Cole could be trusted. At the meeting, Cole warned Sallie that Federal agents might be closing in on her and offered to burn any letters she might be carrying. Grateful for this warning, she revealed a cornucopia of correspondence that had been hidden in her bosom, her pockets, and under her dress. Cole then arrested her. She confessed that she had been carrying mail across the river since she was fourteen years old and asked to be treated "as a lady."

Among the many letters hidden about Sallie's person was one to Jacob Gassman from "Belle" of Cumberland. The envelope had the printed return address of a Cumberland hotel, near the railroad depot. In the letter, Belle tells Gassman, "General Sigle [sic] is boarding with us, has number 60," and later reveals her pro-Confederate sentiments: "We have a fine little boy, ten months old. His name is Lee. I hope he may be as great as the man he is named after." It would indeed have been a major stroke for the Confederacy if Major General Franz Sigel had been captured from Room 60 of a Cumberland hotel.

At her trial, in April 1864, Sallie pled not guilty but entered no testimony in her own defense. She was found guilty and sentenced to be imprisoned until the end of the war at the Pennsylvania State Penitentiary at Pittsburgh. Although behind bars, she was not devoid of supporters. Within weeks, her friends opened a campaign to free her. Major Abram W. Hendricks, Union paymaster, and Major W. W. Dunn, judge advocate of the Department of the Ohio, wrote to the War Department on Sallie's behalf, citing her youth ("she was a bright sunshiny child") and noting that she was "a person of high social standing," with many wealthy relatives in Pennsylvania and Indiana. Her uncle, a Mr. Moorhead, also urged pardon, citing her "delicate health" and promising that he would take her into his Pennsylvania household and "give any security that might be required."

Secretary of War Edwin W. Stanton referred these appeals to Judge Advocate General Joseph Holt, who was violently opposed to her release. He dismissed the concerns about her health, suggesting that anyone who could repeatedly ford the Potomac River in winter and ride long distances while wet and cold, over a period of three years, was probably not overly delicate. But he reserved his sharpest criticism for her attempted conveyance to the Confederacy of the entire Union plan for the spring campaign. He raised the specter of Union soldiers killed by the accurate information carried by the highly efficient Confederate spy network. He then turned to the problem of women spies: "The accused is one of a class of persons whose very sex and apparent guilelessness enable them to carry on a system of communication between our lines and those of the enemy, and in many cases almost with impunity. Protected by their womanly character, they readily pass to and fro." Holt concluded, "The interests of the service . . . urgently require . . . that she should be restrained from renewing her disloyal practices."

But Sallie Pollock was not doomed to prison for years to come. In her case, the bonds of family loyalty and social class seem to have transcended the opinion of Lincoln's highest legal adviser. On May 25, 1864, Holt had urged her continued incarceration. Just ten days later, a telegram from Secretary of War Stanton to the provost marshal at Pittsburgh ordered that she be released from custody if she would promise not to carry any more information to the Confederacy. Including her time awaiting trial, Sallie was confined a total of seven weeks, a remarkably light punishment for a crime that could have carried the death penalty. Perhaps the same mixture of youthful charm and personal bravery that enabled this native of Allegheny County, Maryland, to serve her beloved South also saved her from the hangman's noose.

A long peninsula of Maryland territory stretches south from Washington, D.C., bounded on one side by the Potomac River and on the other by the Chesapeake Bay. At the extreme southerly tip is Point Lookout, site of the infamous Civil War prisoner-of-war camp. Twenty-five miles northwest of the point, on Breton Bay, is the old port of Leonardtown. There, in April 1864, Mary Elizabeth Gilbee was arrested and charged with smuggling letters to the Confederacy. She was also charged with having smuggled a large quantity of goods from the north to the Confederacy by way of Nassau in 1863. On April 16, 1864, two weeks after her arrest, she was interrogated at Fortress Monroe, Virginia. The setting was one of the country's most imposing and formidable brick forts, bristling with cannon and home to many famous generals. Yet she was anything but intimidated by this setting, as the record of her interrogation reveals:

"Where have you been living, Miss Gilbee?"

"For the last 18 years, I have been living in Georgia. I have been a governess in a family there. Last October, I came to the north to visit my mother, who was living in Baltimore."

"How did you come through?"

"It is not fair for you to ask me such a question. I ran the blockade, of course. I was intending to go back to Georgia to my friends."

"Why did you try to carry letters and information through the lines?"

"I did not try to carry any information through. I would not do it. I have too many friends in the United States."

"You were carrying goods through, such as shoes, dresses, letters, stationery, et cetera."

"They were only my own personal goods. I would not do such a disreputable thing. Look at me now (she stood up) and see if you think I am such a disreputable person. I have a great many friends at the north. I can show you a letter I have to Mr. [Secretary of State William] Seward."

"You and Miss Davidson were going to go south together?"

"We have nothing to do with each other. I met her in Baltimore and made her acquaintance only the day before I came to Leonardtown."

"There was a carpetbag belonging to one of you containing a letter. Was it yours?"

"No, sir, it was not mine."

"Who wrote this letter addressed to Mrs. Namine?"

"I am not going to tell you!"

"This letter says, 'Allow me, my dear friend, to make you acquainted with a lady whom you must have heard me mention with affection, et cetera. She will tell you of us here and if she does not start too soon I hope to send you a photograph of a dear relative of yours. If it is not ready in time, the lady will make a third effort to get it to you. This dear relation had a message from "Number One" which gave her good news of you all a month later than her latest letters. Do not mention having received this either at home or in writing. Let me say that a young friend of ours came here from being greatly needed and just in time. It is now never to be mentioned where he is, but you will understand and excuse. Necessity knows no law, you know. Godmother keeps well. I heard from her today.'" [Here she digressed upon a photograph found in the records.]

"Now, then, you brought this letter through, did you not?"

"No, sir. Let me see all those letters, won't you, and I will tell you what I brought through."

"One thing at a time, Miss Gilbee. I want to know if that is not a letter which you took to carry through the lines."

"Yes, sir, it is. I don't know, though, as it is. No, sir, it is not. Yes, sir, it is."

"Well, you have told me three or four different stories about that letter. Now I want to know whether you did not take that letter through the lines."

"Yes, sir, I did."

"Well, here is one which I will mark No. 2, evidently from the same person. Who wrote that?"

"I won't tell you!"

"This one speaks of 'L.' and hopes he may get here to see his mother. Who is 'L.'?"

"I don't know who 'L.' is."

"Who is 'Mrs. J.' that is spoken of also?"

"I am not going to explain these things."

"I know you know. The writers of these letters say that you know her and her family."

"So, I do know her and her family, but I am not going to tell you."

"Well, who wrote this letter (No. 2)?"

"Don't you see it is the same person?"

"That is not answering me. I ask you again who wrote this letter."

"The same person that wrote the other!"

"Where were they going to?"

"To Richmond—I hope they will get there yet."

"Well, they are not very likely to. Who were they going to in Richmond?"

"That's the question."

"Well, that was the question I asked. Who were they going to?"

"That is not a question I will answer."

"Who are 'G.' and 'E.'?"

"I will not tell. That might lead to a desperate clue."

"Who is M. W.?"

"Mary Whittingham, that's all I will tell you." [Here she was asked about smuggling through Bermuda, which she answered with another uninformative digression.]

"Here is a letter signed 'L.' and she says, 'I hope you have forgiven me for ever having a Union sentiment. I am the greatest little "Reb" you ever saw.' Who wrote this letter?"

"Her name is Lee, but no relative to the general. [She repeated this five times and requested that the stenographer put it in.] I believe you are trying to get me hung. I don't see what you ask me such questions for."

"Where does Mrs. Lee live?"

"I don't know. She was in a boarding house."

"What boarding house?"

"I don't know. I think she was going to move."

"Where was she when you saw her last?"

"She was in Maryland."

"Miss Gilbee, is that a proper answer? I read you the letter, which was dated Baltimore. Don't you suppose that I know that Baltimore is in Maryland?" [Here the interrogator asked which street.]

"Perhaps it was in Baltimore Street."

"Now, Miss Gilbee, you know it was not in Baltimore Street, for this very letter twice says, 'My address is 75 North Charles Street, care of Mrs. Gwinn.'"

"What a fool that woman was to write that in a letter. She was a goose!" [Here she digressed again, this time musing on "a handsome young lady."]

"Here is a letter directed to Mrs. Archibald Gracie, Mobile, Alabama, and it is signed 'E. D. Gracie.' Where did that come from?"

"It came from Baltimore."

"You know better, Miss Gilbee, it is dated New York."

"Well, I ain't going to tell you anything about it."

"Miss Gilbee, allow me to give you a little advice. You are laughing and trying to deceive me in all these matters. I think you will find out before you have finished that this is a serious matter, and that you must not trifle with the matter in the manner you have been doing. Here are three letters from some members of Mr. Charles King's family, of Columbia College, New York."[13]

"How do you know?"

"Why, I am a New Yorker and I know Charles King well enough."

"Do you know him and his family? If you do, you see you and I know the same persons and I know you cannot be severe upon me. Then, you know that he is one of your party. He [King] is a Black Republican." [Here followed several more fruitless exchanges.]

"Why don't you say at once then that you won't tell?"

"I am more polite than to say that."

"You did say it at the beginning of this interview."

"I have got softened down a little bit."[14]

Although Gilbee did her best to provide no information to her New York interrogator, her ledger book was far more revealing. A typical page in this thick volume speaks for itself. She carried $695 in gold. Her spending included passage to Nassau, $90; hotel expenses, $28; soap, $61; Irish linen cloth brilliant, $111.38; Bishop's Lawn Parasols, $35; quinine, $4; gossamer silk ribbon, $3.26; one trunk, $6.50; transportation of the above, $7. Another entry, headed "Two hundred dollars in greenbacks," lists "dresses and dressmaking, $186.70, corset, laces and darning cotton, $10.68, hoop skirt, $2.62." These luxury goods, worth at least $18,000 in today's money, were almost certainly contraband, being smuggled into the Confederacy at great profit. And this was only one set of transactions out of many. It would appear that there were still customers in the South willing and able to pay very high prices for luxuries, and daring souls willing to run the blockade to serve this market. On this trip, however, Gilbee was fortunate to have with her only her own clothes. Her counsel pointed out this absence of smuggled goods, adding his thoughts on her personal life. He had known her for twenty-five years, eighteen of which she had lived in Georgia with the family of James Potter, a brother-in-law of Commodore Robert F. Stockton.

In spite of Gilbee's bravado, even impudence, during her interrogation, a slip of paper found in her trunk suggests that she had inner anxieties that she kept from the world. The paper lists two medicines bought from Caswell, Mack and Company, Fifth Avenue and 24th Street, New York. The first was "valerianten of ammonia, one teaspoon per dose, for headache and nervousness." (Valerian root has long been used for hypochondriasis and as a nerve tonic.) The second was a "neuralgic liniment," made of two drams of chloroform, one dram of tincture of aconite root, and sufficient camphorated soap liniment to bring the volume up to two ounces. Today's equivalent might be Valium and Ben-Gay.

Did Gilbee's adventures aid the Confederacy? The answer seems to be "yes." She had provided morale-building comforts and mail to an isolated Confederacy. She had occupied the time of Brigadier General Charles Devens (president of the military commission, who was recovering from two bullet wounds) and three other officers. She had cost the United States the expenses of holding her for five months before her trial, and she had infuriated her interrogator, another small blow against the North in a war of attrition. (Surprisingly, her claimed British citizenship, found in her many papers, was not raised as an issue.) The court convicted her and levied a fine of $500, being "lenient" because her letters were "of a private nature" and the clothes that she had with her were for her own use.

Two more Maryland smugglers diverted Union officers from their other duties. The case of Clara Howard could engage a regiment of detectives, a brigade of historians, and a division of genealogists. It is a tangled tale of duplicity and perjury, in which an inventive Baltimore socialite led the Yankees on a merry chase. It is also a story of two women of elite society, cousins, each held hostage for the other.[15]

Clara, 26, was Mrs. William Key Howard, whose husband was in the Fourth Virginia Cavalry and the First Maryland Infantry, fighting for the Confederacy. Her cousin was Mrs. Patterson Allen of Ohio, an outspoken Union supporter, then being held by the Confederate authorities. In March 1863, Clara was charged with running the blockade, carrying letters into the Confederacy, and avoiding registering with the Union authorities. She was arrested with many letters in her possession, correspondence that reflects a passionate family-wide devotion to the southern cause. A letter from Clara's brother, Arthur Randolph, a student in Brunswick, Germany, began by insisting that if Jefferson Davis and Winfield Scott were both field commanders, Davis would whip Scott, and he expanded upon the theme that all Randolphs were "born soldiers." Then he informed his sister of his difficulty in getting travel papers at the American consulate in London: "We went there and after a great deal of humbug and my being made to swear that I would protect the Constitution of the United States (an oath I have been making all possible haste to forget) I got the troublesome thing, which I never needed, as nobody ever asked me for it." From the consulate, he walked a mile back to his hotel at dusk and was lost only once. "I take great credit to myself for that, as it isn't the easiest thing in the world to find one's way in London," he bragged. Later, he described taking pride in undertipping the porter who moved his heavy trunk onto the steamer for Hamburg. He also wrote of his four college roommates: one was "half crazy," a second had a "weak mind," a third was "a conceited ass," while the fourth was "an ignorant fool." At the time of the letter, Randolph had already beaten roommate number four with his cane and was planning to "thrash" roommate number three.

Another letter, from "Anna," one of Clara's close friends, gives us a glimpse into the drawing rooms of Baltimore's upper classes: "[I] do get so provoked with the Union people that I feel as if I never wanted to see or speak to one again. Today, we had an animated talk about the 'niggers,' which subject always makes me mad. I said the people here considered the blacks on an equality, and if so, ought to treat them as such, marry them, visit them, et cetera, et cetera, which provoked my opponents highly, and they said they did not consider them equal and so on, one thing led to another until we got excited, but I say exactly what I think of their party."

A long Union intelligence report about Clara Howard reveals that the Howards were a violently secessionist family. In April 1861, Clara and her husband went south; she secreted his pistols under her skirts. In early spring 1863, she came north, escorted to Point of Rocks by Fitzhugh Lee (probably Robert E. Lee's nephew). There she was stopped by "Colonel Schley" (probably William L. Schley, Fifth Maryland, Union). Schley let her proceed to Baltimore after she promised to register with the authorities upon her arrival. She eluded the officers sent to escort her and registered at Barnum's Hotel as "Mrs. Randolph." She continued to escape arrest, moving every few days, often as "Mrs. Ogden." As her pursuers grew closer, she spent time in Elizabethtown, New Jersey; in autumn 1863, she went to St. Louis, Missouri, where she stayed until April 1864, when she returned to Baltimore. Again, she failed to register. This time she was soon arrested and sent to Old Capitol Prison in Washington, D.C. As General Lew Wallace wrote to Assistant Adjutant General E. D. Townsend on April 28, 1864:

Today I send up to Old Capitol Prison a certain Mrs. Howard, a troublesome "lady" in the day of General Schenck and now arrested with letters in her trunk for certain parties in Richmond, Virginia. I have to suggest that Mrs. Allen, a Union woman from Ohio, has been subjected to the most atrocious barbarities by the Rebel authorities. She is reported as insane from her great suffering and now a patient in some kind of a nunnery. As Mrs. Howard holds a high social position and has a husband in the Rebel army, it has occurred to me that she could be used to bring about the exchange of Mrs. Allen, for whom she might be in the meantime held as a hostage.

This shocking suggestion of women as hostages was followed six days later, on May 3, by another letter from Wallace:

> Further information about her [Clara Howard] convinces me of her complicity in many transactions in the way of giving information to the enemy, smuggling goods, conveying mails, et cetera. I do not know what amount of proof may be obtained, but I have instructed certain parties to submit all their knowledge of her acts to me in writing— When received I will forward it to you. I think one thing can be accomplished by keeping her in close custody and that is the release of Mrs. Patterson Allen. . . . Mrs. Allen is a near relative to Mrs. Howard. . . . Mrs. Allen is known to be a strong Unionist and for that reason mainly was incarcerated in the southern prison . . . a strong effort is being made by the friends of Mrs. Howard to obtain her release.

One of these friends was D. S. Turner of St. Louis, who wrote Wallace in late May: "Mrs. Howard is a near connexion of my wife's family and has been residing in St. Louis for several months past with her uncle (my brother-in-law). . . . My belief is that the attention of the authorities . . . has been drawn toward Mrs. Howard by communications from Mrs. Patterson Allen of Richmond, induced by the unfriendly relations known to exist between the two ladies."

On June 7, General Wallace wrote to Colonel John Foster, the judge advocate. Wallace described the difficulty in finding persons to testify against Clara Howard, since most of the likely witnesses were secessionists, her relatives, or both. A month went by. The trial was delayed because two women in New York City who had promised to testify could not be found. Clara's uncle, Henry L. Patterson, wrote to President Lincoln, claiming that she had been in St. Louis all the time from September 1863 to April 1864. He pressed Lincoln further: "My daughter a few days since had a conversation with you on this subject, which was terminated by you telling her that 'If Walter Davis [identity unknown] would send me a written request thereto, I would cause her release immediately.' My daughter went to Stanton, who claimed to know nothing of the case, but I have been told he knew of it weeks ago." Patterson cited his own opposition to secession, gave as his references Postmaster General Montgomery Blair and General Ethan Hitchcock, and ended with this plea: "For God's sake, sir, put an end to such proceedings." Lincoln passed the letter to his private secretary, John Hay, with orders to send it to Stanton. Stanton passed it on to Judge Advocate Foster, who replied on July 23, "The trial was concluded today."

Howard was convicted and sentenced to spend the rest of the war in a military prison, "laboring for the benefit of United States soldiers." Some of the pretrial evidence, given by women who refused to appear as witnesses, strongly suggested that she traveled extensively, even when she was supposedly in St. Louis, and that she was very likely a member of the highly effective, and equally invisible, network of spies and couriers.

The trial records of another letter-smuggler, Mary E. Sawyer, are a veritable gold mine of southern sentiment, because filed with all the usual charges and witnesses' statements are three handwritten poems. And Sawyer's aesthetic interests ranged beyond the literary. Not every Baltimore woman had in her parlor the pictures of forty-eight Confederate generals, but Mary Sawyer did.[16]

This dutiful thirty-four-year-old wife said good-bye to her husband in April 1861, when he went off to join the Confederate army, but in spite of the blockade she managed to exchange over a dozen letters with him. Her war came to an end in 1864, when her case was reviewed twice by Abraham Lincoln and she was passed on to the jurisdiction of General Ben Butler.

Sawyer was charged in June 1864, with "violation of the laws of war," specifically of smuggling letters to the Confederacy from Baltimore. Among the witnesses was Mary's sister, Amanda Dungan, who described a visit by a Mrs. Brill, a Confederate courier: "Mrs. Brill had a pass signed by [Confederate] General [John] Winder at Richmond. I thought Mrs. Brill might be a spy, but I didn't know for which side and I felt contempt for her." The judge advocate, who had read the letters seized in Mary Sawyer's home, said they contained "information of the most treasonable character." Sawyer countered, "The letters contain no state secrets but are of a purely domestic nature." Given that one of her letters included the assertion, "The secessionists here expect to have Lee and Beauregard visit Baltimore this summer, making the north feel some of the injuries they have inflicted on the south," her prosecutors doubtless believed otherwise.

Other witnesses added that Mary Sawyer's husband, Leonard, was not in the Confederate army but was "an agent of [a freight company] the Southern Express." Perhaps this occupation was a cover for numerous travels and servicing of an undercover courier network. In the absence of extant records, however, such an idea must remain a speculation.

Sawyer ended her defense statement with these ringing words of defiance: "My sympathies are now and ever have been with the south. I will not take the Oath of Allegiance to the United States." These bold assertions, seen in the records of so many southern women, are of great interest, but the three poems found among Sawyer's papers make hers a truly unique court record. The first poem, a handwritten document, is "respectfully dedicated to the true-hearted, brave and patriotic Southern girls of the Monumental City," as Baltimore was known:

> Daughters of the Sunny South,
>> Where freedom loves to dwell,
> How rare your charms, how sweet your smiles,
>> No mortal lips can tell.
> Your native hills, the rippling rills,
>> The echo wild and free,
> Declare you born to hate and scorn
>> All Northern tyranny.
> Girls whose smiles are all reserved,
>> The Southern youth to bless,
> Whose hearts are kept for those who fight
>> For Freedom—Happiness.
> Your spirits bold, so now unfold
>> What you would willing do
> Were Yankee spite, the tyrants might
>> Not wielded against you.
> For you your loving brothers rush
>> To o'erthrow the invaders might.
> On martial field, the sword they wield,
>> And Yankee cowards strike.
> "May Heaven bless, with bright success,

Each glorious Southern Son,"
Be this your prayer, O maiden fair,
    And our freedom will be won.
Southern Girls! Ere this we're sworn,
    The South must—shall be free!
No Northern shackles will be worn.
    To them we'll bend no knee.
From hill to hill, exultant, shrill,
    Our battle cry rings forth:
"Freedom or Death" 's on every breath,
    And hatred to the North.
Cease not to smile, brave Southern girls,
    On all our efforts to be free;
Whilst life remains we'll struggle on,
    'Til all the world shall see
That those who fight for home and right
    Can never be enslaved—
Their blood may stain the battle plain—
    Their country must be saved.

A handwritten poem called "The Southern Cross" was another unusual item found in Mary Sawyer's papers. Also published as sheet music during the war, the poem's phrasing strongly suggests that it was intended to be sung to the tune of "The Star Spangled Banner":

Oh, say can you see through the gloom and the storm,
More bright for the darkness, that pure constellation,
Like the symbol of love and redemption its form,
As it points to the haven of hope for the nation.
How radiant each star, as the beacon afar,
Giving promise of peace, or assurance in war!
'Tis the *Cross of the South*, which shall ever remain
To light us to freedom and glory again!
    How peaceful and blest was America's soil.
'Til betrayed by the guile of the Puritan demon,

Which lurks under virtue, and springs from its coil.
To fasten its fangs in the life blood of freemen.
Then boldly appeal to each heart that can feel,
And crush the foul viper 'neath Liberty's heel!
And the *Cross of the South* shall in triumph remain,
To light us to freedom and glory again!
    'Tis the emblem of peace, 'tis the day star of hope,
Like the sacred *Labarum* [banner] that guided the Roman,
From the shore of the Gulf to the Delaware's slope,
'Tis the trust of the free and the terror of foemen.
Fling its folds to the air, while we boldly declare
The rights we demand or the deeds that we dare!
While the Cross of the South shall in triumph remain
To light us to freedom and glory again!

The third poem centers around a Union general, Robert C. Schenck, now mostly forgotten, who commanded the Middle Department and the Eighth Army Corps at Baltimore from September 1862 to December 1863, and his subordinate, Colonel William Fish. After his fifteen months in Baltimore, Schenck served twenty-four years in the U.S. Congress and was U.S. ambassador to Brazil and to the Court of St. James; during the Civil War, he had had his right wrist shattered by a musket ball at Second Manassas while he was commanding the First Division of Sigel's Corps. The permanent pain and stiffening that followed this injury must have made the writing of his best-known book, the definitive text on draw poker, a difficult process. Indeed, the great volume of paperwork incumbent upon him as an administrator probably made every memo and edict a moment of physical suffering. To the Dixie bard who penned these lines (which seem to fit the tune of "When Johnny Comes Marching Home"), however, the Union general was an unalloyed tyrant:

Brave Schenk was walking out one day to view his frowning fort,
Whilst through the hero's brain there poured an avalanche of thought.
He viewed the distant city and he saw the mighty main,
And gazed with pride and pleasure, upon his wide domain.

He looked upon the Heavens & the Earth spread far away,
And exclaimed, "I am the Monarch of all that I survey."
Then he called unto his servant, ever faithful to his will,
A yellow-headed Yankee came, his mandate to fulfil;
With many a low obeisance and scraping of the feet,
He approached his regal Master, whom he well knew how to greet.
Sergeant, look around you and see every living thing,
And tell me if in power, I am not greater than a king.
Yes, indeed, brave General, replied the willing tool,
As sure as worthless Shoddy has taken the place of Wool.
I know I have the power and I'll make this people feel
What a most unpleasant burden is a Yankee soldier's heel.
Yes, I will teach these Christians when to God they bend one knee,
The other bends devoutly in homage unto me.
But if they don't obey me, I'll teach the erring fool,
That I must have obeisance or adopt an ancient rule;
For the Scriptures say that Tobit a fish once brought to light,
Whose liver being roasted restored the blind to sight.
I have a Fish within this fort, a regular Yankee Cod,
Who'll teach my doctrine soundly with aristocratic rod.
Then rising like grim Neptune, he calls his favorite fish,
Who, faithful to his Master's will is present at his wish.
Great Fish, I have an idea, a thought that's all my own,
Invented by my turning brain, whilst I was all alone;
You see these Christian people on Sunday bend the knee,
And think more of Almighty God, than e'er they do of me.
So go into that city, straight to the Central Church,
For there I'll have my banner wave, my standard there shall perch,
And if you have a rocky time, give signals with a drum,
And the whaling I'll give Baltimore will make secession hum.
Should they refuse to place the flag themselves upon their hall
Do you "Scale up" my noble Fish and place in on the wall.
Brave Fish then bowed obeisance and "floundered" from the room
and gathered up his followers by signal from the drum.

On the following Sunday morning, a minister of God
Approached his holy temple to read his sacred word;
And then he spied great Fish's work—unhallowed decoration—
So he took it and subjected it to gospel dispensation.
But for this, he did not seem to know the dreadful penalty,
Invoked by such an insult to the *mighty powers that be*.
Poor man, he little knew he'd be served up as a dish,
To satisfy the appetite of an offended *fish*.
But so it was, and very soon the pompous Major brought
A pressing invitation for a visit to the fort.
And then they told the minister, whose error was to think
That the God of Heaven reigned supreme instead of Genl. Schenck.
Now sir, own that you were ignorant, and on your Bible swear
To own no God but *Abraham* and my allegiance bear,
And if you will not do this, but disobey my wish,
I cast you off like Jonah to the mercy of my *Fish*.
The Minister plead ignorance to such a law divine,
But soon became persuaded, a short parole to sign.
Thus the matter ended, and as for General Schenck
His virtuous indignation subsided with a *drink*.
Moral
Ye clergymen of Baltimore whilst yet ye pray at all,
Pay a little more attention to Salvation temporal,
Your churches are unholy unless dressed in a flag
And your Savior's Cross unholy unless it bears a rag,
For a voice from Fort McHenry declares your creed extinct,
And substitutes for Trinity, Abe Lincoln, Flag, and Schenck.
Now go and kneel devoutly to the General's earnest wish,
Or else be slightly troubled by the presence of a Fish.

Mary Sawyer was convicted and sent to "labor for the benefit of Union soldiers" at Fitchburg Female Prison, a sentence reviewed by President Lincoln, who approved her sentence on July 9, 1864. On July 30, not content with her fate, Sawyer wrote a personal appeal to Lincoln:

I, Mary Sawyer, of Baltimore, Md., was married to Leonard Sawyer of Boston, Mass., in 1854. In 1861 my husband seeking employment as clerk, visited Charleston S.C. where he became and still remains in the employ of an express company. Not having heard from him since 1862, altho having frequently written through the medium of the flag of truce, some four months ago I was called upon by a female, who stated that she was from the South, was about returning, and desired to know whether I wished to send any letters to my husband. I was glad to have an opportunity to write to my dear husband and wrote a letter. At the same time this lady remarked that if I knew of any others that desire to send letters she would take them. At the time appointed she received my letter also the others. To my surprise this lady was a detective. I am informed that I am sentenced to Fitchburg, Mass., for and during the war. My health is at present exceedingly delicate having been imprisoned for three months past. I respectfully request your Excellency to extend the executive clemency. I have never knowingly committed any act detrimental to the interests of the government, and am willing to sign any parole to reside North during the war.

Two days later, Lincoln wrote, "What are the facts of this case?" Assistant Secretary of War Charles A. Dana replied, "It is deemed advisable that the prisoner instead of being confined at hard labor . . . should be remitted to the custody of Major General [Ben] Butler, commanding the District of Virginia and North Carolina, to be transported within the Rebel lines on the first suitable occasion." Perhaps Sawyer was soon reunited with her husband. During his absence she seems to have formed part of a pro-Confederate group, which through images, song, poetry, and correspondence kept southern sentiment alive in Union-occupied Baltimore.

Not every female Baltimore defendant belonged to the elite. Ann Kilbaugh, who supported herself as a washerwoman, was charged with viewing a parade of Union soldiers and remarking that the men were "nothing but black Republican nigger-worshippers." She was also charged with helping a Union soldier to desert. At her trial, the first witness was Mary C. Windle of 30 Amity Street, who testified, "I heard her say that before she would take the oath to the rotten Negro government she would rot in jail.

. . . I am a Union lady. I would like to see the Union kept together and never dissolved and the flag of our country always float over us." Windle recounted being at Kilbaugh's house on February 1, 1864, where she met a soldier from the "Third Union Cavalry," who was about to travel south. Three days later, Kilbaugh told her, "My son is safe in Dixey." Windle's son, Edward, then told the court, "I served with Captain Pettebridge last July and was injured. [Union records show no such captain.] He vividly remembered arriving home after his wounding and hearing Ann Kilbaugh remark, 'It's a pity you weren't killed.'"[17]

Kilbaugh called four defense witnesses. Constable Charles Davis had known Kilbaugh twenty years. He described her as an honest and industrious woman who supported herself and her children by washing and scrubbing. He had arrested Windle and her son at Kilbaugh's request, but he knew nothing of the case. Thirty-year-old justice of the peace Charles Meredith said it was a quarrel among neighbors and that Kilbaugh had asked for a peace warrant. Police Sergeant Charles Handy knew only that Kilbaugh was a poor woman and had complained that Windle had "hallooed" at her. On cross-examination, Kilbaugh asked the sergeant, "Have I seemed to be offensive to the neighborhood?" His reply: "No more so than the others . . . this is kind of a neighborhood spree."

The final defense witness was Kilbaugh's own daughter, Mary, 19, a dressmaker. She denied that her mother had ever helped a soldier to desert and asserted that the real problem was rowdy children on her mother's porch. The judge advocate asked Mary if she "professed to be an unconditional Union lady?" She firmly replied, "No, I do not. I have brothers in the Confederate Army."

The court sentenced Ann Kilbaugh to six months of hard labor. But General Lew Wallace thought this too harsh, writing, "In view of all the circumstances of this case, and the character and position of the accused, the commanding general thinks proper to mitigate the sentence into imprisonment . . . for 30 days."

Carri Weaver and her two grown daughters, Susan and Annie, all from Maryland, found that their southern sympathies led to their being deported. It all began with an attempt to buy railroad tickets from Martinsburg, West Virginia, to Wheeling, West Virginia. To buy a ticket, you needed a pass. To get a pass, you needed to take the oath of allegiance and have your baggage examined.[18]

Lieutenant David Miller of the 123rd Ohio was in charge of administering the oath of allegiance. At first, Susan refused to take the oath, saying that she was from Maryland, "a loyal state," so there was no necessity of an oath. Lieutenant Miller disagreed. Finally, Susan raised her hand and the clerk read the oath, but when it came time for her response, she lowered her hand and said, "I will not do it." The situation escalated. Captain William Walker of the 13th Maine spoke to Susan. As he later recalled, "She told me the president of the United States did not enjoy the confidence of the American people." Captain Albert Corey of the Second Eastern Shore Maryland Infantry, and Martinburg's provost marshal, was summoned. "Susan Weaver told me that Abraham Lincoln and his cabinet are an unprincipled set of tyrants, and that the reelection of Abraham Lincoln . . . was a sham and disgrace to the nation."

Walker was soon having trouble with Carri Weaver as well: "I was examining the contents of her trunk . . . she said that because of the treatment she was receiving in having her trunk examined that she would gladly shoot the president of the United States. She added, 'I really mean it; this is not just an impulse.'" Annie Weaver made a similar statement, refused to take the oath, and called Lincoln "an old fool." Their interrogators, and the military commission that tried them, were clearly disturbed by the defiance of these women. All three were "to be sent into the Confederate lines until the end of the war," a sentence approved by Brigadier General John Stevenson.

War is intended to inflict casualties upon the opponent, to reduce the number of fighting men available to him. It is a rare commander who can cause a 62 percent casualty rate among enemy forces. Yet this degree of success was achieved by Annie Johnson of Prince George's County, Maryland, without the use of a single ounce of gunpowder and without endangering the life of a single Confederate soldier. The site of Johnson's success was Camp Stoneman, which the Federal government had established in 1863 along the eastern banks of the Potomac River, at what was then called Giesboro Point. Camp Stoneman was an enormous facility for the inspection, purchasing, and training of horses for the cavalry and artillery of the Army of the Potomac. In 1864 alone, 170,000 horses passed through the camp. Acres of stables and hundreds of tents spread across the riverside plain. Thousands of permanent staff, both military and civilian, lived there, along with thousands of men convalescing from wounds and disease, who mingled with other men receiving training and awaiting new mounts. A mile east, just inside the Maryland border, lay a quite different type of establishment, the little bordello run by Annie Johnson. In July 1864, she was charged with enticing men to desert, selling civilian clothes to soldiers, and possession of stolen property. Tried with her was Miles Johnson. Annie refused to say if she was legally married to Miles, leaving their true relationship a mystery.[19]

The initial testimony established that the Johnsons "kept a house of ill fame near Camp Stoneman, to which the enlisted men much resorted. In one company of cavalry, 52 of 84 men deserted, nearly all of whom had frequented the house of the Johnsons." Four months earlier, military police had closed the brothel because of its disruptive influence, but Miles had made many promises of reform and it was allowed to reopen. Now he and Annie were in trouble again. As Private Charles Brown of the 25th New York Cavalry told a court stenographer:

On Wednesday, the 8th day of June 1864 he [the] said Brown went to a Brick House, about one and a half miles from the camp of the 3rd Division Camp Stoneman for the purpose of seeing some women, and there saw a man by the name of Johnson who I recognized as a man that I had been acquainted with in Albany, N.Y. I asked him if he could help me away; and he answered that he had done such things before. I then asked him how much (he the said Johnson) would charge me to take me to Washington; he answered from $100 to $200. If he furnished a new set of citizens clothes he would charge two hundred dollars and for the sum of one hundred dollars he would furnish me with a second handed suit. I then told him I would give him two hundred dollars if he would furnish me with a new set of clothes and carry me to Washington he then told me to go to a barn nearby and remain there that night and I would find blankets to sleep on and he would come with a carriage for me at daybreak in the morning and take me to Washington. I spoke to him about the patrol and he said they would not trouble him as he had everything arranged with them. After this conversation, I left him.

Perhaps inspired by this discussion of desertion, Brown deserted a few days after giving his deposition. Further evidence regarding Annie Johnson's brick house was provided by another soldier from the 25th New York Cavalry, George Johnson, who described "a certain house about a one mile and a half from these headquarters where two or more women [prostitutes] . . . engaged in furnishing citizen's clothing to enlisted men."

This evidence alone was enough for a conviction, but other witnesses shed a little more light on the Johnsons. One testified that Annie maintained four girls in rooms upstairs, and added that Miles used to keep the New York Saloon in Alexandria, Virginia, just across the river from Camp Stoneman. Robert Greene, "colored," told the court that George Cox and Terrence Ryan hung around the Johnsons' place "without visible means of support." Ryan himself told the court that there were four rooms upstairs with a girl in each room, adding, somewhat disingenuously, "I don't know if they are prostitutes."

Miles Johnson was a native of Albany, New York. He had a chance to visit his hometown again when he and Annie were sent to the state prison at Albany until the war ended.

By 1864, volunteers for the Union Army were scarce, and huge bounties were given out to encourage enlistment. Payments of $300 were not uncommon, and a few as high as $1,000 are on record. The fifty-two men that Annie Johnson encouraged to desert not only depleted the Union ranks, but also cost the Federal government somewhere around $400,000 in today's money, without even counting the cost of their training or the expenses of catching, trying, and punishing them for desertion. Her activities were certainly a significant benefit to the Confederacy.

Although Maryland remained in the Union, Maryland women contributed mightily to the Confederate cause. They raised the morale of their fellow Rebels; they obtained confidential military information; they conveyed this information to the Confederate secret service; they sowed dissension and encouraged desertion. When captured, though armed only with a burning desire for southern freedom, they stood unintimidated in the face of Union bayonets, stout oak prison doors, and grim-faced prosecutors in blue.

Emma Kline was arrested and guarded by the Fifth Iowa Infantry. She was smuggling across Mississippi's Big Black River around August 1863.

*Courtesy Michael J. McAfee*

The penalty for cutting telegraph wires was death. Major Jeremiah Hackett,
Second Arkansas Cavalry, arrested Mrs. H. M. Gibson and her
daughter as they cut wires near Bentonville.

*Courtesy Karen P. Chionio and Wilson's Creek National Battlefield Park*

Many outspoken Baltimore socialites were sent to the women's prison at Fitchburg, Massachusetts, where they broke furniture and decorations.

Emily Sparks, a mail smuggler, was carrying letters to aristocratic Confederate officers. Her employers' affluent lifestyle can be seen in this photograph: the bombazine skirt, the little girl's pantellettes, and the harp all indicate wealth.

*Courtesy National Archives (RG153, MM2049)*

The Scott sisters of Falls Church, Virginia, betrayed Connecticut captain Abram Kellog to the Confederates, who took him captive. The sisters were arrested. *Harper's Weekly* (August 1, 1861)

# 3

# TENNESSEE

ALTHOUGH TENNESSEE OFFICIALLY seceded and joined the Confederacy, one-third of its population voted against secession, setting the stage for bitter military conflicts and an even more vicious invisible war of sabotage, bushwhacking, summary executions, spying, and spy catching. Adding to the complexity of these small-scale conflicts, so different from the huge set battles in Virginia, was Tennessee's geography. The state is four times longer from east to west than it is from north to south and can be divided into east, middle, and west Tennessee. Each area played a different role in the Civil War, with resulting differences in both the number of women tried by Union military justice and the types of crimes with which they were charged.

East Tennessee is part of southern Appalachia, a largely mountainous region that also encompasses northern Alabama, northern Georgia, western North Carolina, eastern Kentucky, and western Virginia. Its inhabitants, whether they favored the North or the South, soon found that the Civil War quickly diminished their families and depleted their economic resources. Disenchanted deserters, men avoiding conscription, common criminals, home guards, militia units, and regular troops all roamed the region's roads and trails, murdering one another, burning farms, and confiscating increasingly scarce food.[1]

The inhabitants of east Tennessee were divided by economic fortunes. Most small subsistence farmers in isolated areas had strong Union sentiments, fueled in part by resentment of the incursion of wealthier men from Virginia and middle Tennessee. The latter, who possessed flat, fertile land in the area's larger valleys, favored both slavery and secession. There was a mutual contempt and an increasing polarization between the wealthy, slaveholding aristocracy and the class of poor but proud small farmers. However, many other factors also played a part in east Tennessee's tilt toward Unionism: identification with the growing nation; geographic isolation; minimal contact with the lower South and its cotton economy; the influence of the Whig Party, which favored public works; a sense of uniqueness; resentment over uneven distribution of internal improvements; and the relative absence of slavery. The Federal government had hopes of bringing the east Tennessee loyalists into the Union fold, but for two years was unsuccessful because of the isolation caused by steep, roadless mountains. Troops could march in but could not be resupplied, especially during the harsh winters, and the surrounding Confederate states left no easy way of entry.

Union loyalists in east Tennessee were led by future U.S. president Andrew Johnson and William "Parson" Brownlow, the fire-breathing editor of the Knoxville Whig, who promised to "fight the secession leaders till Hell freezes over and then fight them on the ice." Johnson railed against the secessionist gentry as "not half as good as the man who earns his bread by the sweat of his brow."[2] Inspired by such rhetoric and the unrealized hope of a Union invasion, east Tennessee loyalists rose against the Confederate government in late 1861, attacking outposts and burning railroad bridges. This wave of defiance was quickly crushed by the troops in gray, who hanged five bridge-burners and put hundreds of Tennesseans in prison. Liberation by Federal troops had to wait another two years. In these tightly knit communities, everyone knew everyone. This nearly universal mutual surveillance, combined with the Confederate military presence, may explain why east Tennessee generated only two women tried by the Union military legal system, one at Knoxville and one at Chattanooga.

In May 1864 Anna Law was tried for "smuggling secret mail under an assumed name." Unfortunately, however, the testimony in her trial leaves unanswered some major questions about the Confederate courier system. The chief prosecution witness was Captain William Sanford of the 14th Illinois Cavalry. In response to the judge advocate's questions, Sanford testified:

I've seen her twice or three times, 1st at Mrs. Parkers house near Motley Ford, Tenn. [thirty miles south-southwest of Knoxville] 2nd The next day at the same place 3rd She was riding by Hd Qrs. in a buggy towards Madisonville. This was on Wednesday after her arrest. . . . I caused her arrest. . . . Sunday night the picket at Niles [?] Ferry told me that a lady crossed from Blount Co. and went to Mrs. Parkers. He suspicioned she was not all right. I sent a guard down immediately and surrounded the house. Monday I enquired who she was from neighbors but failed to find out anything. In the afternoon a man from Morgantown came there and I went with him to Mrs Parkers. When we got to the house, accused was playing on the piano, no one else was in the room but Mrs Parker. We having no introduction thought it strange. We stayed half an hour. I then took my hat and started. The man with me then turned to accused and asked if her name was Anna Law; she said no it was Frances Lynn. He made a remark that he had word from Miss Law's friends why he asked the question. We passed out and went away together. The next day I went there and informed Mrs Parker of my suspicions She told me the reason she did not introduce us was that she would not give the lady an introduction to any one under an assumed name. [Parker also told Sanford that Law had been there the year before "with Longstreet."][3]

One of the two letters carried by the defendant was addressed to Annie Jones of Morgantown, Tennessee, a village near Motley Ford. Annie was called to testify and said that the letter was from A. Y. Jones, a Confederate soldier. The return address was "care of Major W. E. Gibbs, Baker's Brigade, Stewart's Division, Hood's Corps, Army of the Tennessee," and the letter was dated April 9, 1864. In it, Jones described his unit's move from Lookout Mountain, Tennessee, to Dalton, Georgia, where he was assigned to gather forage. He complained of the deteriorating postal service in the Confederacy, writing that her last letter to him had come by way of Selma, Montgomery, and Atlanta, and had taken six months to reach him. He told her of the troops' high morale and of men who had reenlisted for "99 years," and he predicted that peace would come only when Lincoln gave up and allowed secession. He concluded with a note of affectionate concern and hopes for a bright future: "I hope that you all can get along without suffering. I will be well satisfied when we get our indipendance if I find you with one dress only. I think I could soon get the second one, and two dresses, a wife and indipendance I think will make a world of pleasure."

Anna Law was convicted and sentenced to stay out of the Union lines until the end of the war. From Knoxville to Dalton is a two-hundred-mile round trip through hazardous mountain country. Would any sane woman have made such a journey to carry nothing more than a love letter for a friend? Anna was a self-professed Rebel, used a false name, and had known General James Longstreet. It seems highly likely that she was part of the vast network of volunteer Confederate couriers, whose tireless activity kept the Rebel army informed of every Yankee move. However, the actual evidence against Anna Law consisted of a love letter, conveying no military secrets. Based on this, banishment seems harsh.

The little town of Ooltewah is twenty miles east of Chattanooga. There, in April 1864, a Federal witness feared for her own safety as she gave evidence about Mary Lewis, accused of being a spy and of "lurking" around Union camps. The witness, Elizabeth Adams, was a resident of Ooltewah; she knew many people who seemed to be involved in espionage and counterespionage. She told the court that Lewis had come to her house through Julian Gap and was a frequent visitor. She identified Hayward McKeehan as captain of the Confederate spies in the area and said that when the Rebels came to Ooltewah they would spare Woodson Fitzgerald and Jo Varnal, but that they would kill William Fitzgerald. Adams also told the court that the Rebels had plenty of money to hire spies, and she concluded that her own life was in danger for having testified.[4]

The wife of the alleged Confederate spymaster, Mrs. McKeehan, had little to say. She had known Mary Lewis for nine years and claimed that the defendant lived in Red Clay, Georgia, and was known as a shrewd businesswoman. Lewis herself confirmed this testimony, stating that she had come to Ooltewah to collect business debts, not to spy. She said her mule teams were to haul the lard that she bought and sold. She also traded in currency, giving two Federal cents for one Confederate dollar.

The court found Lewis not guilty, but ordered her held in jail until the Union troops moved on. Since the timing of troop movements was unknown, this amounted to an indefinite sentence. The general reviewing the case, David Stanley, noted the illegality of holding someone who had been acquitted and ordered Lewis released. (During the Civil War, Stanley was disabled by a broken ankle, diarrhea, a painful groin injury, and a bullet through his neck.) It seems very likely, however, that a friend of the wife of the "captain of the Rebel spies"—a businesswoman who frequently crossed the lines and who asked Union soldiers questions about their numbers and supplies—might have been a Confederate spy or courier. If such was the case, Mary Lewis not only successfully evaded Union prosecution and helped the Confederacy, but also prospered in the lard business.

## MIDDLE TENNESSEE

Middle Tennessee is dominated by Nashville, which even in 1860 was a major center for commerce. A new suspension bridge linked the city with lands to the north, and the new telegraph system brought instantaneous communication between the city and the larger world. Four railroad lines joined Nashville to the entire mid-South, and the steamboat landing on the Cumberland River played host to hundreds of watercraft. Colleges, publishing houses, seminaries, and a medical school all gave the city reason to call itself "the Athens of the South."

On February 15, 1862, the Union capture of Fort Donelson made Nashville strategically impossible for the Confederacy to defend. Ten days later, with hardly a shot fired, the city passed under Yankee occupation. The Confederates, who had neglected to plant "sleeper" spies in Nashville, swiftly compensated for this oversight. So effective was their embryo spy network that it enabled the South to retrieve many important documents left behind in the hasty evacuation.[5]

Relying on family friends and safe houses, both male and female spies and couriers swarmed over Tennessee territory—familiar to them since childhood—that was ostensibly under Union control. The example of Coleman's Scouts suggests the scope of southern activities, which extended over most of the war years. This small intelligence unit, never more than fifty men, was commanded by a former steamboat owner, Captain Henry B. Shaw, who used the alias of Coleman. Before Union forces took Nashville, Shaw had already been supplying information to Confederate generals Nathan Bedford Forrest, Earl Van Dorn, and Joseph Wheeler. Oscar Davis and his older brother, Sam Davis, aged twenty-one, were two of Shaw's agents. These men and their often anonymous associates brought General Braxton Bragg remarkably complete information about Union plans, timing, and morale at Chickamauga, Georgia—information that they thought Bragg did not exploit fully.

In the winter of 1863–64, three of Shaw's men were captured; two were tried as spies. Both were offered life in exchange for their secrets. Both chose death. At the foot of the gallows, Sam Davis was given three chances to save his own life by naming his comrades. He remained silent, and five minutes later he was dead. David O. Dodd met the same fate as Davis. Dee Jobe met a harsher fate: his captors knocked out his teeth, strangled him, and dragged him until his neck broke, all without benefit of a trial.[6] Despite these active counterintelligence efforts, very few middle-Tennessee women appear in the trial records, suggesting a high degree of success in their undercover activities. Only six trials were held, two of which were for events after the end of the war.

Sallie Hodge was boarding on Summer Street at Nashville when she was arrested on suspicion of being a spy in December 1863. Her trial was adjourned twice because the courtroom was too cold to do business, but finally enough firewood was procured to keep the prosecution and the defense (as well as the ink) from freezing. The principle witness was Lieutenant Colonel George Spalding, provost marshal for Nashville, who testified, "I know these letters. This letter (A) was taken from the pocket of Miss Sallie Hodges, the prisoner, by myself at a private boarding house . . . in this city sometime in August last, I think. . . . This letter (B), at the time I took possession of letter (A) and while reading it I noticed her take a piece of paper out of her pocket supposed to be the letter marked (B) and tear it and throw it out of the window. It was picked up by an officer boarding there . . . who was standing on the porch and handed to me."

The two letters, submitted as evidence, revealed much about Hodges's associates.[7]

The first letter, dated August 24, 1863, is from an Alabama cavalry officer "under arrest in Nashville." Addressing a "Dear Friend," he writes:

> It is with the greatest pleasure that I find myself alone to answer yours of the 17th. I was glad to learn that you all was doing so well over there. The time has been gloomy with me. I have been under arrest since I have been at this place though relieved and am willing to do as much as ever. Tell cousin there are no force at the place you were speaking of more than a guard. [Major General Joseph] Wheeler can take it at his ease. Tell him all he has to do is to let me know in time to lead the way, & send me one of his best horses for I can't get about well afoot. Be careful not to let the Yankees get him for I want to see him some time this week if possible for I need money. I am here at this place & can't get away. The best way is to make an attack here on this place in order to draw troops from Murfreesboro & I will join him here & and go up with him so come week after next, though I recon I will see Morgan before then. Rosecrans is about 15,000 strong—I am sure he will have to fall back & if Johnson will attack his forces with him, he will compel him to fall back to Ky. Oh, they think they have got the whole Confederacy. I suppose they have got Dick McCann. I am agoing to try and release him if I can. I can get me another dress and bring him out in disguise.

The letter goes on to describe the writer's plans to visit "Tom" at Columbus and emphasizes the large number of secessionists at Murfreesboro. The writer closes by saying that "Willa" had sent him a revolver, and he offers to send his correspondent a newspaper every day.

The second letter is from Willa Strong—presumably the same woman who sent the revolver—to her sister and is dated August 19, 1863, from Chattanooga. She writes: "I find myself permitted to drop you a few lines to let you know that Wheeler is going to make a raid in Murfreesboro soon. So be on your guard and don't let him have trouble for he is depending on you, and if he is defeated you will be to blame, so stir around and get the ketch of all the particulars . . . write us word if you think it would be a good policy to attack Nashville first or not."

Willa made many other revelations. "Tom," she writes, is now using a fictitious name; she warns against a stepsister who might have him arrested. She speaks of some wild times, though it is not clear whether the activities are social or military: "You know what a fine time we had last year though that was nothing to what it is now. We stay out all the time both night and day." She also gives advice to her sister: "Don't depend on none of the Yankees for no favors. If you don't find no friends and [are] without money, take a walk and the first officer you see, shoot him down and take whatever he has got. Sallie, play off them. I know you are one that can do it, for when at home you are quick and fast. It takes a wise person to act the fool."

Willa closed with some purely military information: "Morgan's recruits is about 500 strong. Wheeler is about 1900. Forrest about 1400, so I am sure we will have them in the right place someday . . . be careful how you write, for Joseph E. Johnston will read every word you send back." The specificity and earnestness in these letters point to several nodes in a very real network of spies and couriers. The men trying Sallie Hodges's case took it seriously. They found her to be "a dangerous person, disposed to do mischief," and recommended that she be sent north of the Department of the Cumberland for the duration of the war.

Two women were arrested for smuggling revolvers to the southern loyalists who surrounded Nashville, concealed among familiar woods and hills. Marina C. Wright, Amelia Hunt, and George W. Clements were each charged with smuggling six revolvers through the Union lines at Nashville. Wright told the court that the revolvers were not intended for "the enemy," but as a convenience for Henry Kerr, a "loyal citizen" who wished to have the guns without being troubled by the Union authorities. She added that she had been induced to join the smuggling scheme under pressure from a U.S. government detective. Hunt's defense followed a similar pattern, with some further details. Henry Kerr was "very sick." The pistols had been left at his house by two U.S. detectives, "under a colorable sale." Hunt also claimed that Clements had bought the revolvers and that a U.S. detective "induced me against my will to carry the pistols."[8]

The court gave little credence to these stories and sentenced Wright and Hunt each "to be imprisoned in the military prison . . . for 90 days and be put at such labor, for the benefit of the army, as may befit her sex and condition." General George Thomas approved the sentences but remitted them, "as they have already been sufficiently punished."

Ten miles north of Bugscuffle is the town of Fairfield, which twenty years after the Civil War had a population of only forty-six; even today it lacks its own post office. The strange trial of Minerva Ballard apparently thus involved more than 20 percent of Fairfield's inhabitants. Ballard was charged with assault and tried by a military court headed by Captain Ethan E. Thornton of the 12th Indiana Cavalry. The chain of events leading to her trial began when Caroline E. May went to the Federal authorities, accusing her neighbors, George and Minerva Ballard, of feeding bushwhackers and of trading in Rebel horses during General Joseph Wheeler's recent raid. Another neighbor, Mrs. Floyd, recalled, "Mrs. May told the Union soldiers to go and destroy the Ballards." This ill will escalated a few days later, when "a Negro who lives at Mrs. May's" was sent to the Ballards' house to bring back a horse that May claimed as her own. Up to this point, the two antagonists had avoided direct confrontation. Given that they lived within a hundred yards of each other, however, a clash was inevitable.[9]

It occurred in yet another household, where Rebecca Kidd's son had badly cut his foot. Kidd's screams summoned neighborly help and brought Caroline May and Minerva Ballard face to face. Without a word, Ballard lifted a chair to strike May. Mrs. Floyd, who was also present, jerked the chair away. Ballard seized a second chair, which was pulled from her grasp by Rebecca Kidd and her older son, Leander. Ballard broke free and charged May, slamming her up against a bureau and scratching her face until the blood ran down. The neighbors separated the two women and notified the authorities.

Was this simply a neighborhood feud, or were the Ballards actually aiding the southern cause? At Minerva Ballard's trial, Rebecca Kidd said, "Mrs. Ballard always treated the Federals well when they came by, but I suppose the Ballards are in sympathy with Jeff Davis. I hear they are going to move as soon as they get their corn gathered." Leander Kidd added,

"Most people around here think the Ballards are Rebble [sic] sympathizers." Mrs. Floyd, too, had an opinion: "The horse that Mrs. May sent her
Negro to get was one which Mr. Ballard had bought from Mr. Lane's black
man. I hear that the Ballards are planning to move to the other side of
Hillsborough in the Cumberlim [sic] Mountains." No one presented any
direct evidence that the Ballards were helping the Confederacy.

The final conclusion of the case was just as confusing as the testimony.
The court found that "Minerva Ballard is guilty of treason and is in sympathy with Jeff Davis and the Southern conspiracy." There is nothing in the
record showing any evidence of treason, nor is there a recorded sentence
or punishment. Whatever the Ballards had done or not done, it is clear that
the Civil War could inflame passions in even the tiniest hamlet. There is no
record of a trial of George Ballard.

Edgefield, a slightly larger village two miles northeast of Nashville,
was the postwar scene of two more southern women facing Union military
justice. The events of Maria Martin's case occurred in a boarding house
on Edgefield's main street, Spring Street. The house was owned by the
"Widow Brian," who had contracted with Mrs. S. E. Hunter to collect rent
and manage it. Three of Hunter's daughters—Mary, Pauline, and Laura—
also lived there. Hunter did the washing for a nearby military hospital.
In early April 1865, Maria Martin joined this group and a few days later
bought the contract for managing the boarding house. Almost immediately, Hunter regretted her decision to sell and asked to cancel the transaction, which Martin refused to do. The three Hunter girls sided with their
mother, and soon the little house on Spring Street seethed with hatred.[10]

Meanwhile, larger events unfolded. On Saturday, April 15, 1865, news
reached Edgefield that President Lincoln had been assassinated. The events
of the next few days brought Maria Martin before the bar of northern justice, charged with disloyalty. As Mary Hunter testified at the trial, "When
she [Maria] first heard it [the news] she said she was glad he was dead and
when the soldiers passed there she would say 'Your daddy's dead and I'm
damned glad of it.' She said the same to negroes when they would pass.
She would holler out to them 'Uncle your daddy's dead.'"

Gideon Niles, a soldier in the Fourth Michigan Cavalry, was another
witness for the prosecution. He had visited the household frequently on

laundry business. He recalled a post-assassination visit: "It was the second day after we had commenced mourning for the president. . . . I heard Miss Martin remark she was glad the old devil is dead. . . . The devil could never has his due till he got Abe Lincoln. She was in hopes that Jeff Davis would be our next president." Niles claimed he was a neutral party and denied saying, "I'll make Miss Martin suffer for what she said about Mrs. Hunter." Upon further cross-examination, however, he admitted that he might have said, "Miss Martin is a God damned whore, a damned dirty bitch who ought to be turned out of doors."

Niles was followed on the witness stand by Maria Martin's star defense witness, Hugh McBratney. He remembered sitting around the table with Gideon Niles and several of the girls when Niles said that he would shoot anyone who spoke disrespectfully of Lincoln, a remark treated lightly by the girls. When McBratney was queried about Martin's background and political sympathies, he said, "I understand she was from Illinois. I never made any particular inquiry as to that. . . . I have never her heard her utter any disloyal sentiments." The judge advocate had some concerns about McBratney's objectivity, and closer examination revealed that McBratney was paying Martin's board and lived with her as husband and wife, although they had never married.

The court was faced with contradictory and probably perjured testimony. Its decision was one seen not infrequently in military court decisions: guilty of the charge, but "without criminality," leaving a final verdict of acquittal, a conclusion approved by General George Thomas. The preponderance of the testimony suggests that Maria Martin did speak out against the dead Lincoln, a daring act in the fevered days of April 1865.

The alleged desecration of the U.S. flag by Emma Latimer, a "schoolgirl," brought her to trial in September 1865, charged with disloyalty and treason. On the Fourth of July, at her parents' home, she had allegedly torn down and trampled on the Stars and Stripes. The witnesses against her were four clerks in the Union quartermaster department, young men who boarded with the Latimers in Edgefield and worked in Nashville: W. R. Adams, John D. Rodgers, W. P. Litten, and Jacob Moore.[11]

The Latimer household contained the two parents and their two school-age daughters. The four clerks who boarded there amused themselves by taunting young Emma about her southern sympathies. They put up American flags in their room, to which their hosts made no objection; but when the indoor flags failed to incite a reaction, the men announced that on the Fourth of July they planned to fly a large American flag in front of the house. Upon hearing this, young Emma impetuously blurted out, "If you do so, I will pull it down."

The clerks had located a boarding house nearer their place of work in Nashville, but they delayed moving in order to discomfit Emma with their planned Fourth of July provocation. Having no large American flag, they borrowed a five by eight–foot one from an Iowa regiment and, early in the morning on Independence Day, hung it from a tree directly in front of the Latimer's house, an act clearly intended to inflame southern emotions. Adams fired his revolver into the air to celebrate the occasion (and doubtless to annoy the Latimers). After this salute, Rodgers and Moore left for Nashville, and Adams sat on the front steps to reload his revolver—and to wait for Emma to respond to their provocation.

Emma soon appeared and pulled the hated symbol out of the tree. Rodgers claimed that he saw her trample it on the ground, an observation contradicted by Emma's sister, Luella, who told the court, "All I saw was that she had took the flag down and said that if it had been put up by gentlemen she wouldn't have taken it down . . . she did not have it under her feet." Rodgers placed the flag back in the tree and dared Emma to touch it, even offering her money if she would try to pull it down again.

Adams then took the stand and confirmed Rodgers's story. Defense counsel Will Brien asked Adams if he had ever served in the U.S. Army. He had not. Brien responded, "Well, then, Mr. Adams, this then was your first fight for the flag?" The prosecution's objection to this question was sustained, but not before counsel's ironic arrow had struck home.

After all testimony had been heard, Brien submitted a 3,000-word defense statement which fairly vibrated with Victorian scorn. He noted that Emma—"who on account of her age could not prosecute or defend a civil suit in her own name, who could not make a legal contract for a paper of sewing needles, whose promissory note would impose upon her no obligation . . . whose language, however violent or injurious . . . would not be actionable"—was being held fully responsible for the crime of treason. And so she was.

Emma, who had sat in the Nashville penitentiary for two months awaiting trial, was ordered to spend another ninety days in prison and pay a $300 fine, the equivalent of two years' salary for a soldier and ridiculously beyond the means of a schoolgirl. This sentence and the trial record arrived upon the desk of Brevet Major General Richard W. Johnson, an 1849 West Point graduate. With ten years of service on the western frontier, and still suffering with chronic diarrhea, malaria, and a liver wound received at New Hope Church, Georgia, Johnson was in no mood for such a verdict. He wrote:

> The sentence is approved . . . but in consideration of the peculiar circumstances of the case, the brevet major general commanding is pleased to remit the entire sentence. It will be well for Miss Lattimer to remember that it will not do to trifle with the sacred emblem of our nationality that in spite of the opposition of all the schoolgirls in the South, the "Banner of Glory and of Beauty" will still wave over the land of the free, and notwithstanding the united efforts of all the rebellious women in the country will continue to float, until time shall cease to be, upon every breeze, the pride and admiration of all thinking persons. She will be released from confinement and restored to her parents, with attention to Solomon's sage remark, "He that spareth the rod, spoileth the child."

General Johnson then he turned his attention to the four clerks: "The conduct of the prosecuting witnesses deserves a passing remark. The testimony shows that they had resolved on changing their place of abode previous to July Fourth, but agreed to remain at the house of Mr. Lattimer until after that date in order to ensnare his little daughter and get her into trouble. Their first battle for the flag was with a thoughtless schoolgirl! The entire transaction looks like the work of children temporarily removed from parental control." Nonetheless, he suggested no punishment for the instigators behind Emma Latimer's trial.

## MEMPHIS

In July 1862, William T. Sherman, later to be famous for burning his way across Georgia, became the military governor of Memphis. It was not an easy task, he noted: "The people are all more or less in sympathy with our enemies . . . all in the South are enemies of all in the North. There is not a garrison in Tennessee where a man can go beyond sight of the flagstaff without being shot or captured." It is thus not surprising to find twenty-two Memphis women tried and convicted by Union military commissions. The year 1862 produced no such convictions, but 1863 was quite another matter.

During the Civil War, surgeons in white regiments reported 73,382 cases of syphilis and 109,397 cases of gonorrhea. The situation in Nashville was so bad that the Union authorities mandated licensure, medical inspection, and treatment (when necessary) for all the prostitutes in that city, and two venereal disease hospitals were established there. The result was a major drop in sexually transmitted diseases.[12]

After two and a half years of Union occupation, the Memphis authorities reluctantly agreed that they had a similar problem and, in September 1864, a nearly identical program of venereal disease detection and treatment got underway. By then it was a little late for the thousands of Union soldiers who had passed through Memphis and, more specifically, for six prostitutes on Memphis's famous Beale Street. The stories of these six women tried by military commission provide a rare glimpse into a long-hidden part of America's history.[13]

The military commission convened to prosecute the prostitutes met in July 1863. All the women were charged with violation of "General Orders No. 13, issued by Lieutenant Colonel Melancthon Smith, and approved by General [James] Veatch, dated April 29, 1863." (The order has never been found, but it seems to have regulated prostitution.) The first woman tried was twenty-three-year-old Kate Stoner, the proprietress of a house of pleasure located in the "Aldridge House" at 115 Beale Street. Fourteen prosecution witnesses were called. Mayer Haller, 45, lived on Beale Street between Hernandez and DeSoto Streets. He testified, "I don't know her reputation, but the reputation of the house, of which she is an inmate, is bad." Fifty-year-old Thomas Warrington said of Aldridge House, "It has the reputation of being a house of easy virtue, or ill fame." He went further, calling it "notoriously a house of ill fame," but denied any "personal knowledge" of such activities. Henry Kirkland, 64, also lived on Beale Street, working as a "market master." He said that Stoner's place had been a house of ill fame for three months. William Milton, who lived at the corner of Beale and Hernando, told the court: "Her house is notorious as a house of prostitution. It is as well known for that as the Gayoso is known as a hotel." John Cheek, from the northeast corner of DeSoto and Beale Streets agreed. A more lively witness was Jerome Martlett, 23. Asked what he had seen near the house, he replied:

> I saw six or seven girls, and some twenty-five or thirty gentlemen came in and went out while I was there. . . . They sat there laughing and talking, and some of the gentlemen had their arms around the girls. I got tired sitting there and went out, and came back after supper and men still kept coming in and going out. About eleven o'clock I went out to get the guards to arrest the inmates. We placed the guards around the house, and went upstairs to the door, and they let us in. In looking around I saw Mr. Cherry [a U.S. detective] in a room with a woman, both of them stripped. I did not see them in bed together. I was not acquainted with the woman. The door was fastened when I first went to this room, and I told them to consider themselves under arrest. They wanted to know what for. I told them they would find out hereafter. They then dressed themselves. I went to another room and found a gentleman in bed, and a woman in the room with him. Her name is Miss Wilson. [Miss Wilson was called and witness recognized her as the woman who was in the room where the gentleman was in bed.] . . . We arrested the men who were in the house, and sent them to the "Irving Block" [prison].

The court had further questions of Marlett. "What did you do in the first hours you were there?" "I refuse to answer." "What is your occupation?" "I have been told not to answer for the good of the service."

Detective Cherry was the next witness. He had been to Kate Stoner's place twice and seen men contracting to spend the night with women.

The court wanted to know what he had been doing during the hours that Martlett was absent. Cherry had a ready reply: "I refuse to answer." He was asked if he knew Florence Knight. He remembered that she worked at Kate Stoner's and had escaped through the kitchen when the guard arrived. The court demanded, "Who went with her when she escaped?" Again he replied, "I refuse to answer."

Witness William McBride, 28, had been to Kate Stoner's three times and had seen her "exercise acts of proprietorship." He knew one of the girls by name: Maria White. Mark Flower, also called by the prosecution, knew that Fannie Gray had previously worked at the Iron Clad, perhaps Memphis's best-known bordello. Sergeant Henry Gans of the Second Illinois Cavalry was with the party that raided Stoner's establishment; he knew one girl by sight, Anna Wilson. She, too, had been an inmate of the Iron Clad. Kate Stoner was found guilty of violating General Orders No. 13. All her furniture was confiscated and she was sent north of Cairo, Illinois.

Five more women from Kate Stoner's establishment were also tried for the same offense. Kate Seamon was twenty-three, the sole support of her two-year-old son. Several Beale Street residents repeated their testimony about the nature of the house and Seamon's role in it. Fletcher Snow seemed to have inside knowledge, testifying, "I was there when we were sent to make arrests." But when asked, "Do you know of your *personal* knowledge that Kate Seamon was a woman of ill fame?" he refused to answer.

Thirty-three-year-old William Cheney was caught in the provost's raid. He said his purpose in going to Kate Stoner's was "to see what was carried on at the house." Remarkably, Stoner herself testified for the prosecution. The former madam told the court, "I've known Kate Seamon more than a year. She lives at my place." Seamon defended herself with dignity:

I am a resident of Memphis, Tenn.—have always endeavored to conduct myself as a quiet and peaceable citizen, have always been compelled to labor hard to support a helpless son, which is the only child I have. My child is two years old and I am his only protection and were it not for my efforts would be subjected to the cold charities of an inhospitable world. I would further state that if my case comes under Special Order No. (13) issued by Lt. Col. Melancthon Smith, and said order was carried into execution, and I was deprived of my citizenship in Memphis I would be entirely destitute of means of support for myself and helpless child and would therefore ask the leniency of the Court and Commission in the consideration of my case.

She was sent north of Cairo, presumably with her small son, and was threatened with prison if she returned.

Maria Wilson, Anna Wilson, and Fanny May all pled guilty to violation of General Orders No. 13, so there was no testimony in their cases. They, too, were sent north of Cairo. For them also, prison awaited if they returned. Florence Knight was charged in absentia, but not tried, as the authorities were unable to find her. Perhaps she was being concealed by Detective William Cherry, who seems to have helped her escape through the kitchen during the raid on the whorehouse.

Fanny Gray had been captured in the raid, pled guilty to "being an inmate in a house of ill fame, kept for purposes of prostitution and lewdness," and was sent north of Cairo with the same threat of prison if she returned. Unlike most of the other women, she left a written statement in the Federal records:

I came to Memphis, Tenn. two weeks previous to Kate Stoner's arrest. I was at the house at the time Mrs. Stoner and the inmates were arrested. I simply came to Memphis on a visit with the intention of returning to Louisville & not anticipating any trouble by my sojourn at Mrs. Stoner's. Did not know of any existing military orders prohibiting persons from visiting Mrs. Stoner, but that inasmuch as she was an old friend, there was no harm in doing so. I would not intentionally violate any order which in the discretion of military commanders and those of the United States government in authority deem necessary to impose for the peace and good order of this community.

The court was not convinced by Gray's insistence that she was "just visiting," especially since one of the prior witnesses had testified that she had worked at two other whorehouses.

There is no accurate way to measure the effect of Kate Stoner's industry on the northern war effort. Certainly the Union soldiers and detectives seemed just as eager to hop into bed with the women as to arrest them. From what is known of the medical history of the Civil War, however, many of these same soldiers were put on the sick list by the bacteria and spirochetes that lurked unseen in Kate Stoner's women. Any Union soldier suffering from venereal disease (or the equally painful treatment for it) was that much less of a threat to the men in butternut and gray.

While prostitution briefly occupied the military courts, smuggling by Memphis women was an ongoing problem. A June 21, 1863, letter from Private Francis M. Guernsey of the 32nd Wisconsin Infantry sheds a somewhat irreverent light on the issue:

> There was quite a laughable affair that hapened on our picket line to day. There has been strict orders issued to search everyone passing out through our lines to see that no smuggled goods pass. To day a man drove up to the picket with an old horse and wagon with two quite pretty women in, and wanted to go through, they of course had to undergo a search there was nothing found on the man but *from under the crinoline of the fair ones were taken four large revolvers*; they were arrested and sent to camp where a more thorough examination took place by the hospital matron. She also found four large revolvers, making eight in all, which these pinks of perfection were trying to smuggle through to the Rebs. They were all loaded and ready to use. I tell you what Fannie, if all women are walking magazines as these were I shall look out, and keep clear of them, for there is no telling when they will explode.[14]

One Tennessee woman, Mary Jordan, was leaving Memphis with her wagon and two gray horses when the pickets stopped her and sent her to Captain Whitney Frank's office. He asked her if she would prefer to be searched by a woman. Jordan replied, "That is not necessary. I will give all that I have." She tore off the skirt from an old dress, from which she removed twenty-nine Confederate uniform caps. She was charged with smuggling.[15]

On Jordan's wagon was a flour barrel. The court asked Captain Frank if she had a permit for the flour. He replied, "She had a permit for a barrel of flour, but when we opened it, it was a barrel of hats." The final inventory of the barrel lists 192 soft hats, 184 cap covers, 159 Confederate uniform caps, and 55 cotton cards. She had no defense witnesses, but made this statement: "I am from Iowa and have had no one to take care of me since 1849. For three years, I had charge of the sewing at Barnum's Hotel in St. Louis, then I heard that a person could make money taking goods out of the lines. I have invested everything that I have in these caps." Mary Jordan had gambled everything—and lost. She was convicted, and her horses, wagon, barrel, and caps were all confiscated. General Stephen Hurlbut added an additional punishment: being sent out of the district. He gave her a choice of north or south. Either way, she would be utterly destitute. But if her journey had been successful, the Confederate soldiers would have had enough new caps for a small regiment of infantry.

Mary Nicholson tried to cross the same picket line using a forged pass, and she was also brought before Captain Frank. He had her searched by a Mrs. Brown, whose first discovery was of a bolt of gray uniform cloth under Nicholson's hoop skirt. In Nicholson's trunk was a girl's hat. Nicholson tried to thrust the hat into the fire, but it was too late. Sewn into the lining of the hat were ten letters. One was addressed to Preston Smith, who had been a leading citizen of Memphis before the war and was now a brigadier general in the Confederate army. (If the letter had reached him, it would have been just five months before his death at Chickamauga in September 1863.) Other letters were addressed to "Lieutenant Henry Jenkins, c/o General Sterling Price," "Captain T. T. Turner, c/o General Ewell at Richmond," "John Newland, c/o Major Quinlon of General Burns' Command," and various citizens of Mississippi. She was charged with carrying communications to the Rebels and was sentenced to four months at Alton Prison. On hearing her claim of being a British subject, however, the court commuted this sentence to being "sent outside the lines."[16]

A Mrs. Hurbard (who also used the alias of Steele) seems to have been more of a professional smuggler. The usual procedure in regulating traffic in and out of Memphis was this: after a trunk had been searched, it received a Federal seal and was allowed to pass through the picket lines. When Hurbard's wagon reached the final checkpoint, a sharp-eyed sentry noticed that the seals on her three large trunks did not look quite right. Back at the police office, a clerk made a list of what was found in her luggage. It included two bottles of powdered opium, a gross of military buttons, a gross of military vest buttons, 6 gross of steel pins, 13,000 needles, 60 pocket knives, a dozen pairs of suspenders, a gross of lead pencils, many reams of paper, 12 pairs of socks, many silk undershirts, a dozen *porte-monnaie* (change purses), 45 yards of "print," 2 pairs of ladies' shoes, 6 bunches of violin strings, 8 pairs of cavalry boots, 290 soft hats, 33 pairs of gauntlets, 13 dozen gloves, 6 dozen toothbrushes, 9 boxes of mourning pins, 36 dozen "fine" combs, a gross of pen holders, 1,000 envelopes, and a few other items.[17]

Hurbard's claim of needing these things for her personal use fell on deaf ears. All her goods were confiscated and she was fined $1,000. In addition, she was ordered to post a $5,000 bond and sentenced to remain in prison until both the bond and the fine were paid. The items that she was carrying would have been of great use in the South, which suffered shortages of every type of consumer goods.

The case of Mary Clemmens precipitated a clash between Lincoln's judge advocate general, Joseph Holt, and the general commanding at Memphis, Stephen Hurlbut. Clemmens had been stopped by the pickets and brought to the office of a Captain Woodward, the assistant provost marshal, who had her searched by Louisa Oldridge. According to the trial record, "Miss Clemmens had concealed about her person about 1,000 needles and a gross of combs, as well as a large number of envelopes and toothbrushes." She was charged with smuggling and convicted. The remarkable collection of items found under her hoop skirts was confiscated, and she was ordered to be "sent beyond the lines."[18]

Paperwork traveled amazingly fast in 1863. In Washington, D.C., a few days after the trial, Judge Holt overturned the verdict on technicalities. He found that the trial record did not show who was the judge advocate or the recorder, nor did it show that the commission was sworn "in the presence of the accused." Moreover, it did not suggest any opportunity for Clemmens to challenge the witnesses. Holt's conclusion: "The sentence is inoperative and the accused should be relieved from its consequences."

Nine days after Holt's decision, the papers were back on Hurlbut's desk. Hurlbut, who himself had been relieved from different things, including field service (due to a painful face infection, possibly combined with alcoholism), was enraged. As he wrote, "The evidence in this case is conclusive that the accused attempted to smuggle goods which were contraband. The commanding officer had full authority to put her beyond our lines for this offense without any trial at all by a military court. If we regard the proceedings of this commission as informal, they were sufficient to justify the order of the general. If the goods are improperly confiscated, let her recover them by civil proceedings." Hurlbut was apparently asserting the power to seize a woman's goods entirely on his own authority, in spite of Holt's directive. The records do not reveal whether Clemmens ever recovered her goods.

Fannie Duke, another woman who fell afoul of military authority, was not new to the Union justice system. In October 1862, she had been arrested for smuggling, and she was sent back to her native Arkansas and ordered not to return. But she did, whereupon she seems to have fallen into the hands of U.S. detective A. B. Morey. On March 4, 1863, Duke, who had never taken the oath of allegiance, obtained a permit from R. Hough, Memphis surveyor of customs, to carry a barrel of salt, a gallon of brandy, 25 pounds of coffee and 5 pounds of tobacco to any point "ten miles out." For this merchandise, she paid thirty dollars. However, when she was arrested on the Pigeon Roost Road, a barrel marked "Salt" and a box marked "Candles" were both found to contain liquor, later determined to be brandy. The record noted, "She also had a jug of liquor, about 2 gallons." Another box held six bundles of combs.[19]

In her trial, defense witness L. C. Hardwick told the court, "Mr. Morey procured her a wagon and a black boy to carry goods through the lines." Testifying for the prosecution, Morey himself continued the story: "Mrs. Duke asked me to help her get outside the lines. We met at the Hardwick House and went to Henry Ashner's grocery. I helped her pack the whisky and seal the barrel. The whisky cost $28 and the empty keg was $1.25." The grocer appeared as the next witness, saying, "I saw Mr. Morey pack the barrel. After Mrs. Duke was arrested, Morey came back to my place and told me to put up $25 to stay out of trouble. He also said he was sorry that she was caught because he could have made $1,000." Fanny Duke was convicted; she lost her property and had to post a $5,000 bond. Meanwhile, Morey—the crooked cop and agent provocateur—went unpunished.

Two women, Elvira Mitchell and Barbara Ann Dunavan, each tried to conceal and smuggle out of Memphis four Navy revolvers. They were represented by the firm of Vollentine and Woodward, who prepared brief but elegant defense statements. Elvira's record read, in part: "I am a very poor woman and widow with one child. The sum of money offered being to me large, in my ignorance of military rules it was accepted. This being my first attempt of the kind, and it being done without my knowledge of the enormity of the crime, I hope and pray to be released from further confinement." Her prayer was not answered. She was sent to Alton Prison until the end of the war. The defense of Barbara Ann, who pled guilty, was nearly identical, except that it made no mention of a child. She, too, went to Alton.[20]

The trial of Mary Moore, the last of the March 1863 cases, is unusual for its light sentence. She was stopped and searched by the pickets on the edge of Memphis. On her wagon were two large barrels, one marked "Salt" and another marked "Flour." The former contained ten gallons of whiskey in metal cans, while the latter contained even more whiskey. Under the cans of whiskey were several cases of officer's buttons and two dozen cotton cards. Her whiskey was confiscated (and no doubt drunk by the Yankees), but all her other goods were returned to her and she was released. General Hurlbut was impatient with such a mild penalty. He called the sentence "too lenient," but confirmed it and asked that she give bond "in such sum as she can afford."[21]

The case of Anna Johnson involves not only a female spy but also a female detective, a rare entity in the Victorian era. Even more unusual was Johnson's mode of carrying secret documents—which would prevent detection, she bragged, "even if I was stripped to the skin."[22]

It is difficult to assign a home base to Johnson. Various documents and testimony place her at Vicksburg, Cincinnati, Richmond, and Memphis. Her trial was set in Nashville and began in November 1863. She was charged with being a spy. The first witness against her was Federal detective Mary E. Truesdale, who testified:

Sometime in the latter part of May 1863 I was requested by Captain Hempner [an aide to General Burnside] to make her acquaintance. . . . He sent me for the purpose of ascertaining her intentions for the future. I consequently called on her at her fathers residence, 105, Clinton Street Cincinnati; In order to accomplish the object for which I was sent, and ordered to go. I stated something about my husband being in the rebel army, represented to her that I was strongly in sympathy with the rebels myself, and in their movements. After she had satisfied herself, and questioned me how I ascertained where she was, her remark was "who told you of me & how I had known such a person, and all about it," [sic] "who told you there was such a person." I told her was glad to hear the Bonny blue Flag sung there, and told her she must be a Southern lady, if she had that there. It seemed to satisfy her. Then she asked me what I wanted her to do. I commenced by requesting her to take money and clothing for me to my family where she could take them into the rebel lines. After some, not very important conversation, about things that I do not definitely remember, she stated to me that she intended to leave the fore part of the next week, and was going through to Chattanoog[a]. She didn't know how fast or by what route but she was going when she started. She would not be stopped. She then told me of having come from the south within a few months. I cannot state exactly the length of time. Being arrested at Memphis, she mentioned the treatment of General Hulburt [Hurlbut]. I think he had her confined and searched and kept some length of time. She told me then that she had her news hid where news could not be found, she carried it still,—she carried it where he could not find it. She intimated very important business she had to transact in the south, but did not give the particulars. She also stated that she must reach Chattanooga before Bragg made any further movements, as she had news of the greatest importance—in fact that it involved the salvation of his army, respecting Rosecrans resources and movements. I complimented her for her achievements which she had accomplished for the rebels, and told her that they ought to pay her all that money would compensate. She stated then that she had the rank and pay of a colonel in the Confederate Army, for services rendered as a spy. She said she had been through the Federal Army in Virginia, three times and took dispatches to Richmond, and delivered them to Jeff Davis, president of the Confederacy, in person. After that conversation, I left, promising to furnish her with the money and clothing by the next Monday. On Monday morning, I sent, by introduction, John M. Palmer, whom I knew to be a loyal citizen. I introduced him by representing him to be my brother in law, and by the name of T. R. Truesdale. After a few hours he called and told me that she requested to see me. She told him some things respecting my family, in which she sympathized with me and wished to see me. I called on Mrs. Johnson, she supposing he had brought [illegible] word. He brought her word that I had lost a child and my children were small, that I had a son dead in the Southern army, and his coming had changed the plans. I went to see her and rather encouraged the imposition that he was my brother in law, was a bachelor; was from Alabama, and very wealthy, in order to give her an opportunity, as she had told me before that, to flatter the Federals, by receiving attentions—that was one way she did, allowing them to court her—which led me to send this man as a bachelor. The second meeting after she had seen Capt Palmer we had a very important conversation, as it was mostly about him as a bachelor and his wealth, his being a good secessionist, and his capacity to serve the rebel Government. She remarked that she liked his movements better than any secessionist she had come across. I still intended to leave in order to give him an opportunity to watch her movements; I pressed her that she should accept, or advised her to let him assist her in any of her movements that she intended to carry out. I merely did this to get clear of furnishing the money.

Mary Truesdale stepped down from the witness stand, after reiterating Johnson's claim of having Jefferson Davis's authorization to sell six hundred bales of cotton in the North. She was followed by Captain Palmer. He confirmed Truesdale's narrative and added several details to it. He had told Anna Johnson that he had a pass issued by Confederate general Joseph Wheeler and that his travel north had been via Huntsville, Alabama, and the Charlotte Pike. She seemed to find this very credible. She had told him of a plot to exchange large amounts of southern cotton for Union commissary goods, a plot endorsed by the then-Union commander at Memphis, in collusion with a man in Richmond and a man in New York State. Johnson was to receive a large commission out of the deal. "She said that Jefferson Davis had sanctioned the operation to the amount of one million of bales," Palmer testified. She had told him that she had been arrested by two different Union generals, Jeremiah Sullivan and U. S. Grant. She also had said that a Union officer, a Colonel Forbes, had warned her that Federal detectives might be following her. She had looked forward to meeting General Burnside, as he was "a ladies man," and she had anticipated no problem in handling him. She had carried passes signed in Richmond and by General Braxton Bragg, but she had had no fear of their being found, as she had carried them hidden in "the lower part" of her body. Palmer concluded that she was very dangerous and would not hesitate to kill.

Four defense witnesses told a very different story. M. A. Barrett, the mother of "Annie," said that her daughter had gone to Memphis to retrieve her horse and buggy and had traveled south only to settle her husband's estate. The defense provided a document from the Probate Court of Warren County, Mississippi, dated September 2, 1861, naming Anna Johnson as the executor of the estate of Lucius B. Johnson. According to the trial report, "Annie never lived in the south, but her late husband was from Vicksburg." Three more witnesses described her as utterly loyal to the Union.

The court found Anna Johnson guilty of conveying information to the enemy but not of being a spy. This puzzling decision was rendered even stranger by General George Thomas's note, which remitted her sentence because of "various circumstances brought to the notice of the general commanding since the trial."

Yet this isn't necessarily the end of Anna Johnson's story. A few months later, an Anna Johnson was tried for spying in Tennessee. An Anna Johnson was tried in Maryland in July 1864 for possessing stolen Federal equipment. Did all these trials involve the same woman? Or were there two or three women of the same name who fell into the hands of Union military justice? Unfortunately, the Federal records do not say.

James H. Cox, 14, seems to have been a worldly wise, cynical young delinquent. He was a star prosecution witness in the last 1863 case in Memphis, which involved Eliza and Julia Stillman, who were both accused of smuggling bales of cotton. The smuggling of cotton bales into the North was a great boon to the South, since the Union blockade of southern ports had cut deeply into the Confederacy's trade with Europe. While the smugglers had profit as their motive, the Confederate economy received a vital boost even from discounted and illegal sales. Moreover, the smugglers' purchases and bank deposits within the seceded states increased the cash in circulation.

According to Cox's rambling narrative, he had been ordered by his parents to go with the Stillmans. After a wagon trip through Tuscumbia, Alabama, and Bolivar, Tennessee, the Stillmans purchased three bales of cotton but took delivery of only two, because the mules could not haul more. Cox had been promised that if he paid his own way and put up the money for a hundred-pound share of the cotton, he would get his profit once they returned to Memphis. When the Stillmans changed their minds and cut him out of this illegal scheme, he not only left them, but also asked the court to give him $75 ($2,000 in today's money) for his failure to make money breaking the law.[23]

The next witness was twenty-one-year-old Charles Anderson, a cotton-permit clerk in the Memphis office of the U.S. Treasury Department. The Stillmans' counsel, R. B. Brown, made a vigorous, almost frenzied attempt to discredit Anderson's authority to issue cotton permits. The court overruled Brown, and the young clerk went on to testify that only cotton grown in Tennessee was covered by the permits. Osborn Criden, a U.S. detective, arrested the Stillmans on the Hernando Road. As he recalled, "They had a permit for rope, salt, coffee, and tea, but none for cotton."

A defense witness, Sallie Nutter, seemed to discredit young Cox. He had told her that he would receive $70 after the trial, but from whom was unclear. The next witness, hack driver Frank Maynard, was less helpful to the defendants. He said he had been hired by the Stillmans to go fifteen miles east of Memphis, but was later told to go south, towards Mississippi. In the end, the court acquitted Julia Stillman but convicted Eliza (the reasons are unclear), ordering her to pay a $500 fine and sentencing her to a year at hard labor. She probably never served this time, as neither she nor her counsel appeared for sentencing.

In 1864 the war moved further south, and only five Memphis women were convicted by military justice. The most explosive case was that of Rebecca J. Thompson, who had smuggled 50,000 percussion caps to the Confederacy. When she was arrested, a little research on the part of the provost marshal showed that she had taken the oath of allegiance eight times, not only as Rebecca Thompson, but also as Jane Franklin, R. F. Giles, Martha James, Martha Sharpe, Fanny Logan, and Mary Link. Handwriting expert Sergeant William J. Cammity of the 72nd Ohio told the court that all these forms had been signed by the same person. His views seemed confirmed by the fact that all these women were described as five feet, four inches in height, with blue eyes and auburn hair.[24]

Charles Fyfe, who searched Thompson's house, found incriminating papers behind a loose brick in the chimney. More incriminating still was the testimony of Sergeant F. W. Dygert, of the 114th Illinois, who was on detached service as a U.S. detective. He had posed as Frank Cook, a Rebel spy, and had heard from Thompson that she had smuggled ammunition every day in a hidden compartment of her buggy. The delivery was made to Rebel forces near Nonconnah Creek. (The creek runs east to west, just south of today's Interstate 240.) The sergeant was asked, "What amount of money have you been paid to produce the conviction of Mrs. Thompson?" His answer: "I get only the pay of a soldier."

Three days after Thompson's arrest, she wrote to Union general C. C. Washburn from her jail cell, alleging that she was the victim of a mistaken identity and that the real spy and smuggler was her cousin, a Mrs. Cook. This note was sent as a sworn statement. Based upon it, a charge of perjury was added to the prior charges of smuggling, disloyalty, and taking the oath under assumed names. The court found her "not guilty" of all four charges, which annoyed General Washburn mightily. As he wrote: "Findings disapproved. The testimony raises so strong a presumption of guilt of the accused, that it almost amounts to positive evidence, her own confession amounting to an admission of the whole charge made, without inducement or duress, is strongly corroborated, and she furnishes no explanation whatever, does not even attempt to overcome the presumption of her guilt." Washburn sent her north of Cairo, Illinois, as "an extremely dangerous character." He was probably right to do so. Any woman who brought the Confederacy 50,000 percussion caps was certainly a threat to the Union war effort.

Florence Lundy and an ex-slave who bore her a grudge were the key players in a July 1864 trial. Lundy was charged with smuggling cotton cards out of Memphis. Cotton cards, which looked like a pair of stiff dog brushes, were used to straighten cotton by hand before it was spun. The brisk trade in such cards suggests that the Confederate manufacturing sector was incapable of producing an adequate supply of even these primitive tools. The prime prosecution witness in the trial was a "colored boy," thirty-three-year-old Joe Lundy, formerly a slave of Florence Lundy's father. No longer a slave, he was serving as a soldier and wagon master at Fort Pickering, in the Memphis suburbs. He told the court that Florence Lundy had offered him two dollars to carry goods outside the lines in one of his government wagons. He and a Lieutenant Halam set up a sting operation to catch her. In the cross-examination, Joe Lundy was asked, "How long were you and Lieutenant Halam fixing up the trick to catch Miss Lundy?" His reply: "I told Lieutenant Hallam about it in the evening about three oclock the day before I took the boxes." As soon as the wagon crossed the picket line, she was arrested for smuggling. Thomas H. Williams, himself a convicted smuggler, had sold her 288 pairs of cotton cards, which were duly discovered. Williams recalled that "she had a black get them."[25]

Lundy's defense was that she had been entrapped. The court did not buy her story and sentenced her to a $3,000 fine and six months at Alton Prison, with more time in prison if the fine remained unpaid. A few weeks before Lincoln's assassination, a John S. Berry of New York wrote to a D. H. Ogden on her behalf:

> You will observe by the [enclosed] notes, that the term of imprisonment without the fine expired on the 18th ult. She however, is utterly unable to pay the fine or any portion thereof. Her father died previous to the Rebellion, and her only brother Capt. Lundy of the Confederate

service, was killed in Forrests raid on Memphis. . . . Miss Lundys health is in very delicate condition. Since her confinement she has had two hemorages of the lungs, and if compelled to remain much longer . . . she will undoubtedly be carried out feet foremost. In all respects other than her "impulsive indiscretion" for which she was sentenced Miss Lundy is a lady of unimpeachable character, also a person of refinement and cultivation.

Berry closed with "Fraternally yours." The letter reached the Executive Mansion, and on March 21, 1865, Lincoln's private secretary John Hay referred the question to Judge Advocate Joseph Holt, who saw no reason to remit the sentence.

Northerners were often surprised by the care and concern felt by southerners for their former slaves, as is seen in the case of L. G. Pickett of Memphis. She was arrested for attempting to smuggle eight hats, a pair of boots, and sixty military vest buttons. Her remarkable written defense combined contrition with barely disguised contempt for her captors:

I had on my person concealed on the day of my arrest one pair of citizens boots & six or eight wool hats. I do not & never did know the number. I had also in the outside pocket of my dress where I carried my money purse and pocket handkerchief, 60 small gilt military vest buttons. There was no intended concealment of the latter, further than stated but the hats and boots were. I confess with much penitence and humility than I have done wrong—wrong to the military regulation to which I have always been obedient, wrong to my husband & family, who have always opposed & admonished me against such conduct, & I have done wrong to my own feelings in betraying myself to an occupation of so much odium. I am alone to blame, and whatever attaches to the crime of smuggling, none of my family & friends are in any wise to blame, for they had no knowledge of it. But Col, I beg your indulgence to [illegible] that I did not intend to gain by this act to aid the rebellion. I have an only brother in the Rebel army [John J. Jamison, 154th Regiment, Polk's Division] from whom I had not heard directly for many months—in fact I have only heard from him this letter written to my father in which he stated that he was bareheaded and barefooted—that he was suffering severely for want of both boots and hat. He has with him a negro boy raised in the family who has been with him for three years and I desired to relieve their immediate necessities in procuring the boots & hats. The military vest buttons (60) I intended to send to my brother and the negro boy on the first opportunity but more especially for the negro boy who was very fond of dress & display & had sent word to me to send him some buttons. . . . My reliance is only upon the clemency and forbearance of the military authorities. I beg forgiveness & pardon for this offense under the most solemn determination never to be guilty again of any infraction for military orders, wholy denying that this has been perpetrated with any *criminal* or *wicked intent*. I have a large family & an afflicted husband, who is a loyal man utterly opposed to my conduct—I alone have sinned against the law, & I beg again to be forgiven.[26]

Clemency there was none. Even Pickett's intent of aiding her young slave did not lighten her sentence. She was sent to the disease-ridden Alton Prison for six months, not to be released until a thousand-dollar fine was paid.

Mary Head, 22, an orphan, and the sole support of herself and her four younger siblings, was arrested on the road out of Memphis. Concealed under her clothes were brown drilling (a coarse cloth used for trousers), gray cassimere (a thin, twilled woolen cloth), gray uniform cloth, military buttons, and "many other articles of a like contraband nature." She had no permit for any of these. Arrested with her was her sister Isabella, age seventeen. Suspended under her skirts were gray plaid cassimere and women's shoes.[27]

Did loyalty to the South or desperate poverty move these two young women to risk the wrath of Union justice? In the trial, a Mrs. S. E. Beck testified that Mary had an "excellent character." Other witnesses described Isabella as "nothing but a poor, sickly child . . . she is consumptive and is a constant invalid . . . ill for three years." Mary Head reminded the court of what seems to have been a broken promise: "The prisoner here stated that she had no further evidence to offer and did not wish to make any written defense, but did wish to claim the benefit of the Asst Provost Marshall,

Capt [Samuel E.] Rankin 8th Iowa Infty. that if she would make a confession that she should be granted the privileges of a witness & not be subject to a prosecution, under which promise she did make a full confession and did fully and freely testify in the case of the United States vs Lindauer [another smuggler]." Did her cooperation help her? The records are silent on this point. Captain Rankin, who seems to have betrayed Mary's trust, was promoted to major. Mary and Isabella Head were sent to prison, where they were to stay until they paid fines of $1,000 and $500 respectively—amounts impossibly beyond their means.

Love and a sharp-eyed detective were the undoing of sixteen-year-old Mary J. O'Callan, a native of Scotland. On a road leading out of Memphis, Officer John Lewis observed her movements and "thought that she was attempting to pass through the lines with goods secreted upon her person." He ordered her to be searched by U.S. detective Laura E. Pye, but O'Callan removed the hidden items herself: twelve yards of gray cloth, two woolen shirts, and a gold cord hatband. Captain Jacob Swivel of the 21st Iowa asked her why she was smuggling, but all she said was, "It's done now and cannot be helped."[28]

She came to trial in February 1865 and pled guilty. The court called for testimony. Her counsel, W. H. Russel objected: "The accused objects to any questions on the part of the prosecution, for the reason that she has pleaded 'guilty.'" He was overruled twice by a court that seemed unwilling to follow accepted procedure. Character witness Mary E. Rembert told the court, "I do know her reputation. It is the very best. I have sent my child to school to her."

O'Callan was found guilty, adjudged to be "a dangerous character," and was ordered to be jailed until she paid a $50 fine. If she did pay the fine, she was to be deported north. At the time of her trial, the Army of Northern Virginia was bottled up in Petersburg and Richmond, while William T. Sherman's forces were headed north from Savannah, Georgia, on their way into South Carolina. But in Union eyes, even a few yards of gray cloth, a thousand miles from the battlefield, made Mary O'Callan was a threat.

Not every woman arrested was a smuggler. Sarah Clifford sold whiskey. Officers were allowed whiskey; soldiers were not. On February 25,

1865, Clifford sold a pint of whiskey to Private William Smith of the 113th Illinois. Smith's recollections were somewhat vague. Not so those of his commander, Lieutenant Colonel George R. Clarke: "She admitted to me the day she was arrested that she had been selling liquor to my soldiers . . . she said she had sold a pint of liquor to one William Smith of Co. 'F,' 113 Ills. . . . It made him crazy drunk and he got his head pounded up pretty badly." In her defense, Clifford described the difficulties of a widow before the existence of welfare and Social Security. Selling whiskey was her only way of supporting her five children. She told the court that if God permitted, she would find another way of supporting her family. Any divine intervention was delayed a fortnight while she completed her fifteen-day jail sentence.[29]

Another whiskey seller seems to have been a less sympathetic character. It was May 1865, the war was nearly over, and combat was far from Memphis; but a drunk and disorderly Union soldier could be as dangerous as a sober Confederate guerrilla. Bridget McCoy was charged with selling "intoxicating liquor to a soldier at the corner of Fourth and Exchange Streets." Prosecution witness P. P. Higgins, a blacksmith, lived at the same address. He testified, "I saw her dealing out whiskey to soldiers. . . . I know positively that it was [her] for I have been in there several times when she was selling to soldiers. It was whiskey she was selling to them, and the meanest kind." McCoy had no witnesses for her defense. The court put her in prison until she paid her $25 fine.[30]

The final Tennessee case includes a highly unlikely cast of characters: Abraham Lincoln, General Nathan Bedford Forrest, the widow of a Union war hero, and Massachusetts senator Charles Sumner. The story begins with Lionel F. Booth, a private in Company B, Second U.S. Infantry, and Lizzie Way, who were married on September 5, 1861, by a St. Louis justice of the peace. For unknown reasons, the groom signed his name as "George H. Lanning." To add to the confusion, the trial records say that he was a clerk for General Nathaniel Lyon, who had been killed August 10, 1861, at the battle of Wilson's Creek, Missouri—three weeks before the wedding.[31]

Many of the officers for regiments of U.S. colored troops were experienced white enlisted men who had been promoted and commissioned with the understanding that they would command colored troops. Under this arrangement, Private Booth, in 1863, became Major Booth of the Sixth U.S. Colored Heavy Artillery (later the 11th U.S. Colored Infantry). His first position of great responsibility was as commander of the Union post of Fort Pillow, Tennessee. There, on April 12, 1864, during an attack led by General Nathan Bedford Forrest, Booth and hundreds of his men were killed.[32]

Three weeks later, his widow, Lizzie Booth, met with President Lincoln in Washington, D.C. On May 19, 1864, Lincoln wrote to Senator Charles Sumner, "The bearer of this is the widow of Major [Lionel] Booth, who fell at Fort Pillow. She makes a point, which I think very worthy of consideration which is, widows and children in fact, of colored soldiers who fall in our service, be placed in law, the same as if their marriages were legal, so that they can have the benefit of the provisions made the widows and orphans of white soldiers. Please see and hear Mrs. Booth."[33]

In July 1864, Lizzie was back in Memphis, employed to search women for contraband. On Pigeon Roost Road, she found $280 in gold coins hidden on the person of one woman. The smuggler offered a $100 bribe to be let past. Lizzie accepted the bribe—and was caught. She was charged with violation of military orders and taking a bribe. During her very brief trial, she was convicted and sentenced to a year in prison. A sentence to prison was not usually carried out until the finding had been properly published. A few minutes after the trial concluded, Lizzie returned to her room on the third floor of 300 Front Row.

The judge advocate for her trial had been Lieutenant Colonel William P. Hepburn, who, according to the charges in his own trial, went immediately to her room and "when alone with her in said private apartment did then and there with force and violence, and against the will of said Mrs. Booth, tear open the bosom of her dress, and attempt other indecent liberties . . . and attempt to induce her . . . to have sexual intercourse."[34] Lizzie was duly called as a witness in Hepburn's trial. His counsel attempted to exclude her testimony on the grounds that she had been "convicted of an infamous crime . . . and was utterly unworthy of credit." The objection was overruled, however, and she proceeded to tell her story:

At the instance of my friends I make the following statement. Immediately after my trial I was followed home by Col. Hepburn the *Judge Advocate* upon entering my room he put down my curtains and attempted to seat me on his knee and tore open my bosom I indignantly resented his insult when he told me the result of my trial rested with him and it was best for me to *submit* to his wishes I appealed to my situation my distress my husbands memory but he was deaf to everything but his base passions. He even attempted violence when I called for help thinking the occupants of the [*illegible*] should hear me . . . he desisted and with much anger left—telling me he would *call* again. I immediately sent for an officer who loaned me a pistol and told me to *shoot* him which I would have done had he returned. I told the circumstances to Maj. Lachand [?] who advised me to report to you [General C. C. Washburn] but I declined doing so until I was placed here as I believe at the insistence of Col Hepburn I can prove he was in my apartment at the time specified.

Colonel Hepburn's defense witnesses seemed to rely entirely on hearsay. Three officers of the Third U.S. Colored Heavy Artillery—Lieutenant Colonel James P. Harper (himself dismissed in disgrace soon afterwards), Captain Charles H. Cole, and Lieutenant James E. Helm—all stated that they had heard that Lizzie had a bad reputation, but that they had had no direct knowledge of it. Captain Joseph W. Eystra of the Second Iowa Cavalry told the court, "Mrs. Booth was Major Booth's kept woman." At this point, the trial paused for the funeral of Colonel Hepburn's counsel, who had suddenly died. When the trial resumed, Hepburn asked the court for permission to subpoena Colonel Warren Lothrop of the First Missouri Light Artillery, saying, "He has knowledge that Mrs. Booth has been a public prostitute." The court refused the request. General Hurlbut then gave an entirely different picture from those attempting to aid Colonel Hepburn by blackening the reputation of Lizzie Booth. As he testified, "I had intended making Mrs. Booth chief matron of the federal hospital at Cairo, Illinois."

The wheels of justice were now operating in both cases. When Lizzie Booth's trial papers came to General C. C. Washburn, he disapproved her conviction because of insufficient evidence and irregularities in the trial transcript. She was free to go. And so was Colonel Hepburn, acquitted not only of conduct unbecoming an officer and a gentleman, but also of charges that he failed to deliver food to prisoners and that he had been steering legal cases to a crooked judge.

The case of Lizzie Booth leaves many questions unanswered. Why did Private/Major Booth use a different name on his wedding certificate? What was the story behind Lizzie's trip from Memphis to the office of the president of the United States? Was she, the widow of a Union war hero, truly agreeable to bribery by a smuggler? Why, if she and Lionel Booth had been married for three years, were so many of his fellow officers willing to believe that she was no better than a prostitute? Was her claim of sexual aggression by Colonel Hepburn a vicious bit of perjury on her part, or were his acts truly ungentlemanly and his acquittal an injustice? Her initial conviction suggests that she was capable of aiding the Confederacy by allowing smugglers to pass south. But why would she wish to aid the same cause that had killed her husband? History, it seems, never lacks mystery.

# 4

# SOUTH OF THE LINE

AT LATITUDE 36°35′ north, give or take a few hundred yards, a line runs from the Atlantic Ocean along the northern boundaries of North Carolina, Tennessee, and Arkansas. Ten Confederate states lay south of that line. Excluding Tennessee, these states saw the trials of a total of twenty-five southern women during the Civil War. The Appomattox meeting between Lee and Grant did not truly end the war, and some of these cases illustrate the continuing hostilities that marked Reconstruction and beyond.

## TEXAS

About seventy-five miles northwest of Houston, in the town of Union Hill, Mary Boyd was charged with "armed resistance to the authority of the United States government." Her son, Samuel Boyd, a "notorious desperado," was accused of murdering a member of the "Garrett mob," and a detachment of the 29th Illinois Veteran Volunteers had been sent to the Boyd house to arrest Samuel. On a July evening, Lieutenant Arden Ray knocked on the door and announced his identity and his business. He might have been surprised at the response, but he retained a very full recollection of those minutes. As he later testified:

> I know them. Their names are Augustus Boyd and Mary Boyd. I saw them first at the residence of Mrs. Boyd (the accused) in Washington County Texas about 16 miles from Brenham on the 25th of July last in the evening. I went there under orders from Comdg. Officer, Post of Brenham with ten men for the purpose of arresting Saml. Boyd and others concerned in the murder of Garrett. I got to Mrs. Boyd's prob-

ably about 10 or 11 o'clk in the evening. I dismounted my men and left the horses in charge of Corp. Fowler and Private McDonald in front or near the front of a house. I think the house of Widow Garrett about two or three hundred yards from Mrs. Boyds. I went on foot with 8 men to Mrs. Boyds and surrounded the house sending Sergt Barber with five men round the house, to place the men opposite each window and to watch and let no one out of the house. I then took three men and approached the house in front, and went upon the gallery and placed a man at the left-hand door as you come up to the house from the road and a man between the two windows that were between the two doors in front, and another man at the right hand window near the right hand door. I told my men not to let any one out of the house. Sergt Raber at the time I stepped upon the gallery and had got round the house and said "Is that you Lt," and I replied "All right, it's me." After placing my men I knocked at the door and hailed. I did this two or three or 4 times about the last time I knocked someone apparently on the upper gallery said "Hallo, What do you want there" or something to that amount. I then stepped back off the gallery and some person on the upper gallery walked to the edge of the gallery and asked what was wanted. I told him I was a United States officer there under orders from Houston. I recalled the word Houston and said "Brenham" for the arrest of Saml Boyd and for him to come down if he was in there and give himself up and I would treat him like a gentleman about the same time I stepped toward the gallery and he threw up his arm and fired a revolver I supposed from the report the ball passing near me and hitting Henry Bennett, Co. K, 29th Ill. Vet. Vol. Inf. in the left arm. About the time this shot was fired a shotgun was fired out of the right hand end of the house. I then gave orders for the boys to fire into the windows and the firing commenced which was kept up for I suppose about from 2½ to 5 minutes. I heard talking in the house during the firing and about the time it commenced I heard a voice of a female say "leave there you Yankee sons of bitches" or "Black sons of bitches" I could not state which. I also heard a finer voice which I supposed to be that of a young lady saying "give me the gun and I'll do the loading."

[He also heard a man's voice at the other end of the house ordering "Yankee son of bitches" to leave, and shortly thereafter the screams of a young woman.] About the time the firing ceased Mrs. Boyd . . . looked out of the window and I ordered her to open the door. She said she would not do it, that she has run off 40 or 45 Germans or Dutch from there with brickbats and she said something about . . . ammunition.[1]

The Union soldiers lit candles and searched the house, finding an Enfield rifle, two shotguns, two pistols, and two Bowie knives. As they searched, Mary Boyd abused them "right smart," saying that the man that Sam had killed was not a good citizen. In the firefight, her daughter was wounded in the arm, and her son escaped. Sergeant Levi Raber was wounded in the shooting, but recovered. Private Bennett died of gangrene in his wounded arm. Private William Kirby then took the stand, saying, "I was posted near the smokehouse. I saw a man and a woman with their heads out the window. . . . [One] said, 'What are you doing there, you son of a bitch?'"

The defense presented three witnesses. The first was Julia, Mary Boyd's sixteen-year-old daughter, who remembered:

At suppertime . . . there were at our house my brothers, Augustus Boyd and Sam Boyd, Moses Park, Miss Anna Park, my mother, Jack Conner and myself. After supper, we went into the parlor and amused ourselves playing cards . . . we stayed up until about 10 o'clock. When we went to bed, Mrs. Boyd, Miss Park and I slept in the same room and Mr. Park and my brother Augustus Boyd slept in another room upstairs. Sam and Jack Conner slept on the gallery on a pallet. I went to sleep and was woke up by the firing of guns . . . just as I laid down on the floor I was wounded . . . in the left arm with a pistol ball. [The ball was exhibited to the court.] As soon as I was wounded I went out on the gallery and asked them to please not shoot any more.

The prosecution asked Julia about Mary's role, and she replied, "I did not see my mother doing any shooting."

Moses Park, a twenty-one-year-old visitor from Galveston, was awakened by noises on the night of the search. He remembered Sam Boyd exclaiming that the Garrett mob had come to kill him. When Sam learned it was Federals, Park continued, he slipped out a window and disappeared into the night. Park denied seeing Mary Boyd fire a single shot. Fourteen-year-old Jack Conner, visiting from Austin, told the court that only Sam Boyd did any shooting: "Mrs. Boyd never had a gun in her hand." Based on this testimony, Mary Boyd was found not guilty. Her acquittal seems somewhat curious, considering the testimony of the Union soldiers.

## LOUISIANA

The stories of Louisiana women tried by Union military commissions are of a somewhat different nature. In the first case from Louisiana, Mary Hill of New Orleans had corresponded with a Confederate officer, General Thomas Taylor, who commanded the Confederate post at Clinton. In May 1864, a Mrs. Coulon brought a letter from General Taylor to Hill, who promptly replied: "New Orleans, corner of Hercules and Melpomene Streets. Sir: A communication from you was handed me by a lady, today, bearing date April 12th. I send my address. Communicate and state what you require, and I will do all in my power. I will be here until the end of July."[2]

That same day, Mary Hill wrote a second letter—a long and infuriated one—to her brother Samuel W. Hill, a captain of engineers in the Confederate army:

> I had a most unpleasant journey home, as I had not a pass, I returned to the city. I was along with all else who came on the schooner taken charge of by the Yankees, sent to the ladies' prison, and from thence before a military commission, to render a full and true account of my journey. Two days and a half I was in confinement, and for a week was kept on parole. I trotted about from the provost to the inquisition, and so on, with a guard at my heels, and all the riff-raff they trumped up; imagine how my English blood boiled with indignation at being treated like a criminal. Last day I was asked if I had taken the iron-clad. I had just laid before my interrogator Earl Russell's passport, with which I, of course, had provided myself while in Europe last summer, also the neutral oath, to which I had signed my name on landing here. Miss Hill you need report no more. So Richard was himself again. But not himself, either, for I took the scarlet fever, from

which I am barely recovering; it was evidently brought on by exposure to the sun and the annoyances of every kind thrown in my way. I will never forget it to the Yankees, never. [She then digressed upon family photos and the weather.] We have accounts of the battles in Richmond, but so hatched up to suit Northern palates, you can make neither head nor tail of the affair; but through my spectacles, I see General Grant and his well-whipped army with their faces toward Washington, and their backs to the hated city Richmond, except those who will take their summer residence at the Libby [prison]. Tell the boys, Banks has made a splendid commissary to Dick Taylor's army [the failed Union Red River campaign], and they were so ungrateful as also to whip him, and that very badly.

Mary's counsel, a Mr. Roselius, launched a spirited defense. He first claimed that his client was too well-bred to have written anything critical of the Union authorities: "The . . . commission will not, I trust, be influenced in the least by the abusive and unbecoming rhapsody of vituperative epithets contained in the three letters handed by the accused to Mrs. Coulon. How any lady could, under any circumstances, make use of such language, it is difficult to conceive; and when we learn that she is an Englishwoman . . . but travels under the protection of a passport issued by Earl Russell, secretary of foreign affairs . . . our astonishment is increased."

Roselius next employed a tactic long favored by his legal brethren: dismissal by definition. Noting that Webster's defined "correspondence" as an exchange of letters, he argued that since the prosecution had shown only her letters, and not any replies, they, technically, could not be a correspondence. Then he introduced a psychiatric term—"politico-mensmania"—which, he asserted, "prevails among certain persons in the Southern States . . . a moral epidemic . . . found in the greatest intensity among some of the gentler sex. They are but too often led away by the impulse of their feelings, instead of being guided by the dictates of reason and propriety." Roselius then turned to the letter from General Taylor, condemning it as "a wicked and contemptible fabrication." He pointed to inconsistencies in the handwriting and the dates, and asserted that the letter's only purpose was to entrap Mary Hill. He concluded, "She is charged with giving intelligence to the enemy. There is no 'intelligence' in her letters. They contain only personal opinion and family news."

The military commission was swayed by none of these arguments. Mary Hill was convicted and sentenced to confinement until the end of the war. General Stephen Hurlbut modified the sentence and ordered her to be sent into Confederate territory, where her service to the Confederacy continued. Inspired by the enlistment of her brother, Sam, in the Seventh Louisiana Infantry, Mary labored as a nurse in the Louisiana hospital near Richmond, Virginia, during the Seven Days' Battle, earning the sobriquet of "the Florence Nightingale of the Army of Northern Virginia." After the war, she served as the first matron of the Louisiana Veterans' Home. When she died in 1902, she was buried with full military honors; her coffin was followed to the grave by a long line of aged men in gray uniforms.

The case of Emily Sparks opens a window on the politics and social network of the Pelican State. In March 1865, at Verret Lake, twenty miles south of Baton Rouge, Sparks was arrested with a wagonload of contraband. Colonel Willard Sayles of the Third Rhode Island Cavalry told the court, "I was on or about the 24th of Jany at the foot of the canal near Lake Verret. I found Mrs. Margaret Ivy and Miss Martha Dunning on a mule team with certain packages directed to officers in the Confederate service—one to General Nichol one to Lt. Col. Rightor, and I think, one to Capt Samuel Flower—these packages contained articles of clothing of different kinds—letters to officers in the Confederate service—Pelican Buttons." One package was also addressed to a Captain Winchester. Sparks told him that Ivy and Dunning had nothing to do with the bundles and said that they had been given to her by the wives of Flowers and Nicholls.[3]

The court called upon the women who had prepared the bundles, who proved to be surprisingly talkative witnesses. The first to testify was Mary Flowers, the daughter of Walter Pugh; her stepmother was General Nicholls's sister. She told the court, "I reside about 4 miles from Napoleonville on the road to Thibodaux west side of Bayou Lafourche. . . . I do know her [Emily Sparks]—I have known her some 8 or 10 years—she lives about 5 miles from Napoleonville on the Canal Road . . . we went out [there] to see if we could get some things across the lines." The court asked where the officers were now. She replied, "General Nichols is in Nacodochas in Texas. Capt. Flowers is in Alexandria, La. He is my brother in law. Lt. Col. Rightor, I do not know where he is." The court then asked her how she had gotten clothes past the pickets. "We dressed in them. We took them on our persons," she answered. And why had they not prepared the bundles at the home of the Pughs? She replied, "They had more servants [slaves] at Walter Pugh's, ready to inform on us."

The next witness, Elise Nicholls, first addressed her relationship with the defendant. The court asked, "Since you have been acquainted with Mrs. Sparks . . . have you been on visiting terms with her?" The answer: "No, sir!" Rather, she felt a claim upon Sparks because Sparks's son was a lieutenant in General Nicholls's command. The bundle made up for the general had four flannel shirts, shoes, socks, cod liver oil, and brass buttons with the Louisiana pelican on them.

The many documents still preserved in Sparks's trial record are silent witnesses to the events leading up to her trial: dozens of photographs, letters, and newspaper clippings, many of them in French. Although most of the photos and papers are unlabeled, they nonetheless reveal a compelling picture of life in 1865. An article in French gives Robert E. Lee's views "de l'armement des noirs" (on arming the blacks). A handful of business cards advertise embroidery designs and dentists. A clipping details Grierson's raid. A charming carte de visite, inscribed to "cher Dick," shows a fashionably dressed woman and child standing by a harp. A brief letter begins, "Mon cher cousin, Ci-inclu je t'envoi un petit paquet," while a much longer letter tells of Monsieur M. Gastreau of Bayou LaFourche, who was "shot by one of his own Negroes while at supper with his family . . . this one of the fruits of Yankee interference . . . making the Negroes discontented with their condition." (The fortunate Monsieur Gastreau was wearing two heavy overcoats due to chilly weather and survived the six bullets fired into him.) In yet another letter, the writer speaks of the "mortification" of having to take the oath of allegiance and grieves over losing so many relatives in the war, especially "young Bruyere, so brave and so true a patriot." The writer was further disturbed by the 16th Indiana troops, who were quartered in the sugarhouse, where they had damaged the brass cane-processing equipment. In a brief missive, a child's scrawl proclaimed, "Dear Aunt Fanny, I send by your mother some cartridges and two pairs of spurs."

Sparks's counsel, a Mr. Gentile, told the court that his client conveyed only items of familial and social value, not money, food, or ammunition; nor had she conveyed any military intelligence. The court found her guilty of violating the 56th Article of War, which prohibited providing money or ammunition to the enemy under penalty of death. She was convicted and fined $1,000. General Nathaniel Banks approved the proceedings and ordered her to the "House of Detention for Females" if the fine was not paid within thirty days. There is no mention of penalties for the two upper-class women who had employed Emily Sparks, nor any indication that her social betters ever paid her fine.

The last month of the war saw the joint trial of Catherine Debat and Constance Shawkede, who were charged with bribery, smuggling, conveying letters to the enemy, and violating the oath of allegiance. The court records still preserve the steel pen nibs and common pins that were entered as evidence of smuggled contraband. These small metal items are also mute witnesses to the desperate nature of Confederate home life, for even the smallest conveniences could be had only at great risk.[4]

Debat and Shawkede traveled together, and the court evinced considerable interest in their relationship. One witness was asked, "Did they appear to be mistress and servant?" The reply: "No, they sat together at table, and both danced at the same parties." Debat was from Liberty, Texas (about fifty miles northeast of Houston), while Shawkede lived in New Orleans. They might have traveled together because Debat appeared to be in poor health. Her counsel asserted that she suffered from "fits" and needed a companion. A witness disagreed, saying that Debat had "chills," not fits, and that while persons with fits (possibly epilepsy) might need an attendant, persons with chills (possibly malaria) did not. In the end, neither the women's relationship nor Debat's medical status were clarified, and the court moved on to the actual offense.

The two women had stayed at Proffit's Napoleonville Hotel. While Lucinda Jordan (Proffit's sister) was cleaning their room, she had noticed an unusual bundle and a very thick petticoat. She had promptly notified Major

George R. Davis, Third Rhode Island Cavalry, the local provost marshal. Davis told the court, "At the request of Madame Profitt, I examined the room and found three bags, designed to be tied around the waist and fit under a hoop skirt. In these bags were large quantities of pins, needles, gentlemen's socks, ladies combs, linen thread, cotton spools, hooks and eyes, fifty letters addressed to persons in the Confederacy, and a large number of Negro handkerchiefs, meant to be tied around the head. There were many photographs in the letters. One letter was addressed to Lieutenant Colonel William Claiborne of the Rebel army."

The letters contained damaging evidence suggesting that Debat was not a newcomer to the world of smuggling. A letter to "Dear Kate," praised Debat's skills: "By a stroke of good luck . . . I discovered Madame D. and through her learned news of our dear ones . . . she will give you a small list [of things to buy]." A note from "JDY" informed the recipient that "I have sent by Madame C. Debat three volumes of Tennyson's poems. Cost $13.50." A letter to First Lieutenant Oscar Robin, aide-de-camp to Hebrade DeBlanc, began, "Je profite de la complaisance de Madame Debat pour envoyer les articles suivant" (I benefit from the kindness of Mrs. Debat to send you the following items). The following list included cashmere shirts, silk shirts, and custom-made boots.

Debat's trunk contained yet more goods, but she asserted that the trunk had been inspected, approved, and sealed by the Union authorities in Assumption Parish. Captain John Green, 26th Indiana, provost marshal in that parish, told the court, "Neither I nor my clerk gave them a permit." What were the goods worth? An opinion was rendered by Max Mock, dry-goods clerk, who was sworn in as an expert witness: "Nine handkerchiefs at $4.00 a dozen; five hairnets at $1.50 a dozen; five pairs of gloves at $2.00 a dozen; 15 spools of cotton thread, $2.00; 325 needles, 50 cents." Mock continued his recitation through sixty-eight more items; he then reminded the court that retail prices were 25 percent higher.

The court adjourned for a day at this point to honor the memory of the recently assassinated Abraham Lincoln. When they resumed, Debat asserted that all her goods were for the use of her "servants" in Texas. The court made no comment on the use to which the alleged recipients—most likely recently freed slaves—might put cashmere shirts, pen nibs, volumes of Tennyson, and photographs of elderly Frenchmen. Perhaps Debat should have heeded the final words in one of the letters she was smuggling: "Crois moi—la cause est perdu" (Believe me, the cause is lost). She was convicted and sentenced to two years in prison and the confiscation of her goods. The reviewing general cited "the change in the country" and remitted her prison sentence. Constance Shawkede was tried on the same charges, with much the same testimony. As she spoke no English, a French interpreter was sworn in to translate. Shawkede was sentenced to a year in prison and the confiscation of her goods. Her prison time was also remitted.

Two women were tried for offenses near Baton Rouge. Mary E. Kirby had a permit to carry a few items through the Union lines. When she was searched in November 1864, however, she seems to have exceeded her limit. She was carrying 14 yards of domestic cloth, 8 pounds of candles, 10 pounds of green coffee, 5 boxes of blacking, 11 papers of pepper, a paper of cinnamon, 10 lead pencils, 48 military buttons, a pair of slippers, a Sharp's carbine, 11 bunches of braid, 6 pairs of shoes, 2 padlocks, 4 cans of ground mustard, 2 pairs of woolen socks, 3 pairs of cotton stockings, 18 linen handkerchiefs, 2 remnants of linsey, a remnant of calico, an officer's saber belt, 4 papers of tea, a set of shirt buttons, 22 spools of thread, a corset, 2 woolen skirts, 2 ladies' belts, and a lady's satchel. The charge was "smuggling . . . sundry articles . . . designed for the use of the Rebel army in arms."[5]

She pled guilty and, as was customary in such cases, was allowed to introduce character witnesses who might lead to mitigation. John O'Connor, recorder of mortgages for East Baton Rouge Parish, had known her for eight years and testified, "Her general moral character is very good." Eduard Cousinard, sheriff of the same parish, had known her for fifteen years and described her moral character as "good." He had no opinion on her "loyalty to the Union." The court did, however; it sentenced her to the Female Prison in New Orleans until the end of the war. General William Benton, a veteran of both the Mexican War and the Civil War, approved the sentence.

Florvillei Landry was charged with using "insulting and abusing language toward soldiers of the United States army in the performance of their duties" in December 1864, near Baton Rouge. Her outspoken comments cost her $500, and her sentence was approved by General George L. Andrews, whose years in Louisiana were devoted to the organization and training of troops who had formerly been slaves.[6]

The case of Rebecca Field, who ran a small store at Goodrich's Landing, is a study in conflicting testimony, character assassination, and possible perjury—but perjury by whom? Field's husband, son, and brother were all in the Union army. She had worked as a volunteer nurse in Tennessee and had come to Louisiana when her brother, an officer in the U.S. Colored Troops, became sick. When his regiment (whose designation is not given) moved away, there was no store for the freedmen. She received authority to open a store, which was soon busy with both black and white customers. The surrounding area had few stores, and southern women came to shop for themselves—and possibly for their Confederate soldier husbands. Field was charged with selling contraband goods and helping her female customers conceal the goods they planned to carry through the lines. The first prosecution witness was Eliza Gillison, "a colored woman," who told the court:

> I wash and sew for my living. I have been living for the past four months at Mrs. Field's. . . . I saw Mrs. Bullin, who lives out on Bayou Maçon somewhere, put on a pair of boots in Mrs. Field's room. That was just before the burning by the secesh at Morgan's plantation near here, in August last. The next week, there came in Mrs. Ellen Henry, and went into the store of Mrs. Field . . . and came out from there . . . with a pair of spurs, and I helped to fasten those spurs under her dress, at the waist. . . . Mrs. Humphreys, who lives on Bayou Maçon, near Floyd, got a pair of boots before that, and when she came back, she told me she had got home safe with the boots. I told her she'd have to be careful about packing things away that way out of the lines, or she would be caught. . . . All the ladies, that come in here from the hills on Bayou Maçon, used to carry away spools of thread and tobacco, in their bosoms and pockets. [She was asked about Bullin's boots.] They called them ladies boots. They came out of Mrs. Field's store; and I asked Mrs. Bullin, if her husband could wear her boots, and she said she'd

get a pair larger than enough for her, and then her husband could wear them. I asked her what she was going to do with her shoes that she wore in. She said she would put them in her pocket. [The court asked more about her helping Ellen Henry.] She asked me to hold up her clothes while she fastened them [the spurs]. She couldn't fasten them well and I fastened them for her.[7]

Having just launched her employer on the road to prison, Gillison concluded by describing Field as "a very fine woman." The next witness, Mary Langford ("colored"), told the court, "I do sewing and washing. I've made many pockets for secesh ladies. They tell me the pockets are to carry things through the lines." Another damaging witness was Sergeant Charles W. Emory of the 66th U.S. Colored Troops, who testified, "Mrs. Field lives in a little house by the levee. I went by to get a drink of whisky and I saw her sewing a pair of spurs on a lady's underskirt. The lady held up her dress and Mrs. Field sewed them in."

Several defense witnesses not only supported Rebecca Field, but also described how they had served as volunteer clerks when she was overwhelmed with business. Lieutenant Lucius Morse of the 66th U.S. Colored Troops said, "Her loyalty is unquestioned. She refuses to sell to people who don't have a Treasury Department permit. I have heard her ask Colonel Graham about the permit rules. I have been in her store every day until the store closed and I've often helped her by clerking and selling goods. I write up bills for her when the store is crowded. Mrs. Gillison spends all her time in the kitchen and knows nothing of Mrs. Field's business." John Faun, a government lessee at Terrapin Neck, said, "I made out bills and sold goods when she was short of help. She tried to stay within the regulations. I certainly think she's loyal." L. B. Wilkinson, acting principal for the 51st U.S. Colored Troops school, also helped out in the store and noted that Field had both black and white customers.

The next witness, Colonel A. Watson Webber of the 51st U.S. Colored Troops, asserted the strictness of Federal policy: "I have never permitted a dime's worth of goods without a reference to the Treasury Department and a permit, and I issue no permits at all to the back country people."

Five "colored citizens" questioned Eliza Gillison's veracity. Abe Davenport, who had known Gillison for ten years, described her "bad character." Solomon Wilkens said, "I have never heard any good of her from black or white," while Albert Kean from Outpost Plantation commented, "She was so disagreeable that the man who employed her turned her out." Alfred Wyatt, who also farmed at Outpost, termed Gillison "mischief-making, quarrelsome, dissipated and untruthful." He added, "She has got fowl from me, then refused to pay." The court asked, "Would you consider her worthy of belief under oath?" "No, sir, I would not," Wyatt replied. The prosecution then produced fifteen rebuttal witnesses, who all avowed Gillison's fine character and excellent reputation for truthfulness. The defense returned fire, describing the fifteen prosecution witnesses as "field hands . . . of the lowest order of intellect, easily molded in their testimony. The defendant has been defamed and vilified by persons of no social standing."

The court found Rebecca Field guilty of "selling goods, contraband of war, without proper authority" and "smuggling and assisting to smuggle . . . contraband of war through the lines of United States forces." She was fined $1,000 and ordered to be imprisoned until the fine was paid. In view of the inconsistent testimony presented and the questionable degree of her involvement in any smuggling, the penalty seems harsh. Perhaps she had Confederate affinities not perceptible in the written record. Certainly, the existence of her store had made life more pleasant for local inhabitants in her small part of Louisiana.

One of New Orleans's places of incarceration was the Union Press Prison. Like many Civil War prisons, it was an improvised affair, housed in an industrial building. (It most likely had been a cotton press, where loose cotton was squashed under great pressure into bales.) Unlike today's penal institutions, only a wall—and not a very good one—separated in from out. In September 1864, Mrs. William Denison, who lived very near the prison, was charged with throwing a bundle over the wall into the prison and concealing Confederate prisoners who had escaped through a hole in the wall.[8]

Second Lieutenant Henry Schumpe, of the 56th Ohio, testified first: "I saw a bundle thrown from her residence. The bundle was in a handkerchief. I did not see who threw it. When we came to her house, she ran out and seemed confused. I searched the house and found one escapee in the kitchen and two in the stable. We found that they had sawed through the prison floor and dug out into Mrs. Denison's yard." A piece of carpet covered the hole in the prison wall. On cross-examination, Schumpe conceded that he had not seen Denison at the prison or in conversation with any of the prisoners. His testimony was followed by that of Private Jacob Bender of the same regiment, who said, "I assisted Lieutenant Schumpe and found an escaped prisoner hiding in Mrs. Denison's house behind the door in a downstairs bedroom. When we first came to the house, she said, 'Go ahead and search the house.'" The defendant summarized her case: "They searched my house four or five times. I know nothing of it." Based on this rather slender testimony, Denison was convicted of hiding escaped prisoners in her house and sentenced to twelve months of hard labor in the "City Work House." The reviewing general, E. R. S. Canby approved the sentence.

## ARKANSAS

During the Civil War, malaria was found in nearly every American state, but it was far more common in the South than the North. Over a million Union soldiers contracted malaria and were badly weakened by its symptoms of intermittent chills and fever. Over four thousand Union soldiers died of the disease, mostly of the *Plasmodium falciparum* type, which even now is often fatal because of its damage to the brain and kidneys. During Grant's siege of Vicksburg, 13 percent of his troops came down with new cases of malaria each month. The suffering of Confederate troops was, most likely, even greater.

In 1861, the only useful treatment (or preventive) for malaria was quinine, a derivative of the bark of the cinchona tree, found in South America. Quinine for the Confederacy had to pass through the blockade and was always in short supply. Ten grains of quinine (600 milligrams) each day will prevent malaria in a person. A soldier without chills and fever could march farther and shoot straighter than his shivering comrade. Six ounces of quinine would keep most of a regiment healthy for an entire day, and that was the amount Fanny Foster smuggled south at Pine Bluff in October 1864. In her trial, prosecution witness Obodiah Flynn, a farmer, said, "I know she brought six ounces [of quinine] down to my house . . . she left it with me to sell for her."[9]

Watchmaker Eugene Wordman had known Foster for eight years. He testified, "In October 1864, I saw Mrs. Foster near the lines. She had came outside the lines in a buggy. I was arranging seats for her and others in Mr. Flynn's wagon, and told Mrs. Foster her carpet sack would make a good seat. She said she could not sit on that as she had some quinine in it and might break the bottles." The final witness against Foster was Treasury Agent Charles Godden, who confirmed that she had no permit to take quinine beyond the lines. Foster herself made no defense. She was fined $500; if she failed to pay this amount within ten days, she was to serve six months in prison. The severity of the punishment suggests that the military value of quinine was well understood. To whom farmer Flynn sold the quinine is not recorded, but the life-preserving white powder was certainly not going north, where medicines were in relatively abundant supply.

## MISSISSIPPI

Why did the Confederacy want Spanish fly? Known today as a legendary aphrodisiac, this substance was widely used by doctors in the 1860s. Civil War surgeons hardly needed to incite lust among the soldiers, and indeed Spanish fly is not only useless as a love potion but is also rather poisonous. Yet it was thought to have beneficial properties as well. Spanish fly, *Cantharis vesicatoria*—literally, the "beetle that blisters"—was made from the pulverized bodies of the beetles and was used to raise blisters on ailing soldiers. The prevailing medical notion was that if painfully reddened skin was good, then red and blistered skin must be even better. Some soldiers who resisted this painful treatment (now known to be useless) were court-martialed for failure to obey orders.

Jennie Shenkle had contraband cantharides and morphine in her baggage when she tried to pass through the Union lines at Vicksburg. The full text of the August 1864 trial is now lost, but the remaining material reveals that Shenkle used the alias of Jenny Shulers and that she was sentenced to twelve months in military prison. The reviewing general, Napoleon J. T. Dana, had some doubts about the justice of imprisonment; as he wrote, "Inasmuch as the evidence fails to establish an absolute certainty that this person was a full partner in the guilt . . . of her associates, her sentence is commuted to banishment from the district, with orders not to return during the war . . . she will be landed at Cairo [Illinois]."[10]

More extensive records from the file of Maggie Kelly tell us of her associates. Shenkle, Kelly, and a Mrs. Reynolds had traveled together. The trio had begun their journey in Union-occupied New Orleans, where a woman had hired them to smuggle cantharides, morphine, and other items into the Confederacy. Kelly (also known as Maggie Oliver) was provided with a trunk, the false bottom of which was packed with these medicines. The three women were to meet a contact at Natchez, but that mysterious person did not appear, so they took the next steamboat north. What they did not know was that their smuggling plan was no longer a secret.[11]

Captain Jacob S. Curtiss, 72nd Illinois, provost marshal at Vicksburg, told the court that his contact in Natchez had warned him of the smugglers. He testified, "I stationed a watch at the landing and on their arrival here had them arrested when leaving the boat on the 18th of August 1864. On taking them to the Provost Marshal's office and having their baggage searched I found a quantity of contraband goods (as per exhibit) therein. The accused [Kelly] admitted to me that she and her two friends had made arrangements to take the said goods through the Federal lines at Natchez."

The list of concealed items is quite remarkable, covering 63 types of goods. Domestic items included spools of thread, shirts, dresses, linens, hats, bonnet frames, cologne, collars, ribbons, combs, hairpins, a hoop skirt, and "32 boxes of Lily White" (the nature of which has remained a mystery). Items of potential use to an army included two pounds of cantharides, four ounces of morphine, 72 boxes of Radway's Pills, 72 boxes of Wright's Vegetable Pills, and hundreds of sheets of writing paper. General Dana approved Kelly's sentence: twelve months in prison. Whether Kelly was motivated by money or patriotism, four ounces of morphine would have provided 12,000 ten-milligram doses, relief from misery for a whole field of wounded Confederate soldiers.

Mary A. Russell, tried at Vicksburg in October 1864, seems to have been the victim of a deliberate misreading of a Confederate document. The issue was whether she had taken an oath of allegiance to both the United States of America and the Confederate States of America. Captain Curtiss, who had testified in the Shenkle case, appeared in Russell's trial as well. He confirmed that she had a pass from the proper Union authorities to go to Mobile, Alabama. Defense counsel E. W. Chamberlain asked, "Do you swear positively the accused said she had taken the Oath of Allegiance to the Confederate States government[?] . . . Do you know of the accused having taken the Oath of Allegiance to the so called Southern Confederacy while at Mobile?" Curtiss replied, "I saw an oath in her possession which I took to be such."[12]

This oath, issued by the Confederate provost marshal in Mobile, is still in her records. The wording seems clear: "Permission is granted to Mary Ann Russell to proceed to Vicksburg and Memphis through our lines, upon oath not to communicate, in writing or verbally, for publication, or otherwise, any fact ascertained, which, if known to the enemy, might be injurious to the Confederate States of America." Nowhere is allegiance to the Confederacy mentioned. An apparently intentional misreading of the clearest possible language gave the Union an excuse to confine her for a year in Jail No. 1 at Vicksburg, with General Dana's approval.

Mattie Patterson seems to have been an industrious, if incautious, spy for the Confederacy. At her June 1863 trial for conveying information about Union troops near Jackson, Mississippi, she refused to speak, even to enter a plea. The presiding officer, Colonel Joseph W. Burke, 10th Ohio, admonished her, "It would be much more pleasant for this commission and much more to conduce [sic] to justice being done . . . if [you] would lay aside your recusant manner, and consent to conduct a defense . . . you should procure counsel." She refused to do either, and the court entered a plea of "not guilty" on her behalf.[13]

Captain R. M. Goodwin, assistant provost marshal general of the District of Cumberland, spoke: "All parties passing through our lines . . . are examined by me . . . we gave her a pass to Centralia, Illinois . . . merely to throw her off guard . . . because of information from a female detective."

That person was Carrie King, a resident of Murfreesboro, Tennessee, some forty miles southeast of Nashville, who then told the court of her surveillance of Patterson:

> I met the prisoner first about Thursday, last about the 27th; I called on her the next day as a friend . . . she had just come through the lines and was going to Nashville, I told her then that I had been in pretty much her situation but had obtained a pass, was going to Nashville, and would be glad of her company. I told her to call at my boarding house and I would accompany her to Nashville. She said she would call; she did not call, and I came round to where she was staying to see her. I engaged in conversation with her. She told me she had not yet obtained a pass to go to Nashville. . . . She also said she had parents living in Illinois. I told her I was detained here but had a friend in Nashville, a northern lady, who could be of advantage to her if she would call on her. She said she . . . should go south again. She also said that considering her situation she did not think the officers here had treated her well and that she should do them all the harm in her power. [She wanted to] send a note out through the lines to a Major [William] Clare [on Braxton Bragg's staff] . . . that from her observation they would be attacked and for them to be on their guard and not be taken by surprise. She then wrote a note [that King promised to carry south]. She . . . folded it and put it in an envelope and gave it to me sealed. The envelope here shown me (marked exhibit B) is the one she gave me . . . her whole interest and sympathies were with that side.

King added that the defendant had told Union officers wildly exaggerated tales of southern fortifications and had destroyed any incriminating papers, saying, "They must think me a fool to carry such things." At their next talk, Patterson had told her that they both must be on guard against Union detectives posing as southern sympathizers. King concluded her testimony by noting Patterson's claim that she was well acquainted with General Cheatham. Cheatham, Tennessee's most beloved Confederate commander, was a hard drinker, rumored to dally with women, and was and an implacable foe of both Braxton Bragg and John Bell Hood. He was slightly wounded at Shiloh.

On hearing King's narrative, Patterson dropped her stance of mute defiance and announced that she had hidden relevant documents under a rock near the trial location. The court sent her under guard to retrieve the papers, which she did. (Sadly, the papers have been lost from the trial record.) Patterson's next act was to request counsel, and Captain James Warnock, Second Ohio, was appointed to assist in her defense.

Upon cross-examination, King was asked if she had concealed her identity as a detective. This she readily admitted, noting that such concealment was an essential part of her occupation. At this point, Patterson asked for a continuance and made a most remarkable request: she wished to obtain a deposition from Braxton Bragg's provost marshal, then at Shelbyville, Tennessee. The court rejected her request on the grounds that it would be very difficult to obtain a deposition from an enemy officer during wartime and that any such testimony was unlikely to be accurate.

The documents that tied Patterson to Jackson, Mississippi, are absent from the record, but it would appear that they revealed her to be a formidable spy. And for that, she received a formidable sentence: life in prison. On review by General Rosecrans, however, her jail term was reduced to three years in the military prison at Jeffersonville, Tennessee.

### ALABAMA

In the heyday of Caribbean piracy, two female buccaneers bestrode the stage of history: Anne Bonney and Mary Read, a pair of hard-drinking, cross-dressing, bisexual, pistol-toting women with murder in their hearts. Surprisingly, the little town of Larkinsville, five miles west of Scottsboro, was home to the larcenous, cross-dressing, pistol-toting Maggie Johnson, who under a variety of aliases (including Marcella Rains and Maggie Rains) struck terror into the hearts of peaceable citizens, especially Union men.[14]

On the night of March 23, 1865, Maggie, dressed in a Union soldier's uniform, with two male companions, all carrying revolvers, burst into the home of T. E. Harris, "a loyal citizen," and took at gunpoint sixteen women's dresses, a silver watch, a razor with its strop, and a variety of lesser items. Maggie was soon captured and sent to Nashville to stand trial. Harris's daughter, Laura, recalled that night: "I am personally acquainted with [the defendant]. I am shure she could not so disguise herself that I wouldn't readily recognize her." The robbers attempted to keep their victims literally in the dark, using a candle only in a separate room. However, the alert Laura peeked into the room where theft was underway. She testified that Maggie "held the candle in her hand and I had a clear and plain view of her countenance. . . . I would know her at any time or place."

Maggie's reputation is reflected in a letter addressed to the provost marshal of the District of Tennessee, "with the request that the lady be disposed of in some manner so that we will not be troubled with her in this district, not having the slightest use for that kind of truck." The writer's prayers were answered when Maggie's sentence of three years in the penitentiary at Nashville was approved by the commanding general. She fared better than her Caribbean sisters who were both sentenced to hang, although they escaped the noose by "pleading their bellies," that is, pregnancy.

In Alabama, July was a prime time to acquire malaria. Jane Burleson hoped to alleviate this situation (and make a little money) by carrying "a large amount" of quinine to Athens, Alabama. In addition to the quinine that she brought through the lines, she also carried a letter, 9 pairs of ladies shoes, a gross of hooks and eyes, 44 spools of cotton thread, 42 yards of Irish linen, 8 yards of black calico, 31 yards of dackonette, 32 yards of brown linen, and a dozen handkerchiefs. How she hoped to conceal all this remains a mystery, but it certainly confirms the shortage of consumer goods in the South in the summer of 1864. After finding her guilty, the court sentenced her to be sent south of the Union lines until the end of the war. All her goods were confiscated. The exact amount of quinine does not appear in the records, but its value was well known.[15]

## GEORGIA

On December 21, 1864, Confederate forces withdrew from Savannah. The following day, William T. Sherman sent his famous message to Abraham Lincoln: "I beg to present you, as a Christmas present, the city of Savannah, with 150 heavy guns and plenty of ammunition and also about 25,000 bales of cotton." Savannah became a city under occupation, with all the problems of an economy half military and half civilian.

Annie Egan was one of those problems. She and her husband Patrick ran a small grocery at the corner of Drayton and York Streets. (A "grocery" was often a liquor store, but the Egans sold "nothing stronger than soda water.") In October 1865, they were tried for possession of stolen goods, in particular a hospital bedsheet and part of a bedspread. J. S. Allen, a hospital detective with the occupying Federal forces, told the court: "I found a sheet marked 'Hospital Department' and . . . a green spread which had been cut up." Allen returned to the Egans' grocery with four people—the hospital steward, the commissary sergeant, a U.S. detective, and a policeman. "We then made a search but found nothing more," he testified. The cut-up spread matched common hospital bedspreads. The Egans had a few shirts they said they had bought from soldiers, and a discharged soldier said that he had sold them a flannel shirt.[16]

The defense produced one witness, Lewis Jacobs, a "colored man," who had seen Annie Egan buy drawers and a shirt from a man who showed his discharge papers. However, Jacobs conceded that Annie could not read and therefore could not tell a discharge from any other piece of paper. The Egans' counsel argued that they were not in the military and could not legitimately be tried by a military court. Moreover, according to the laws of Georgia, the Egans' offense was liable to prosecution only if they knew the goods to be stolen; and since neither of them could read or write, they could not read the purported discharge sheet. Finally, the Egans made no attempt to conceal the items and were innocent of any crime.

The court, however, thought otherwise. The Egans were each fined $35, which they were unable to pay, and as a result they were marched off to spend sixty days in the Chatham County Jail.

## SOUTH CAROLINA

Charleston, the legendary cradle of secession, was the site of two trials in September 1865. Both trials centered around the symbol of northern occupation—the Stars and Stripes. The defendants were two women, tried separately for a crime in which both had allegedly participated.[17]

Emma Jones was charged with dragging the American flag in the dust, trampling and kicking it, while exclaiming, "Here is what I think of your

flag . . . you would serve our English flag the same way, if you could."
Jones, who ran a boarding house on Wentworth Street, came to the United
States from Ireland at age sixteen.

There was intense interest in this apparent desecration of the symbol of
a reunited nation. The first prosecution witness was thirty-eight-year-old
Oscar Van Tassel, a machinist and engineer, who boarded at Jones's place.
As he testified:

> I have a room in the house of Mrs. Jones. On that day [August 18,
> 1865] at 12 o'clock or thereabouts, when descending from my room,
> Mrs. Byer, the accused, and Mrs. Jones were at dinner. I was invited by
> the accused to take dinner with them. The invitation I accepted. After
> dinner, I was about to retire from the house, when the accused told me
> she had received a present the evening before from a friend in Phila-
> delphia, and that if I would remain a few moments, she would go and
> bring the present and show it to me. She brought in a small American
> flag, the Stars and Stripes. I examined the flag telling her it was very
> beautiful. About this time, the daughter and niece of the accused came
> into the room. Whereupon, after an introduction, the accused threw
> the flag over her niece's head saying that she would make a Yankee of
> her and kissed her through the flag. The flag then dropping upon the
> floor, the accused picked it up, folded it and laid it carefully in her lap.
> I then retired from the dining room to the parlour, the accused passing
> then through the parlour, made the remark that she must take her flag
> home, meaning the next door. I remarked to the accused, she must take
> good care of the flag, it was all she had now to protect her. Whereupon
> she replied in a laughing manner: go away with your old flag. I know
> that it's all I have to protect me. The flag then dropped on the ground
> between the house and the gate, the accused stood upon it—all in a
> joking and pleasant manner. After she [illegible] up the flag and walked
> toward her house outside of the gate. Mrs. Jones then passed through
> the parlour to the gate, after which I heard none of the conversation or
> what they had done with the flag. The accused returned some ten min-
> utes afterwards. I then remarked to her, that it was wrong to do what
> she had done: should there have been a United States officer or friend

passing by, they would have taken the flag away from her. The accused remarked, "They wouldn't be so foolish as to do that when she was only in fun or playing with it," saying at the same time she wouldn't take $200 for it, that there wasn't money enough in Charleston to buy it.

Three soldiers from the 47th Pennsylvania were the next witnesses. Levi Wagner had been sitting on the porch of a theater across the street. He saw both Byers and Jones trample the flag. When he crossed the street and spoke to them, Jones "talked so saucy," that he left and returned with twenty-three-year old Peter Allen, who had much to say:

> I was on King Street, I suppose when the thing occurred. I was go-ing down Wentworth Street. I then met a man by the name of Wagner. He stopped me and said there was an awful thing occurred up here. I asked him what it was. He said, two ladies trampling on the flag in the street. I requested of him that we would return & see what they meant by it. I asked the accused when we got there what she meant by doing what she had done. [Wagner seems to be speaking of Byers.] She said she had just done it to tantalize a friend, pointing to a friend sitting on the settee. I told her that was very poor sport, doing so. She replied "She knew it but didn't think any no harm of it." She said the flag was made a present to her by a friend in the naval department—she thought she would have a little fun over the flag as it was made a present to her. I remarked again I thought it mighty poor fun, trampling on the flag. We then went down to the Provost Marshal's and got two file of guards and arrested them. . . . She remarked to me if she had done wrong, she was sorry.

Jones reacted very differently. According to Allen, she stepped right up to him and said, "What of it? That's no more than what you have done with my flag." He continued, "I told her if I heard any more of her talk I would arrest her. She stamped her foot and said she was an Englishwoman. I asked her why she didn't stay in England. She replied she'd go to England but that the Yankees had stolen all her gold and silver. I said that her gold and silver was like mine—damned little." During her arrest, she asked Al-len what the Union would have done without the help of British subjects.

"I told her that the few British subjects that came here were deserters from the British Army and were bounty jumpers in the United States."

With her counsel, L. W. Spratt, Jones prepared a very long defense statement. A few excerpts convey its essence:

> It is perhaps not altogether frank to say that I did not sympathize with the individuals in this city who suffered from the late unhappy war, but I can say with perfect frankness that I did not in feeling or in fact become a party to that war, and ever hoped for the return of peace and the restoration of the Union . . . my obligation is to the Queen of Great Britain. . . . I am a woman with three small children and my funds were dependent upon a letter from my husband. I took the Oath of Amnesty solely to get my mail at the Post Office. . . . Trusting to the indulgent consideration of this honorable court and that they may deal gently with the faults of a woman . . . the mother of three small children, who without her will want the care necessary to them.

She was fined $100, the equivalent of $3,000 today.

Jane Byers was charged with the same crime. Oscar Van Tassel repeated his testimony, adding, "When I told Mrs. Byers to take care of the flag, she deliberately dropped it on the ground and stood on it. Then she picked it up and went home." Private Wagner, whose primary language was German, recalled Byers rubbing the flag with both hands, trampling it on the pavement, and kicking it. Her attorney cross-examined Wagner, suggesting that his imperfect English caused him to misunderstand her. Wagner was quick to reply that he understood English well enough to know what she was saying.

A different picture emerged in the defense testimony of Captain Henry J. Inwood, provost judge and member of the 165th New York Infantry, who had visited her in jail:

> She was sent to jail by mistake before the sentence of the court was approved. I called at the jail to know why the accused had been sent there & found her in a deplorable state of depression, but the only request she made was that I should send her the flag I had taken from her and wished I had shot her rather than to have sent her to jail. [The court

asked of her past character.] Having a doubt of the guilt of the accused, implied in the charges, I visited her house repeatedly. I found the circle of visiting acquaintances [*illegible*] but select. I never at any time heard seditious language or slurs cast upon the Federal authorities uttered by anyone in the house. I also learnt they were much respected neighbors. . . . I have been informed that three Federal prisoners were secreted by Mrs. Byers [during the Confederate occupation] in her house, fed, clothed & then furnished with money to make their escape. This I heard from her daughter. . . . I consider her guilty of the act [of desecrating the flag] but not of the intent. I deem it an act of thoughtlessness, not of the impulse. I never knew her before this incident.

The Reverend William B. Yates, seaman's chaplain at the Mariner's Church of Charleston, also spoke on Byers's behalf: "She is a member of my church and is of unblemished character. . . . She makes statements playfully which would go to show that she had lost the balance of her mind. She has taken no part in [politics] at all."

Guided by her counsel, Mrs. Byers prepared a truly remarkable defense. After a three-paragraph introduction, she arrived at the heart of her argument:

Gentlemen, let me assure you, as a woman, as a mother, and as an American citizen, that before my God I intended no insult to the flag or to the nation. Gentlemen, I cannot and will not deny the act, on the contrary, I blush to admit that I trailed that flag on the ground, but with no malice or criminal intent. I have often, in admiring a fine piece of cloth, held it in my hand and taken the shades of light as reflected upon the colors, as a source of pleasure, and I have judged the harmony of colors in this manner. In this manner, gentlemen, did I take this new flag, that had just been presented to me by a Federal officer, and a friend of mine and of my family.

After several hundred words on the theme of her loyalty to the United States, she returned to the issues of the trial: "I am not guilty of insulting the American flag, nor of an intent to do so, but, gentlemen, I am guilty of wicked indiscretion, without any intent to do wrong." She ended with a plea for clemency, asking the court to keep in mind the "mortification and disgrace" that would fall upon her children if she were convicted, which she was. Her fine was $100. The whole case was then thrown out on a technicality (the court had not been sworn in the presence of the accused) by Brevet Brigadier General W. T. Bennett, and Byers was released from jail.

## NORTH CAROLINA

Before the Civil War, relationships between blacks and whites were well defined, both by law and by custom. The heart of the matter may be seen in the words of the U.S. Supreme Court's Dred Scott decision, which proclaimed that blacks were "beings of an inferior order, and altogether unfit to associate with the white race, either socially or politically; and so far inferior that they have no rights which the white man was bound to respect." This 1857 opinion, which enraged northern abolitionists and comforted southern slaveholders, was soon made irrelevant by the Emancipation Proclamation of 1863 and the Thirteenth Amendment of 1864. However, the North had no clear plans for what to do with millions of people without education, wealth, or land, suddenly set adrift in a ruined South. The trials of two North Carolina women illustrate the fatal possibilities in this historic moment of wrenching adjustment.

In Davie County, the Neely plantation was presided over by the widow Providence Neely and her daughter, Temperance Neely. In July 1865, Temperance was charged with murder, accused of killing "Galina, a colored woman, formerly the property of Providence Neely." The trial was presided over by Lieutenant Colonel Reuben C. Kise of the 120th Indiana. Temperance's attorneys began by denying the jurisdiction of military courts now that the war was over. Failing in this objection, they cited chapter 107, section 71, of North Carolina's law code, which prohibited blacks from testifying against white persons. This objection was also overruled, and Sallie, "a colored woman," began her testimony.

> She [Temperance Neely] did have a pistol and she fired it on the day you mention and she fired it at Galina. The hands were in the field harvesting—they got through at 4 o'clock. Miss Providence asked Galina's daughter [Ellen, age ten] after she got through why she did not come to the house as she had plenty of work for her to do. She then

told her to go after a bucket of water, if she did not she would not give her any supper that night. She [Ellen] replied to Miss Providence that she would have supper, and that she could not hinder her either. Then Miss Providence told her that she would whip her when she came back, for talking to her so—the girl said back to Miss Providence "nor you won't whip me" when she came back Miss Providence went to whipping her. Then Galina the mother of the girl being whipped laid down her child and went into the big house, and pushed Miss Providence down. The prisoner [Temperance] told her not to come in there—if she did she would shoot her. Galina said she was going to have her child—then Galina got her child and came on out and the prisoner fired at her as she was going out with her child. Galina said something in reply to the prisoner which I did not understand and thereupon the prisoner jumped down run around her and shot her in the breast. [The court asked if Galina had struck either white woman.] No sir, she just pushed Miss Providence down and got her child.[18]

Sallie added that Temperance had always treated Galina and Galina's five children more kindly that the other blacks on the plantation, which had provoked jealousy in the quarters of the former slaves. A few months earlier, Providence had told Galina to leave the plantation, but Temperance had told Galina that if she left, her children would be put in the woods to perish.

After the defense counsel's usual objections, Henderson, "a colored man," was allowed to testify: "I was sitting by my back door and heard shots. Galina said, 'Miss Temperance has shot me.' Those were her last words. . . . She died in about 15 minutes. Miss Temperance seemed in great distress. She caught a horse for herself to go to the doctor." Cassandra, another former slave, told the court, "I was hauling wheat. I saw her kick Ellen before Ellen went for water."

Providence Neely then took the stand. She testified that she had called Ellen three times, but had gotten no response until the fourth call. When threatened with the loss of supper for her insolence, Ellen had been quite unrepentant. As Ellen was getting water, Providence had broken off a peach-tree switch. Ellen had delivered the water and started to run. Providence had grabbed Ellen's arm. The girl had tried to bite her. Providence had grabbed both of the girl's arms and had dragged her into the dining room where the switch lay. She had released one arm and had begun beating Ellen, who in turn had tried to scratch her face. At this moment, Galina had arrived, pulled Ellen away, and had thrown Providence down. She was going down the steps when Temperance had fired the first shot, which missed. Providence had caught up with them near the cookhouse and had begun to beat Ellen again. Galina had whirled around as if to push Providence, and Temperance had fired the fatal shot. Galina had been able to reach Henderson's house, where she had collapsed. Providence remembered that "Temperance was in a very distracted condition, crying out such things as, 'What shall I do? I never expected to have my hands in human blood. Galina was my favorite Negro!'"

Arthur Neely, 60, was the next defense witness. He stated: "Providence is my brother's widow. He died in 1842 or 1843. Providence has always been very easy with them [her slaves]—clothed and fed them well, never had an overseer." John D. Johnson, a neighbor, added, "She is remarkably kind hearted both toward white and black. Her treatment to her negroes has been very good, protecting them when they were hired out." Both men called Sallie, the first witness, a liar.

A written defense statement, dozens of pages in length, cited as its centerpiece the words of a then-celebrated Justice Foster in a similar case: "I have been longer upon this case because accidents of this lamentable kind may be the lot of the wisest and best of mankind, and commonly fall amongst the nearest friends and relatives . . . the forfeiture of goods . . . would be heaping affliction upon the head of the afflicted, and galling to a heart already wounded beyond cure." The court, apparently swayed by the argument that the murderer is the true victim, ordered Temperance Neely to pay a fine of $1,000. The reviewing general, Thomas A. Ruger, a future commandant of West Point who had been wounded in the head at Antietam, was appalled. As he wrote, "To a person of property, such punishment is the very lightest which could be inflicted, and the affect . . . is simply to encourage crime."

A hundred miles to the east, a parallel story was played out near the town of Henderson, where Elizabeth Ball was tried for the murder of James

Thomas, "a colored man." William Hendricks, "a young white man," was called by the prosecution. Hendricks, who could read and write, had been sent with a note for Ball from Captain Benjamin Evans of the 28th Michigan. He was to read aloud the note on behalf of Thomas. It appears that neither Thomas nor Ball could read. Hendricks testified:

> I went up to Mrs. Ball's house with Jim Thomas—and Mrs. Ball said you are come to kill me with your guns. I said, Oh no Mrs. Ball I am coming to read a note. She said I don't want to hear your note, Mrs. Ball then came out of the kitchen and got a gun and came out to meet us . . . myself and the deceased. When she got in about ten steps of us I said don't go to shooting this way—and she said then get out of the way; I went close by the chimney. I just run out of the way ten or fifteen steps. Mrs. Ball then sprung the gun, and snapped once at the deceased Thomas. And then the deceased went up to Mrs. Ball and caught hold of the muzzle of the gun she had, and pushed it away from him. Then Mrs. Ball got the gun out of the deceased hands and shot him—The deceased after he was shot staggered as if you had stuck a hog—and fell. I went to Mrs. Ball and told her I didn't come there for any bad intentions, and that is about all I know about it.[19]

When asked about the recent plan to end the Union occupation of North Carolina, Hendricks was pessimistic: "The Yankees were about to leave Raleigh and I expected a good number of the Negroes would be killed." Captain Evans added further testimony: "The note was from my office. I told Mr. Thomas to go with a white man and he would have nothing to fear." Sixteen-year-old former slave Martha Scott had been at the house on the day of the killing. As she recalled:

> I was in the house and saw Jim and young Hendricks coming into the yard and heard Mrs. Ball tell him to go back, and he kept coming into the yard. He was coming with Mr. Hendricks. I heard her tell Jim if he came into the yard she must shoot him. She said she had sent him word two or three times that if he came into the yard she intended to kill him, and she asked what he came for, and Jim said, Mrs. Ball, I didn't come for a fuss, and he told her that he came after his things.

She asked Mr. Hendricks what he came for, and he said he came to read the paper, as he was sent, she went into the house then, after her gun, she went out then with her gun. Jim was standing still when Mrs. Ball went out with her gun. I didn't look at them any more, but turned my head away from the window. [After I heard the shot] I heard Mrs. Ball tell Mr. Hendricks to get out of her yard, that she would have him taken up for bringing the nigger into the yard. Mrs. Ball said there he was, that she had shot him, and she told me to go and tell some of the neighbors to come there and carry him out of the yard.

A dozen other witnesses added their perspectives. Frank Parrish said that Jim had worked several months for Ball, apparently without being paid. A Mrs. Harris claimed she was there at the shooting and said that it was "self-defense." Emily Lewis recalled that "Elizabeth Ball's husband said the Yankees was leaving and I'll hang Jim up and you can shoot him." Ball's daughter, thirteen-year-old Rebecca, reported, "Mother said they [Jim's possessions] wasn't there, that Mr. Rolin had them." Neighbor John Wiggins added his opinion of Hendricks: "I only know what I have heard. I think his character is bad. Mr. Ball has paralytic fits. . . . Mrs. Ball is peaceably disposed, honest and truthful." U. A. Quincy said, "Hendricks has been a liar since he was a boy," an opinion voiced by four other witnesses.

Richard Saintsing, 22, had been at Ball's house four days earlier, arresting Jim Thomas. Although Thomas was told that his clothes were at Rollins's place, he insisted that Ball had to be the person who would return them. Betsy Elizabeth, "colored," who did not know how old she was, heard him say, "I'm going to Mrs. Ball's and kill or be killed, and die and go to hell," a recollection shared by the final witness, listed only as "black boy Lee."

Ball's twenty-four-page defense included this mélange of mixed metaphors: "Inspired with this confidence [in the judicial system], she tremblingly flings her little barque upon the untried sea, hugging to her aching bosom the fearful yet consoling thought, that there still lived in the heart of an American soldier the yet-sleeping fires of ancient chivalry, whose strong right arm was at once the shield and avenger of woman's wrongs." Unswayed by this efflorescence, the court sentenced Ball to three years in prison. General Ruger reduced the sentence to one year and sent Ball's case to Judge Advocate General Joseph Holt in Washington, D.C. Holt was not sympathetic to her "aching bosom," as shown in his legal opinion:

> A review of all the papers, including the record, has satisfied this Bureau that, notwithstanding the representations of the petition, there is nothing in the case to recommend it to favorable consideration. The guilt of the prisoner was clearly established, and her punishment is in conformity with the statutes of the state. It is believed security for order and obedience to law will be best promoted by permitting penal justice to take its course in all cases of crimes like this, and that a pardon would be inadvisable. This woman, whose character is better seen in her bearing while committing the homicide, than in any of the testimonials filed in her behalf—has been imprisoned but about two months; and it would be a low estimate, indeed, of the value of the life of a freedman, to hold that the taking of it, under such circumstances as have been detailed, could be atoned for by so slight a punishment.

Perhaps mindful of the two North Carolina governors and fifty-two "influential citizens" who had petitioned him on Ball's behalf, President Andrew Johnson issued her a full pardon, just three months after James Thomas was shot down in her yard.

The final North Carolina case, that of Caroline Campbell, alias Mrs. George Van Slyck, raises many questions. Was she a loyal Union citizen, keeping track of Confederate guerrillas and blockade runners in the largely unpopulated stretches of Currituck Sound? Or was she pulling the wool over the eyes of Ben Butler and his minions while provisioning the Confederate swamp rats who harassed Union patrols and supply boats as they steamed along the inland passages of the Virginia–North Carolina border country?[20]

In Campbell's January 1864 trial, she was charged with trading with the enemy. The trial record itself is lost, but surviving correspondence between 1865 and 1875 reveals many of the issues. In February 1865, Campbell's husband, George S. Van Slyck, wrote to Judge Advocate General Holt, complaining that under orders from General Ben Butler in November 1863, his and his wife's goods and all their money had been seized and that they had been imprisoned for nine days before being told it was "all a mistake"and released. The money and goods were not returned, however, and in February 1865 his wife was tried and convicted for "trading with the enemy." Van Slyck asserted that such trading was impossible, since the lines separating Union and Confederate territory were sixty miles from her store. Nonetheless, his wife was convicted and fined $5,000, which she was unable to pay since the Federals had seized all their cash. Van Slyck appealed to Judge Holt on patriotic grounds, explaining that the witnesses against his wife were secessionist guerrillas opposed to her Union sentiments and her providing of valuable intelligence to Union general John Foster (who was in constant pain from an 1847 leg wound at Molino del Ray).

Holt ordered an investigation. In March 1865, he received a lengthy reply from Major Joseph L. Stackpole, who had been the judge advocate for the Department of Virginia and North Carolina. Major Stackpole told of Campbell's four-day trial, in which she was represented by the Honorable L. H. Chandler and Messrs. Ellis and Ford, of Norfolk. He noted that "Currituck is not 60 miles from the enemy lines, as Mr. Van Slyck says, but is in a position most admirably suited for this trade, being situated in an country sparsely occupied by our troops, filled with smugglers, blockade-runners and guerillas." Stackpole went on to explain the basis of Campbell's financial success: she gave enough intelligence to Union authorities to retain their support, while selling enough goods to Confederate supporters to guarantee their good will and protection.

On April 6, 1865, Holt issued a strong and clearly-worded opinion. His opening phrases would seem to spell doom for Campbell: "A careful examination of the mass of testimony . . . leaves no doubt whatever that the accused during the years 1862 and 1863 repeatedly aided the enemy by furnishing them with large amounts of goods from her store situated near Elizabeth City, No. Ca. and though contriving to remain on good terms with our officials, was constantly and most efficiently serving the Rebels." But all was not lost for Campbell. Holt continued, "It is equally clear, however . . . that the provost court had no jurisdiction of a crime of this character and that it was not legally empowered to pronounce a sentence of confiscation, or expulsion, or even a fine of the magnitude here imposed." He went on to recommend that she be released from custody and that her goods and money be returned to her, in whatever degree possible, closing with a general admonition about the jurisdiction of provost courts: "It will be observed that this is one of that class of cases over which provost courts have unwarrantably extended their jurisdiction and which have recently given much embarrassment to the government." Holt's opinion was endorsed by Secretary of War Edwin Stanton. (In 1875, Campbell attempted, without success, to reopen the case.)

From the records available, it would appear that the Campbell–Van Slyck business was of considerable help to the Confederacy, whatever Campbell's motivation. What is puzzling is Holt's opinion that the provost courts had exceeded their authority, while in hundreds of military commission cases, no such concern is apparent. Was a provost court different from a military commission? Perhaps some future legal scholar will unravel this apparent mystery.

# 5

# NORTH OF THE LINE

## KENTUCKY

KENTUCKY, ALTHOUGH A border state where slavery was legal, generated remarkably few trials of women by Union military commissions. However, Kentucky did produce that rarity—a woman sentenced by a military commission to be hanged.

Jane Ferguson was charged with "lurking as a spy" near Lebanon, Columbia, and other Union army posts in Kentucky. To further this activity, she "disguised herself as a Union soldier, calling herself John F. Lindley." Her November 1863 trial got underway with the testimony of Lieutenant Colonel Israel N. Stiles, of the 62nd Indiana, who commanded the post at Lebanon:

> The accused was brought to my Head Quarters, some two or three weeks since by a guard from the 13th Ky Cavalry, having been arrested by Lieut Col Weatherford on suspicion of her being a spy for the enemy. When I first saw her, she had on a soldiers uniform, with the exception of the hat, which was a broad brimmed black felt hat. In reply to questions which I propounded to her, she stated that her name was Jane Ferguson, that she was married, her husband was a soldier in the rebel Hamilton's command. She said she was furnished by Hamilton with male attire, horse and equipments, and directed to visit Glascow, Columbia and Lebanon, ascertain the number of troops at these localities, their situation and whatever other information she could obtain, and if necessary to join some of the regiments stationed at these points,

that she was directed by him to return as soon as possible with whatever information she obtained. She states that she crossed Cumberland River below Burksville, and came through to Lebanon, stopping on the way not far from Columbia at the house of a citizen. She left her horse and equipments in his charge until she should return. She also stated that she had enlisted in the 13th Ky. Cavalry, I think the day before her arrest, under the name of John F. Tindsley [Lindley?] that Tindsley was her maiden name. She also gave the names of several females whom she said were sent out at different times by Hamilton, to visit the interior portions of Kentucky on the same mission with which she was charged. She gave a description of them, their real names and the names by which they went when on this business. The conversation which I had with her was held in the presence of Capt. [John] Robinson of Genl. Hobson's staff, Lieut Col Weatherford, 13th Ky Cavalry and, I think, one or two others.[1]

Colonel Stiles added that Ferguson's husband was unkind to her and that once she had crossed the Cumberland River, she had resolved not to return. No threats or promises were made during the interview. Captain Robinson, of Company E, 27th Kentucky Mounted Infantry, then testified that she was married to Isaac Ferguson, who was a cousin of the notorious murderer and guerrilla Champ Ferguson. Before she joined Hamilton's group, she had served with "Kilbreth."

Ferguson produced two defense witnesses. Private Elisha Keaton, 13th Kentucky Cavalry (Union), had known her for a year. He stated, "She has tolerable good character and is considered a Union woman." Samuel Jeans of the same regiment said, "I have known her ten months. She always bore the name of a good Union woman and has always talked Union." Ferguson was unable to read or write, so her written defense was done with help and signed with an "X." As it read:

I was married to Isaac Ferguson. I had known him about one year. I had gone to school to him. After marrying him, I remained with him about five months. He was then living at home. He joined Capt. Hamilton's guerrilla company. I then went home and remained there.

My husband came after me. I went with him to Greensborough and remained there about three months, part of the time in camp, and part of the time at a boarding house. Capt. Hamilton . . . wanted somebody to go to Lebanon. I volunteered to go, owing to my husbands ill treatment. I desired to get away from him and his control, my intention being to remain here. His treatment from the time I was first married to him has been unbearable. I had a few hundred dollars of my own, and he desired to obtain possession of it, which I always refused to allow him. On several occasions he has stated that all he wanted with me was the twelve hundred dollars that belonged to me. He was fully aware of my union sentiments, nevertheless, was willing to let me go on this expedition believing that I was too much afraid of him to disobey him. Immediately on my arriving among the Federal troops I gave them warning that rebels might come upon them at any time. Through my general ignorance of how to act, and prompted by a desire of safety, I enlisted in the regiment to avoid again coming in contact with unnatural husband. After my sex had been discovered I then made the voluntary statement of what I had been sent there for, at the same time disclaiming my intention of again returning to those that had sent me. I cannot read nor write and am innocent of any evil intention. I was sent on a mission that was repugnant to me, and I embraced the opportunity to escape.

Ferguson was found guilty and was sentenced to be hanged. A note in an unknown hand states:

Proceedings examined and found correct, but the evidence would hardly seem to warrant the finding of the court the conviction evidently resulting from the prisoner's own confession, which confession should be taken *as a whole* to warrant the finding and this it does not do, for a portion of this confession was, that, although coming through our lines by direction of a rebel captain under pretense of obtaining news; *she never intended returning*—her only object being to get away from a husband whom she loathed. I therefore recommend that the proceedings be forwarded to the Adj't Gen'l of the Army.

Two months after the trial, the badly rheumatic Brigadier General Stephen Burbridge recommended mercy for her. A full eight months passed before Major General John Schofield, in October 1864, ordered her released.

Like so many records of long ago, what is missing can be as intriguing as what is there. Why the eight-month delay before Schofield acted in Jane Ferguson's behalf? Although he was badly injured when his horse fell on him on May 25, 1864, he resumed command a few days later. In 1856, he had suffered from yellow fever (which A. P. Hill, the future Confederate general, had treated with a brandy mint julep each morning), and in 1862 he had contracted typhoid, but he seems to have recovered from both illnesses. All of which leaves unanswered the reason for the long delay in Schofield's decision. Did Ferguson spend those eight months of waiting behind bars, or was she free to come and go? If Isaac Ferguson had been less greedy and less of an "unnatural" husband, would Jane have flown home to him, bearing the military dispositions of Kentucky's Union troops? Isaac Ferguson seems to have unwittingly injured the Confederate cause.

The efforts of other female quinine smugglers pale in comparison with the audacious Ann Trainor, whose enterprises included buying 1,018 ounces of quinine. According to modern dosage recommendations of ten grains every eight hours for seven days to treat active, acute malaria, she had enough for a seven-day course of treatment for 2,327 men, or several depleted Confederate regiments. She also bought nearly two hundred pounds of opium, sufficient for over a million one-grain doses. Opium was and is the best treatment for diarrhea, which was the most common disease in the Civil War—and Ann Trainor had enough opium to dose more than half of the entire Confederate army.[2]

These two acts certainly qualified her as a stalwart Confederate supporter, but her final blow against the Union was that of concealing a Union deserter, Private E. R. Davis of the 15th Pennsylvania Cavalry, who showed his gratitude by testifying against her. As he told the court, she had concealed him for two months, and he had seen her with a packet of quinine.

Her purveyor, Dr. Charles Taffel, a St. Louis drug wholesaler, testified, "She asked me for one thousand ounces of quinine and two hundred pounds of opium. I bought it [quinine] for three dollars and seventy-five cents per ounce and charged her four dollars. . . . [Opium] cost me eleven dollars and 85 cents [per pound] and I charged her twelve dollars and twenty-five cents for it." He was able to supply all the quinine she ordered, but only 149 pounds of opium. The entire transaction was worth nearly $200,000 in today's money. The records do not reveal how or where she obtained such a large sum of money.

U.S. detective Thomas Settelier recalled Trainor's case clearly. He had arrived at her house as the wagon was being loaded and had arrested her, Private Davis, and Dr. Taffel. "She said if I had not been so quick she would have had them out of my reach . . . she said her object was to make money, that as everybody was doing it she thought she had as much right to it as anybody else," Settelier testified.

The court found Trainor not guilty. The reviewing general, George Thomas, the Rock of Chickamauga, expressed amazement at the verdict: "The evidence clearly indicates a certain degree of guilt under the second charge [quinine and opium sales]. The general commanding cannot perceive upon what ground the commission have given an unqualified acquittal." If Ann Trainor's shipment had escaped the Union's grasp, it would have been a vast boon to the blockaded Confederacy, with many thousands of southern boys restored to health.

The case of Meta Mason, of the town of South Bend Mills, is unusual in several respects. She was tried by a court-martial, not by a military commission. She was a seventeen-year-old orphan from a slaveholding family. She was labeled as a "traitor," and she was sentenced to prison on Johnson's Island, near Sandusky, Ohio, a prisoner-of-war camp used for Confederate officers. Her crime? On April 30, 1863, she wrote a letter to her brother, Sergeant Dean K. Mason, Second Kentucky Cavalry (CSA), who was serving in General John H. Morgan's brigade. The letter, which never reached Sergeant Mason, was full of news and opinions, and was the basis of "giving comfort to the enemy," and of "giving the position and conduct of Federal soldiers." As she wrote: "I am happy to say we are all well . . . but the Feds are making sad havoc with the property of some. Dr. Brown and Mrs. Beard have suffered greatly. They have taken 37 Negroes and a great many of her work mules . . . they are pressing all the horses through the country. . . . Mr. Gunn's Negro and one of Mr. Barbus' run off last week and rode Harriet Ann's buggy horse. I hope he killed him. The Feds took Uncle Gram's Old Jim . . . four of Mr. Grimes' [former slaves] has run off this week."[3]

Mason advised her brother not to visit home because of the danger of capture and gave details of other neighbors having their horses and former slaves taken by the Federal troops. She closed with this thought: "I know there is a day coming when these rascals will receive their reward, if not in this world, they will afterwards. I heard you had sold [slave] Harrison. I expect you had better exchange the money for Tennessee [money] if you can, if not for South Carolina or Georgia money . . . write soon to— your sister."

Communicating with the enemy was one of the activities forbidden by General Burnside's General Order No. 38. Mason's counsel opened the defense with these words: "Her only concern was love for her brother. Repeating neighborhood gossip is hardly conveying military secrets. As to her talk of retribution, her thoughts were applicable to those who had perpetrated outrages. She throws herself on the mercy of the court, pledging the honor instilled into her youthful mind by her now-deceased parents."

Brigadier General James M. Shackleford (whose foot had been shattered by a Confederate bullet at Geiger's Lake, Kentucky) interrogated her. She admitted writing the letter. He reminded her that under General Order No. 38, the penalty for communicating with the enemy could be death. When she claimed that she had never heard of such an order, he pointed out that her own brother had been arrested for violating that order. She replied that she did not think such an order would apply to "ladies."

B. W. Bevier, "a Union man" who lived in Mason's neighborhood, told the court that General Order No. 38 was widely discussed and was common knowledge. The judge advocate for the trial, Captain John Arthur of the Eighth Kentucky Cavalry, wrote, "This case . . . is of great magnitude as a precedent for the future conduct and behavior of the very large female rebel population that infests this portion of the Department of the Ohio. You have before you the case of a woman who has always identified herself with the cause of the rebellion and regarding Orders No. 38 . . . did grossly and willfully violate them knowing at the time that if detected she would be liable to a punishment of death."

In her defense summation, Mason told the court that she lived far from the railroad and that it was difficult to find a newspaper. "Many women wrote to men in the Confederate army. It was not considered a matter of importance. How could it be supposed that a girl of tender age . . . should be so well versed in the rules of war?" she asked plaintively.

Although Mason was convicted, her case aroused considerable sympathy. The president of the court-martial, Lieutenant Colonel Thomas B. Fairleigh, 26th Kentucky, and three other officers who had convicted her all petitioned for mitigation, describing her offense as "bad but not willful." Further, they noted, "she is young and inexperienced . . . her entire neighborhood is intensely Rebel . . . and exercises a decided influence on her." They opined that the stress of six weeks of legal proceedings would deter her from further offenses.

Forty-five citizens of Russellville, Kentucky, wrote to General Burnside asking for clemency, as did fourteen members of the 26th Kentucky Infantry (Federal), including their colonel, Cicero Maxwell. The ailing Brigadier General Jeremiah Boyle (his illness was not specified) also wrote to Burnside, recommending that "on account of the extreme youth of Miss Mason . . . that she be released . . . and permitted to return to her home on taking the Oath of Allegiance. She is now in this city [Louisville] on her way to Johnson's Island . . . but I have permitted her to remain here until these papers could be referred to department headquarters."

Meta Mason signed the oath of allegiance, promising to be "faithful and true to the State of Kentucky" and to "disclaim all fellowship with the so-called Confederate States." A few days later, General Burnside ordered her release. It is doubtful, however, that either her love for her brother or her affection for the Confederacy were diminished by signing the oath of allegiance.

## VIRGINIA

It will come as little surprise to find that the Old Dominion State produced some women who opposed the Federal forces. One of the five Virginia cases revolved around the Great Greenback Raid. For most of the war, a portion of northwest Virginia was under the control of Confederate John Singleton Mosby, the commander of Mosby's Rangers and a brilliant tactician. The South regarded him as a dashing cavalier, *un beau sabreur*, a modern-day Robin Hood. The North viewed him and his men as thieves, brigands, highwaymen, murderers, and cutthroats. Both sides agreed, however, that Mosby's crowning achievement occurred on Friday, October 14, 1864, at 2:00 A.M. The night express out of Baltimore, filled with passengers, was speeding west and had just passed Duffield's Station, West Virginia. The silver rails sparkled in the night air—except where Mosby's men had removed one section of rail. When the onrushing locomotive hit the gap, it veered wildly, smashed into an embankment, and came to a violent halt. The still-moving baggage car crushed the boiler; escaping steam badly scalded the engineer and his son. Even as the last car was grinding to a halt, Mosby's men were rushing aboard.[4]

The rangers killed the one Union officer who resisted, robbed the women of their purses and jewelry, stripped the male passengers of all except their underwear, and set fire to the splintered wooden cars. A car full of German-speaking emigrants had fearfully refused to leave the train, but the approaching flames needed no translator; they fled into the night. The rangers viewed their escapade as a fairly normal train robbery until they found the Union paymaster's box, with $168,000 in cash inside. This was real money, Union money, not the rapidly depreciating paper currency of the beleaguered South.

When the rangers divided their loot, each man received roughly $2,000 ($60,000 in today's currency), and soon Loudoun County was awash with stolen cash. At this point, Mary A. Klein entered the story. Klein was a resident of Snickersville, Virginia, but she was arrested and tried in Baltimore in January 1865. The charges against her were feeding Mosby's guerrillas at Snickersville, holding stolen money, and violating the oath of allegiance.

The first witness in her trial was Second Lieutenant H. B. Smith, Fifth New York Light Artillery, who recounted Klein's arrest. "She told me that she had a quantity of money belonging to her son—that it was at the Eutaw House [a better-than-average hotel in Baltimore] in her room. I sent an officer with her to get the money. She went outside the door and shortly returned and said she had the money with her and if I gave her a room she would take it from her person and give it to me. I gave her a room and she handed the amount—the sum of $1600 I think. She stated when she handed it to me that one roll she handed was her own money." It seems not to have occurred to Smith that she could have escaped through a window or that she could have some money still under her hoop skirt.

The provost marshal of the Eighth Army Corps, Lieutenant Colonel John Wooley, interviewed Klein after her arrest. She told him that she was at Harper's Ferry [about ten miles east of Duffield's Station] the day that Mosby captured the Union payroll, and that she had three family members with Mosby's command. In his office, she produced about $1,600, but said that it belonged to her son, who had borrowed it from one of Mosby's men. She said that her son was going to use the money to open a photographic business in Loudoun County, and she insisted that she was a loyal woman. Wooley asked her how she could be loyal if she possessed money stolen from the U.S. government, but she reiterated her declaration of loyalty. She added that her son had been in the Confederate army and that the Mosby's men had assembled for the raid on the train at a place about four miles from her home. She also knew that the total amount stolen from the train was $180,000. The provost marshal demonstrated great interest in the serial numbers on her paper money. Most of the bills were in sequence, beginning with the number 112896.

The first defense witness was Klein's own son, Dr. John A. Klein, 27, who lived three miles from Snickersville. He claimed that any cash in his mother's possession was from a debt owed to her, and he denied that she knew of large sums of cash "floating around" the area. Dr. Klein made a special point of the Union's inability to protect citizens in that area, which is known even today as "Mosby's Confederacy."

Annie O'Bannon lived in nearby Jefferson County, West Virginia. She recalled that Gibson, one of Mosby's men, had given Mary Klein some money. S. B. Caldwell had known Klein for forty years but had not seen her since the war began. He described the "delicate condition" in Loudoun County: "Whichever side comes to the house, we must feed them or suffer depredation, so we treat both sides with equal politeness. As they say, 'If we have our hand in the lion's mouth, we must get it out as quietly as we can.'"

In her written defense, Klein claimed to be only a boarder and house-keeper in her son's house and said that she was powerless to resist Rebels who wished to be fed. She blamed any feeding of Rebel men on her son, and characterized the large amount of money she had received from Gibson as merely the repayment of a prior business debt. She claimed no knowledge of where Gibson had gotten the money. She further insisted that the rules of war made the capture of the money legitimate, and that if Gibson had taken it from the train, he was entitled to it. She concluded, "I am a lady of character and respectability." Her self-proclaimed respectability did not persuade the court. She was found guilty of holding stolen money and of violating the oath of allegiance and was sentenced to spend the rest of the war in the Female Prison at Fitchburg, Massachusetts.

The entrance of Chesapeake Bay is surrounded by towns of historic importance—Hampton, Newport News, Norfolk, and Portsmouth. The waters that lie in the center of this cluster were the scene of the clash between the *Monitor* and the *Virginia*. Just to the south, the sounds of North Carolina and the Great Dismal Swamp all contain thousands of acres where clandestine activities could go unobserved, making them a perfect home for blockade runners and smugglers. And murderers.

It was there, in April 1863, that four women came to grief. Mary Hall and Ann Cuthnell of Norfolk were tried together, charged with carrying letters to the Rebels. They both pled guilty but offered statements that they hoped would mitigate their sentences. Hall told the court:

> I reside near Great Bridge about 1½ miles from Miss Cuthnell. I remember the circumstances of the death of Frank Bromfield, a soldier, at the house of Miss Cuthnell one week ago today. On the morning of Tuesday of last week Miss Cuthnell was at our house on a visit. She went home and I went with her. At her house we met Mr. Harry Williamson, Mr. James Randolph and Thomas Nottingham. We had been there about one hour and a half when a soldier came. We were sitting around the fireplace and the soldier came directly in and asked for the

man that was just from Richmond and he went to Mr. Williamson first and asked "if he was the man." Mr. Williamson replied "He was not." He then went to Mr. Randolph and "asked if he was the man." Mr. Nottingham during this conversation got up and went into the adjoining room. The soldier said "he would arrest all three of the men." The three men followed the soldier out. Mr. Nottingham came from the adjoining room and we all went out together. Mr. Nottingham asked Miss Cuthnell and myself, "What must he do?" My reply was to "go with the soldier." Mr. Nottingham said "he would not," then Mr. Nottingham went into the house and got his coat, came out, and went around the house—the soldier said "what had become of that other man"—the soldier said he "did not believe that Mr. Williamson or Mr. Randolph were either of them the man who came from Richmond—the other man was the man he wanted." The soldier went round the house to look for him. Both went out of sight. We did not know any more until we heard the report of a gun. We did not see Mr. Nottingham any more. When I first saw the soldier after the shot was fired he lay dead on the ground, his head toward us. We went out to the road as soon as he was killed and there in the road we met a teamster. I saw him when he first came in sight. He stopped his team as soon as he heard the report of the pistol or gun. Miss Cuthnell and myself went to this teamster and related the accident to him. He told us to remain at a house nearby until the guard came. We remained as directed. The teamster went to the Great Bridge.[5]

Further testimony established that Nottingham was a known blockade runner who had brought letters to Hall from her brothers in Richmond and Fredericksburg. In the moment before the soldier's body was discovered, Nottingham had taken the dead man's gun and money.

Cuthnell then had her say. She told the court that she lived near Norfolk about a mile from Great Bridge, with her old mother, and claimed that all the letters that had passed through her hands were of "a personal nature." She confirmed the story of the murdered soldier. Both women were convicted of "assisting in forwarding letters across the Rebel lines," although neither had actually carried the letters. In April 1863, Ann Cuthnell and

Mary Hall were sentenced to prison for the duration of the war. The reviewing officer, Major General John A. Dix, ordered both women "retained in the custody of the Provost Marshal at Norfolk until further orders." Those further orders are not evident in the record.

The unusually brief records in the case of Maria L. Tabb hint at a very sad story. In April 1863, she was charged with "carrying letters and money . . . to and from enemies in armed rebellion against the United States, at Portsmouth, Virginia." Her plea of guilty precluded the introduction of testimony, so nothing is known about how long she served as a courier, her routes, or the types of money and letters she carried. Nor do we know if she worked directly for the Confederate government.[6]

Tabb entered a statement asking for leniency: "All I did was to oblige others. My husband, a blacksmith, is in North Carolina. I have three small children. I own in my own right a house and lot in Portsmouth between County Street and Crab Street. As this is my first offense, I hope the court will be lenient." They were not. She was sentenced "to forfeit all her real estate and be imprisoned during the war."

To many southerners, Major General Benjamin F. Butler was a beast, Satan incarnate. Thus, it must have been an extraordinary experience for spinster Amy F. Cormick when, in April 1864, she was interrogated by Butler himself. Cormick was faced with three charges: spying, carrying treasonable letters, and carrying goods and supplies to the enemy. She was a native of Princess Anne County, Virginia, and told the court, "I live with Mr. A. W. Bell, 20 miles from Norfolk, near London Bridge." She pled guilty to carrying goods and supplies but denied spying and letter carrying.[7]

Lieutenant Colonel Abial G. Chamberlain, 37th U.S. Colored Troops, was a witness for the prosecution. He was in charge of the "entrenched camp" two miles northeast of Norfolk. He had heard that Cormick was carrying contraband and ordered her to be arrested. She did not wish to be searched, but her request was denied, and she was moved into a tent where she was searched by Mrs. Lieutenant [Samuel] Day and Mrs. Lieutenant [Calvin] Mixter. Under her skirts the women found carrying bags with four pairs of ladies' boots, calico, letters, and medical powders. The defense counsel asked Chamberlain if he had seen these articles when they were found. The colonel seemed shocked at the question, replying, "It could hardly be possible that a gentleman could be present when a lady was searched!"

Second Lieutenant John C. Davenport, in charge of the Bureau of Information and the Examination of Refugees, Deserters, and Spies, recalled Cormick's words when arrested: "I have not taken the Oath of Allegiance, so I have never deceived you." She refused to identify the persons mentioned in the letters that were hidden under her clothes. She was then brought before General Butler, who asked her, "Have you used any other name lately other than Cormick?"

> "Any other name?" she asked.
>
> "That was my question," replied the man whose legal skills had earned him millions.
>
> "I think I have used several [other names]."
>
> "Such as what?"
>
> "I could not tell you, sir."
>
> "You mean you won't tell?"
>
> "Yes, sir."
>
> "Confine this woman on bread and water until she can tell!"

Thus ended her visit to General Butler.

The many letters seized from under the hoop skirts of Amy Cormick are a fascinating, albeit fragmentary, peephole into the wartime life of ordinary folks. A November 1863 letter from a Richmond family asks for silk and flannel goods and reveals that it cost a dollar to have a letter smuggled. A mysterious note describes "Lieutenant Johnson professing to be a Confederate prisoner but really a Federal nephew of General Butler."

Two notes seem to relate to the defendant herself. Elizabeth Taylor Selden wrote, "Mr. Tabb will pay to Miss A. F. Cormick any sum which she may require for my use and she will give receipts for same." Another note says, "Bought by me in the month of March 1863 a pair of shoes for Negroes Roger and Dick, belonging to the estate of Major John Cormick, deceased. $4.00 each. Settled with Miss A. F. Cormick, admix. [administratrix] April 11, 1863." (The Confederate roster lists no Major John Cormick.)

Wartime social life was described in another letter: "It is bitter cold here. If there is any fun in Norfolk, the Yanks have it all to themselves. . . . Mary Newton was married the day after the snow, under mysterious circumstances, to Dick Jones, who had been summarily kicked out of the 'Atlantis' a few days before for drunkenness and breaking up the crockery. They were married at 11:00 A.M. in old clothes, and he ended the day by getting drunk and going to the theater. . . . This [war] has demoralized every class of society. . . . Lucifer is holding Carnival here."

In effect, Cormick's smuggling had taken the place of peacetime commerce, peacetime postal service, and peacetime legal transactions, as the Confederacy tried to maintain the workings of a modern economy in the face of growing pressure from Federal military power.

## DISTRICT OF COLUMBIA

During the Civil War, Washington, D.C.—with its stinking canals, half-finished buildings, pox-ridden whorehouses, lurking lobbyists, and grasping contractors—was a true sinkhole. It also was the setting for the trials of seven women. In 1864, the city's provost marshal compiled a list of over eighty houses of prostitution in the capital. For each, he listed the name of the madam, the address of the house, the number of inmates, and a rating of quality on a scale of one to four, one being the best and four being the worst. The house of Louisa Koener, with five "girls" was rated as a "three" and was located at 540 12th Street Northwest. It is probably not a coincidence that Rebecca Smith and Maria Kelly gave that as their address, even though they were not charged with prostitution, but with helping soldiers to desert. Their military commission was headed by General Abner Doubleday, who was still recovering from severe headaches after a neck injury at Gettysburg the year before.[8]

According to the trial record, the two women "did purchase three suits of citizens clothes for three enlisted men, namely, Private John Kooch [or Cook], unassigned substitute, Private John Fox, 12th Maryland, and Private Charles Fablich, 22nd Massachusetts, well knowing them to be deserters . . . on or about the sixth day of August, 1864." The testimony in each case was almost identical and was confined largely to statements by the three deserters.

Private Fox testified first. "I first saw her [Smith] at 154—12th Street. . . . I asked her to get citizen's clothes." He told her a lie: "I was free from the service. . . . I had no intention of deserting—I paid about ten dollars for the clothes, changed clothes and was arrested coming out of the house. Misfortune drew me to Washington." Private Kooch, who spoke only German, told his story through a translator: "A gentleman on the train gave me brandy. When I got to Philadelphia I was perfectly drunk. When I came to, I was in uniform. I had 300 guilders in my pocket." Private Fablich [or Frielich] told a similar story, also in German. Fablich, who did not seen overly bright, insisted that he went into that house for no reason at all, but he did recall that "Mrs. Kelly, the lodger, asked the old lady if it was all right to buy clothes for the men." Equally plausible was Rebecca Smith's defense statement: "I didn't want to buy clothes for them, but they insisted. We paid $60 for three suits down on Seventh Street."

The mention of "lodgers" and an "old lady" who had to be consulted seemed to confirm the defendants as prostitutes, making a little extra money by helping soldiers to desert. Judge Advocate General Holt, who reviewed the case, shared this opinion, remarking, "It appears to be a house of ill fame." Both women were sentenced to six months in the Female Prison at Fitchburg, Massachusetts.

The women of 12th Street were not the only women in the garment business. At least five others were in trouble for that offense, including two who helped their husbands to desert. Private Lawrence Kelley of Company I, 25th New York Cavalry, was one of those husbands. He was a deserter, hiding in Washington, D.C. Bringing civilian clothes, his wife, Jane, traveled from Schenectady, New York, to the District of Columbia, where she bought him a train ticket out of town. When a government detective stopped them at the depot, she offered him a $100 bribe to release her husband. Private Kelley and his wife were both taken to the central guardhouse, he for desertion, she for aiding desertion and attempting to bribe a Federal officer. The military commission, headed again by General Abner Doubleday, ordered Jane to prison for two months plus a fine of $250. In an unusual turn of events, the case came before Secretary of War Edwin Stanton, who reduced the fine to the $100 already in the hands of the provost marshal as evidence of bribery.[9]

In November 1864, Private William J. Sheehan [or Sheehen] was a member of the "First New York Heavy Artillery Regiment." His wife, Florence, charged with providing him with civilian clothes, told the court, "My husband wrote a letter to me telling me to fetch his clothes and I brought them to him [at Washington]. . . . He had been a soldier but I didn't think he was one when he wrote me." She pled guilty and offered no witnesses.[10]

At this point, two members of the commission intervened on her behalf. General Francis Fessenden (who had lost a leg at Cane River, Louisiana) asked Florence Sheehan, "You simply obeyed your husband's instructions?" "Yes," she replied. General Doubleday told his colleagues, "I think she ought to withdraw the plea of guilty and enter a plea of not guilty. She does not plead guilty in the sense of criminality being attached to the act." She then entered a modified plea: "I am guilty of fetching the clothes but I deny any criminal intent." This change does not seem to have helped her much; she was sent to the prison at Albany, New York, until she paid a fine of $200. In February 1865, Secretary of War Edwin Stanton ordered her immediate release.

The difficult handwriting and confusing story of Mary Melwell's trial present challenges in interpretation. She appears in the record as Mulwell and Melville as well as Melwell, but that only begins the story. She and a male companion were arrested at Washington's Baltimore and Ohio railroad depot by U.S. detective A. Hitchcock. Her male companion gave his name as James McFadden, a member of the Second Connecticut Heavy Artillery. Hitchcock interviewed the two separately. Melwell told him that McFadden's name was John, not James. When Hitchcock spoke with McFadden alone, he said that Melwell was his sister. As Hitchcock testified, "She said first that he [McFadden] was employed in the city as a teamster on the city cars. After she found out that he had owned up, she acknowledged to her bringing a coat from Philadelphia."[11]

The defendant told the court that she was married to a soldier in the Fifth New Jersey Light Artillery who was at the front at Richmond. When asked about the true identity of her companion in the railroad depot, she replied, weeping, "I have been more than a sister to him." Her testimony was later borne out by a letter written in November 1864, a month after the trial, in which Margaret Green wrote that Mary Melwell's true name was McIlnee and that it was her half brother to whom she had furnished the civilian clothes that he wore at the depot. "Mrs. McIlnee furnished him those clothes owing to the promptness of her affection," Green asserted.

Melwell closed her case with the statement, "I was foolish and ignorant." The commission fined her fifty dollars and sentenced her to six months in prison, but its members asked the reviewing authority to lessen the sentence because of "the peculiar circumstances of the case."

In the next case, it appears that the Union army tortured witnesses until they cooperated. Andrew Allen and Francis Brassell were wearing civilian clothes when arrested. They denied being soldiers. The provost guard took them to the prison in Georgetown, where they were "showered" until they confessed to being members of the Third Massachusetts Heavy Artillery. An officer of that regiment was summoned and visually confirmed their identity. However, Allen and Brassell refused to say where they had bought their clothes. The major commanding the prison found an easy solution to this troublesome detail: "I will have you showered until you tell me." The men then swore under oath that the clothes had been furnished by Elizabeth Buckley, of Uniontown, D.C. First Lieutenant Walter P. Beaumont (Third Massachusetts Heavy Artillery) told the court that he had sent the guard to her house, where they had discovered two pairs of pants. He added, "I have been told that Mrs. Buckley keeps a house of ill repute."[12]

The trial of the twenty-four-year-old, pregnant Elizabeth Buckley began. Privates Brassell and Allen were the first witnesses. Brassell reported that he had been to Buckley's house seven or eight times and had bought civilian clothes from her for $30. Allen had been to Buckley's house only twice. When he ordered a suit, he gave her his size and two greenbacks—a $20 bill and a $10 bill.

Buckley claimed that the men had urged her to buy them clothes and had promised her that they would not desert. "They just wanted to cross the [unspecified] bridge," she asserted. Captain George R. Walbridge, assistant provost marshal, asked for speedy action in the case, "as it is reported to me that she is enciente." Speedy, indeed. Off she went for a year of prison at Fitchburg, Massachusetts, a place not known for its maternity facilities.

All this was unsettling news for her husband, Private Thomas E. Buckley of the First District of Columbia Cavalry, who was busy skirmishing with the Confederates near Richmond. He wrote to Abraham Lincoln, asking for executive clemency. The letter's phrasing suggests that he had help with it:

> Your petitioner Thomas E. Buckley begs to state that his wife Elizabeth F. Buckley, is now in confinement at Fitchburg, Mass. charged with furnishing a soldier with citizen's clothing—to be retained in confinement a period of one year. Your petitioner is at loss to account for this conduct on the part of his wife—and humbly petitions your Excellency's executive clemency in her behalf. Your petitioner is a soldier in Company "B" 1st District Columbia Cavalry devoutly zealous in his attachment to the union and the suppression of rebellion—his wife a laundress in said company, and her fidelity equally true. . . . Ardently attached to her—my wife—I humbly petition your Excellency to mitigate her punishment if not restore her to her widowed mother, her husband and freedom.

Six officers of Private Buckley's regiment endorsed his petition.

Seven months passed. On May 31, 1865, President Andrew Johnson freed Elizabeth Buckley from prison. Her case is puzzling. Was she the victim of perjured men, anxious to avoid another shower? Did she help men to desert, thus aiding the Confederacy, while her own husband was fighting for the Union? Was she pregnant by her husband or by another man, and did she give birth during her seven months at Fitchburg? And if she did, what became of the newborn child?

An apparent sting operation was the downfall of Mary Ann Connor, who ran "a sort of grocery" on L Street, between First Street and New Jersey Avenue. John Langley was a soldier in the 91st New York. He was also a member of "Captain Potts' detective force." As he testified at her trial, "I told her I was going to take the 6 o'clock train going North and that I wanted to get the clothes for that purpose. . . . I took dinner there [Connor's house]." He told the court he had paid $10.50 for civilian clothes.[13]

Connor's counsel, Frederick H. Norton, introduced his only witness, "Martha Smith, colored," Connor's servant. Smith had lived with Connor for four months. She claimed that Langley had purchased no clothes: "He came in and asked for his dinner. He paid half a dollar for it and walked out." Private Langley was recalled and confirmed his previous testimony, which was clearly different from Martha Smith's. Which story was true?

The judge advocate for the trial gave his opinion: "The defense was in the testimony of the colored servant, but she must be mistaken." Connor was found guilty of selling citizen's clothes to a soldier, fined five dollars, and sent to prison for a year. Her husband immediately wrote to President Lincoln. After a preamble in which he outlined the case, he told the president: "She was committed to the military prison in said city to await the publication of the sentence of the court. That his said wife Mary is in a very poor state of health and he fears imprisonment may endanger her life. That about three weeks since she was confined to her bed and gave birth to a child and her life was despaired of by the two physicians attending upon her—and that she had but just recovered from her illness." With this letter came two affidavits certifying him as a man of good character. Lincoln sent the letters to Assistant Secretary of War Charles A. Dana, along with a letter from Dr. C. M. Ford, a surgeon at Washington's Carroll Prison, who wrote, "Mrs. Connor is in very feeble health, owning to recent confinement." Judge Advocate General Holt added his legal opinion: "There is no reason to doubt her guilt."

On December 5, 1864, Connor's counsel requested a review of newly submitted affidavits. Seven days later, a memo from the War Department ordered her release. Her pregnancy and delivery had endangered her life, but had also freed her from prison. And what of the evidence gathered by a police spy, an employee of an agency so secret that the U.S. Treasury was not allowed to audit its books? Was Mary Ann Connor treated fairly? Or was she the victim of a largely hidden bureau whose workings are barely known even today?

The final case raises again the question of work opportunities for women, as well as the question of what constituted a disorderly house. It also illustrates another barrier to the recovery of wounded soldiers, especially at Lincoln General Hospital, a Federal government facility on East Capitol Avenue at 14th Street.

Julia Rosell faced three charges: selling liquor to soldiers, theft, and "keeping a disorderly house." At her February 1865 trial, the parade of witnesses began. Second Lieutenant J. J. Toffy of the Veterans Reserve Corps had searched her premises. He testified, "By order of Dr. McKee ast surgeon in charge of Lincoln Hospital, I went to search the house of the prisoner, in the latter part of July last, I found a pint bottle of whiskey under her bed, and about a quarter of a keg of lager beer." In response to a question about hers being a "disorderly house," Toffy told the court, "Yes, I have seen her house full of soldiers, drunk and noisy, I have been called there twice to surpress [sic] a disturbance, once by the prisoner, and once upon the report several of my men." He added that her house was about forty rods (600 feet) from the hospital. The term "disorderly house" usually indicated the practice of prostitution, but at Rosell's place Toffy found no whores, just alcohol. The stolen items seemed mostly from the hospital: two hospital blankets, four government blankets, one rubber blanket, a bedspread, a pair of pants, and a shirt.[14]

Hospital Detective W. P. Jenkins gave his observations. "Some six months ago she and her sister kept a shanty about one hundred yards from the branch of Lincoln General Hospital. There was a riot in that neighborhood houses were burned and a soldier killed. She and other parties were arrested. At that time, I found whiskey and beer in her house, since then, they [Mrs. Rossell and her sister] have dissolved and have two shanties, one on each side of the hospital." Prosecution witness S. W. Krinkrum was concise: "I often saw sober men going into her house and drunken men coming out." There was one defense witness, Rosell's sister, Mary McGill, who told the court that the defendant was just a laundress, trying to make a living. "I have seen drawers and shirts there, belonging to soldiers, to be washed," she testified.

The defendant asked for mercy, asserting that she had no way of making a living except by keeping a shop. Her son, who was also her only support, was a soldier from the "1st District Cavalry," then being held in a Rebel prison. Julia Rosell was found guilty of all three charges and sentenced to two months in prison. The case was reviewed by Major General Christopher Columbus Augur, who was still crippled by a gunshot wound he had received at Cedar Mountain, Virginia, and by dysentery he had acquired at Port Hudson, Louisiana. Augur remitted the prison term, provided she leave the city until the end of the war.

The purpose of Lincoln Hospital, like all other hospitals, was to return sick and wounded Union soldiers to duty. Riots and drunken brawls certainly delayed this process, and thus aided the Confederacy. While Julia Rosell's motivations seemed largely those of economic survival in an era when legitimate work for women was woefully scarce and badly paid, they actually impaired the Union war effort. In a final turn of the wheel, her disorderly shanty worked against the very cause for which her soldier son was fighting.

# 6

# IT TAKES A VILLAGE

MOST OF THESE stories of women tried by military commission concern individual women or small groups, but on at least two occasions hundreds, even thousands, of southern women worked together to overturn a decision by the authorities of Union military justice. This chapter thus considers not women on trial, but two examples of women resisting the judgments of trials. In both cases, Confederate soldiers had been convicted of murder. One had been sentenced to life in prison, the other to the death penalty. The women rallied networks of relatives, friends, and neighbors to petition the president and the judge advocate general. Especially in Virginia, many of the petitioners were persons with names famous even today.

The triumph of mother love over military justice is seen in a Maryland incident involving a young son of Old Virginia. John W. McCue, of Mosby's Rangers, lay in Clinton Prison at Dannemorra, New York, serving a life sentence. His mother, Mrs. John H. McCue, and 204 other elite Virginia women spearheaded a movement to free him from the looming decades of incarceration. His worried mother began this campaign by writing to President Andrew Johnson in August 1865: "Now that the angel of peace is again rustling her wings over our country that for four years has been drenched in fraternal blood and under your benign influence the prison doors are being thrown open . . . may I not hope that my darling and noble son may likewise have his shackles broken?"[1]

What had McCue done? His story began in the hamlet of Croom in Maryland's Prince George's County. It was the evening of April 3, 1865. South of Croom, the Confederate government had abandoned its capital, and the Army of Northern Virginia was struggling west toward Amelia courthouse. William T. Sherman's troops were fighting at Snow Hill, North Carolina, and Nathan Bedford Forrest's cavalry were holding back the encroaching Union troops near Selma, Alabama. The war seemed finished and far away; at Croom, all was quiet.

Croom's mercantile needs were provided by Jeremiah Coffron's small convenience store. Around 8:00 P.M., Coffron's usual closing time, two young men wearing long gray overcoats entered the store and purchased a bottle of brandy with a twenty-dollar bill. Slouch hats partially concealed their features; their overcoats had no trimming or insignia. Coffron gave them change, closed the store, and went to his home for supper. As he ate his evening meal, a neighbor summoned him, saying that there was a late customer. Coffron put aside his dish, went to the darkened store, and lit a lantern. The same two young men sprang from the shadows, pistols in their hands. In a flash, the cold muzzles were pressed to Coffron's head. As he later testified, "They demanded of me my money or they would blow my brains out." Coffron protested that he had recently been to Baltimore, where he had deposited most of his money. They did not believe him.

After collecting the little cash in the store, the two men marched Coffron to his house, still at gunpoint, and robbed him of his few valuables. Then they marched him back to the store. One robber kept the pistol close to Coffron's face while the other filled his pockets with penknives and watch chains. At that moment, there came shout from outside: "You scoundrels, we have got you at last!" The voice was that of Detective Ryan.

The next few seconds were filled with flashes of gunshots and the sound of running feet. One robber, who was never captured, vanished into the night. Detective Ryan lay in the road, bleeding from several bullet wounds and uttering his last words: "Oh, Lord. I am shot. I think he has killed me." Coffron, though badly wounded, disarmed and captured the second robber, John W. McCue, who immediately capitulated: "Treat me as a Christian, not as a brute. I am your prisoner." A few weeks later, a Union military commission found McCue guilty of murder and of violating General Orders No. 100, which forbade southerners from entering Union territory without permission and also prohibited armed robbery. By mid-July, McCue was locked in Dannemorra.

Within a few days of the prison doors slamming shut behind her son, McCue's mother had circulated a petition in Virginia, asking for his release. She quickly collected over two hundred signatures. Mary Custis Lee is the best-known signatory, but the names of Trout, Stribling, and Cabell stand out, along with dozens of names less well-known today. Nor were the menfolk far behind. Over two thousand prominent Virginians added their names to the petition, including the mayor of Staunton, several Breckenridges, and General Jubal Early. The prisoner's father, John H. McCue, bridled at the notion that his son was not a soldier, but a common thief and murderer; he was reassured by a lengthy opinion by Confederate brigadier general John D. Imboden that the young man was indeed a soldier. Robert E. Lee wrote to the senior McCue, assuring him that Mosby's command was "regularly organized under the laws of the Confederate Congress, was governed by the same regulations, and subject to the same control as any other part of the Confederate army." William D. Cabell also wrote John H. McCue on the young prisoner's behalf: "My Dear Sir, General Lee writes me that he will do what he can for the release of your noble son."

The same theme was taken up in the printed heading of the petitions signed by over three thousand Virginians: "McCue is a native of Augusta County, his family has for many generations resided among us, and for all that time has borne a name distinguished for integrity and moral worth, and unstained by a single act of violence or crime . . . to such a youth, the command of Mosby presented many attractions of a field of wild and romantic adventure."

This voluminous outpouring of popular support soon reached the desk of President Andrew Johnson, who sent it on to Judge Advocate General Joseph Holt. In an eight-page legal opinion, Holt showed little sympathy for McCue or his supporters. Holt noted the distinguished roster of petitioners and their high social position, but he dismissed the opinion of Robert E. Lee as merely that of a "leading traitor" and described Mosby's men as an irregular assembly of bandits and horse thieves, a "party of highwaymen" who were not soldiers at all. Holt did concede that Mosby's group was "composed of the best blood of the country," but he concluded that this merely showed the extent to which the Commonwealth's aristocracy had sunk to "unmanly and even depraved conduct."[2]

When captured, McCue had said that his purpose in entering Maryland was "to rob and see what we could make." This confirmed Holt's view that McCue was no more than an opportunistic common criminal, with the shallow motivation of the morally stunted. The judge advocate general concluded that life in prison was too lenient and that McCue should have been hanged. But the efforts of hundreds of southern woman and thousands of southern men outweighed legal opinion. On November 8, 1865, Andrew Johnson pardoned young McCue.[3]

Six hundred Louisiana women were involved in the next case, that of Omer Boudreaux, who was charged with rape, murder, and robbery. Boudreaux had been a first lieutenant in the Seventh Louisiana Cavalry (Confederate). Between September 1864 and May 1865, his exact military status varied; records describe him as being on detached service, on furlough, absent without leave, awaiting approval of his resignation, and simply as a guerrilla. Testimony did establish several points.[4]

On the night of May 25, 1865, Boudreaux and his band of five men approached the house of Joseph and Artemise Verret on Bayou DuLarge. While his men held her husband outside, Boudreaux raped Artemise. She later told the court that she did not cry out because she felt her life to be in danger, but that the act was without her consent.

Three weeks earlier, Boudreaux and his men, living in the woods of Terrebonne Parish, had captured Private Andrew Jackson of Company A, 75th U.S. Colored Infantry. The next day, while the group was picking berries, Jackson attempted to escape and was shot in the back by William Buford, a Confederate soldier. Boudreaux, finding that Jackson was still alive, said, "We had better put him out of pain," and shot Jackson in the head. The day before capturing Jackson, Boudreaux had robbed Michel Billot of a shotgun and eight ounces of gunpowder. Boudreaux was found guilty of all charges and was sentenced to be "hung by the neck until dead."

A wave of sympathy swept over parts of southeastern Louisiana, mostly among francophone Confederates, who seemed to believe that rape and

murder, when committed by one of their own, did not deserve severe punishment. Was it because the murder victim was an African-American Union
soldier? Or because the rape victim did not object loudly enough? Among
the many petitions circulated on Boudreaux's behalf was one that began:
"We, the undersigned ladies of the parishes of Lafourche, Terrebonne and
Assumption." It asked that Boudreaux's hanging be suspended until his
case was reviewed by President Andrew Johnson. Among the six hundred
signatories were Eugenie Boudreaux, Marielete Boudreaux, Malvina Boudreaux, Emilia Boudreaux, Arelie Aucoin, Theodile Hébert, Cecilia Caba-
llero, Eugenie LeBlanc, and Adolphina LeBlanc. The prevalence of French
names, including at least four with the same surname as the convicted
man, suggests that Boudreaux had a large network of friends and well-
wishers. Other letters on file reveal varying opinions. The governor of
Louisiana, James M. Wells, wrote to Johnson, "I ask on behalf of the unfortunate man your merciful consideration. His ignominious death will bring
sorrow and woe to a large circle of relatives and friends." A different note
was sounded by James V. Beldon, judge of the Third Judicial District: "At
the request of many of the citizens I endorsed the respectability of many
of the signers of petitions looking to a commutation." Belden investigated
the petitioners more closely: "These adjoining parishes have but few Union
men and the petitions are signed by men and women of most intense Rebel
feelings." He withdrew his previous endorsement.

When Boudreaux's case reached Washington, D.C., Judge Advocate
General Holt urged that the death penalty be carried out. The records of
the Civil War trials contain many opinions by Judge Holt, which are not
only easy to read (his clerk had excellent handwriting) but also provide a
window into the logic of military justice. For this reason, Holt's opinion in
this case is given in full.

Bureau of Military Justice, War Dept. 21st October 1865. The case
of Omer Boudreaux, a citizen of Louisiana now in confinement at New
Orleans, awaiting execution of sentence of death, to be carried into
effect on the 9th November 1865, is respectfully returned to the secretary of war for the president. Boudreaux was found guilty by a military
commission convened at Thibodeaux, Louisiana, 7th August 1865, first

of murder, second of rape, third of robbery, fourth of being a guerilla, and fifth violation of the laws and customs of war.

The proof is that the accused was a first lieutenant in the Seventh Regiment of Cavalry in the Rebel service, and was from and after September 1864, until he surrendered himself to the military authorities of the United States on the 1st of June 1865, absent from his regiment on furlough, and without leave. That during a portion of said period, to wit: from and after the 1st of May, 1865, he was in the Parish of Terrebone, Louisiana, in command of a party of five armed men hovering within and near the American lines, living in the woods, without camp. It appears that during this period he held himself to belong to the Confederate Service, and that after the expiration of his furlough, and during the latter part of said period, his name was carried on the roll of his company, Company C of the Seventh Confederate Cavalry, as "absent without leave." It also appears that during said period he reported from time to time to the headquarters of his regiment and made, through the captain of his company, an application for leave to raise a company within the Union lines; and that subsequently he offered his resignation, which was not accepted.

The accused was found guilty of murder, upon evidence that being with his party of four men, in the woods, near an encampment of Union colored troops, two men from that encampment rambling in the woods, fell in with the accused and his command and were captured by them, they being in Confederate uniforms, and professing to belong to the Confederate army. It appears that the two colored soldiers thus captured were treated as prisoners of war, and that the accused ordered his men to shoot them if they attempted to escape: That on the next day when on a march, the party stopped to pick berries and while thus engaged, one of the prisoners attempted to escape, the other having previously succeeded in doing so.

William Buford, a witness for the prosecution, testified that he was a member of Captain Whitaker's Company in the Confederate service and was one of the party under command of the accused when the colored soldiers were captured: That one of them named "Andrew

Jackson" was placed especially in his charge with directions not to let him escape, that a few minutes afterwards Andrew started to run when he, by direction of the accused, fired and shot him in the back. He fell, and when witness and the accused went to him they found that the ball had passed through his body but that he was still alive. The accused said, "He cannot live: We had better put him out of pain than to see him suffer," and thereupon drew his revolver and shot him through the head.

The "rape" was proved by the testimony of the woman upon whose body it was perpetrated. A party under command of the prisoner approached and entered the dwelling of this woman and her husband in the night. The husband was taken off about 20 paces from the house and kept under guard. The doors and windows of the house being open and the room where the crime was committed near the front door. No outcry or other noise was heard and one of the witnesses testified that the accused came amicably out of the room with the woman and that she remarked that they would say nothing about what occurred. Some evidence was offered to show that the woman's reputation was not good, but it was not such as to destroy the effects of her testimony.

The only one of several specifications of robbery charged against the prisoner, of which he was found guilty, was one committed at the house of Michel Billot. It was shown that the accused with his party entered the house at 8:00 or 9:00 o'clock of an evening in May 1865 and demanded of Billot the arms and ammunition in his possession. He gave up a shotgun and half a pound of powder. On being required to do so, Billot unlocked several trunks which were overhauled and several rooms were searched for more arms and ammunition, but it appears that no more were found and nothing was taken besides the gun and powder mentioned, and a bowl of shot.

The specification of this robbery sets forth that besides the articles enumerated, a watch and $400.00 in money were taken. Neither of the witnesses had any knowledge of money being taken and although a watch was missed on the next morning, there is no evidence that it was taken by the prisoner, but it appeared—on the contrary—that two strangers were in the house all night and were in the room where this watch was while the party of the accused were not known to have been in that room at all. It also appeared that there two other watches in the house and much other property which the party might have taken but did not.

The Court appears to have considered the guilt of the prisoner established of being a guerilla and of his violation of the laws and customs of war by the evidence adduced in support of the other charges. It is conclusively shown that during the month of May, at least, the prisoner and four or five men under his command lived in the woods, in an irregular and predatory manner common to guerillas or bands of robbers, that they had no camp and exhibited no evidence of military organization but the uniform dress of the so-called Confederate army. It appears—on the other hand—that the prisoner was a duly commissioned officer of the Rebel army and that he and his command were recognized as belonging to that army down to 9th March 1865, when S. A. Binger, commanding Seventh Regiment Louisiana Cavalry and J. L. Brent, Brigadier General Commanding endorsed and confirmed a furlough granted by him to one of his men, he being then in command of the small party only, implicated in the present charges.

It is in evidence also, that during the month of May 1865, the small band under command of the prisoner, visited several other houses in the Parish of Terrebone besides that of Michel Billot, in quest of arms and ammunition and that in each case as in that, they refrained from the indiscriminate plunder which has been found generally to mark the course of a guerilla party.

An application for pardon or commutation of sentence in this case is made to the president by J. M. Wells, governor of Louisiana, who represents that if the latter be granted, the friends of the prisoner will be able to show that he is not guilty of the crimes of which he has been convicted. Major General [E. S.] Canby, Commanding Department of Louisiana by General Orders No. 71, dated 30th September 1865, suspends the execution of the prisoner's sentence of death for 40 days from said 30th September and in forwarding the petition of Governor

Wells recommended that the sentence of death be mitigated to ten years' imprisonment.

Petitions to the president, very numerously signed by residents of Louisiana of both sexes are presented for the prisoner's pardon, or to commutation of his sentence to exile for a term of years, on the ground that the acts charged against the prisoner as crimes were committed during the late Rebellion, and while he was a commissioned officer of the so-called Confederate army: And also "that he surrendered himself to the nearest Federal officer in accordance with the Articles of Capitulation agreed on between Major General E. S. Canby and General Kirby Smith."

The recommendation of General Canby that the prisoner's sentence be mitigated to ten years imprisonment is approved by Major General [Philip] Sheridan, Commanding Division of the Gulf.

The first and gravest charge of which the prisoner was convicted is murder. It appears that he and his command captured a colored Union soldier, who, in attempting to escape, was shot and supposed to be mortally wounded: That after he had been so wounded and had fallen to the ground, was speechless and believed to be near death. The prisoner approached him and with the declared purpose of "putting him out of his pain," shot him through the head, killing him. In determining the guilt of this killing, it is not necessary to inquire, for it is immaterial, whether this prisoner and his party were banded together as guerillas and common robbers, or were part of the recognized force of the Rebel army, for though in the latter case the first firing at and wounding the fugitive, as he fled, was authorized by the laws of war, the second shot, after he had fallen and was a disarmed helpless prisoner, dying in the hands of his captors, was utterly unwarranted and criminal in either case and the killing thereby was murder. The life of a prisoner of war is the most sacred trust that can be committed to his captors and no matter how frail may be its tenure or how brief or painful it may promise to be, he has no right to shorten it by a single pulsation, upon any pretext whatsoever, unless it be necessary to do so in preventing his escape. Such necessity is not pretended in this case.

The legal and appropriate punishment of murder is death, and to this punishment the Court properly sentenced the prisoner. This office finds no just ground on which it can concur with Generals Canby and Sheridan in recommending a mitigation of that sentence.

President Andrew Johnson disagreed and wrote the following note to the secretary of war, dated October 27, 1865: "The sentence of the within-named Boudreaux is hereby commuted to imprisonment for life at hard labor in such penitentiary as the secretary of war may designate." Boudreaux was sent to the state prison at Concord, New Hampshire. The Confederate women had won at least a partial victory. It was through their community effort, through their being united, that these daughters of the Confederacy saved a convicted robber, murderer and rapist from the hangman's noose. Such women, and many others like them, have kept alive the cause of the old South and have stood firmly behind their endangered men.

# EPILOGUE

## Where Are the Others?

THERE WERE ROUGHLY 40 million Americans when the Civil War broke out. The women in the preceding chapters are obviously but a tiny fraction of that whole. What is the meaning of their stories in the context of the United States' most consuming conflict?

Are there patterns to their offenses? And how do they fit into the broad panorama of American history in the 1860s? This discussion will focus first on the regional variations in the offenses committed by southern women tried by Union military courts. Secondly, Confederate heroines will be examined within the context of other women tried by military courts, starting with the women acquitted by military commissions and continuing with the many thousands of civilians accused, investigated, and/or arrested by the Federal military justice system. (The Confederacy imprisoned over four thousand of their own citizens for political crimes, but that is another story.)[1]

As can be seen in table 1, some offenses—such as spying—precipitated only a small number of convictions, which were spread almost uniformly across the South. In contrast, smuggling was concentrated in three regions. Tennessee, especially in and around Memphis, was first in the transport of forbidden goods, perhaps because of that city's status as a major river port and its proximity to the Mississippi state border, which provided both wholesale supplies and a ready market. Louisiana had a major commercial port—New Orleans—in Union hands, with nearby areas loosely controlled by the Confederacy. The shortage of consumer goods in the South again created a ready market for those willing to risk the penalties

**Table 1**

CRIMES BY GEOGRAPHIC LOCATION

| | Missouri | Maryland | Tennessee | South of the line | North of the line |
|---|---|---|---|---|---|
| Smuggling | 1 | 5 | 20 | 13 | 1 |
| Spying | 1 | 1 | 3 | 1 | 1 |
| Wire-cutting | 4 | 0 | 0 | 0 | 1 |
| Harboring bushwhackers | 11 | 2 | 1 | 0 | 1 |
| Aiding Confederate escape | 4 | 0 | 0 | 1 | 0 |
| Selling whiskey to soldiers | 0 | 0 | 2 | 0 | 1 |
| Prostitution | 0 | 0 | 5 | 0 | 0 |
| Writing to CSA | 5 | 0 | 0 | 1 | 0 |
| Fraudulent marriage | 2 | 0 | 0 | 0 | 0 |
| Unauthorized travel | 1 | 1 | 0 | 1 | 4 |
| Denouncing the Union | 1 | 4 | 1 | 2 | 0 |
| Flag desecration | 1 | 0 | 1 | 2 | 0 |
| Helping Union deserters | 0 | 2 | 0 | 0 | 7 |
| Armed robbery | 0 | 0 | 0 | 1 | 0 |
| Murder | 0 | 0 | 0 | 2 | 0 |

imposed on captured smugglers. In Maryland, which was relatively isolated north of Washington, D.C., women tended to do their smuggling via the swift ships of the blockade runners or under the guise of legitimate family travelers.

Missouri was a remarkable exception to the patterns of other regions. It contained almost all of the cutters of telegraph wires and nearly all those convicted of harboring and/or feeding bushwhackers. Missouri also had the highest number of women caught corresponding with Confederate soldiers and helping Confederate prisoners of war to escape. Considering the state's geography, these findings are not surprising. The Missouri River runs right across the middle of the state; during the war, it continued to be a major thoroughfare underpinning the slave economy. Fierce guerrilla activity, reprisals, counterreprisals, and political differences wracked the very heart of the Show Me State.

The few cases of southern women helping Union soldiers to desert were confined to the vicinity of Washington, D.C. That city was a major assembly and transshipment point for soldiers, and would-be deserters needed civilian clothes. Army regulations prohibited the sale of such clothing to soldiers, but exceptions were available—for a price.

The five prostitution cases from Memphis are certainly unusual, considering the universal existence of prostitution in the United States in the 1860s. In 1863, there were over 7,000 prostitutes in and around Washington, D.C. Nashville had additional thousands of these women, most working under Union licensure.[2] Later in the war, even Memphis had legalized prostitution. In July 1863, however, the Union commander at Memphis had just issued an order banning prostitution, and it would seem that he intended to make an example of the women of 115 Beale Street.

The final category of local overrepresentation is that of denouncing the Union, often described as "uttering disloyal statements." Maryland, and particularly Baltimore, was the center of such activities, reflecting both the strong southern tradition of that city and the contempt that many Baltimore women traditionally had for northerners.

In brief, these 120 women and their trials tended to fall into a few clusters, reflecting local conditions. But they are so few in number that we might be wise to look at other sources of information about these women and any other women caught up in the Union military justice system.

One such source is military commissions in which the female defendants were tried but found not guilty. There were forty of these: thirteen from Tennessee, nine from Missouri, seven from Louisiana, four from Arkansas and Maryland, two from Kentucky, Florida, and Virginia, and one from the District of Columbia, Kansas, and Alabama. The charges were familiar ones: eleven for smuggling, five for providing military supplies to the Confederacy, and four each of spying, theft, and helping Union soldiers to desert. The remaining charges included concealing Confederate soldiers, selling whisky to Union soldiers, and disloyal speeches. The only cases remarkably different from those of the convicted women were one of arson and another of alleged perjury. In all these cases, the officers forming the court found the evidence insufficient for a conviction. Thus, for every three women convicted by a military commission, one was found not guilty.

Many secondary sources exist about spies, smugglers, and underground figures in the Civil War. Seven of these books were reviewed to see if they discussed the women under consideration here. John Bakeless's *Spies of the Confederacy* lists 46 women, two of whom—Jane Ferguson and Sally Pollock—appear in these pages in far more detail. Louis Sigaud's *Belle Boyd: Confederate Spy* (48 women), Jeffry Wert's *Mosby's Rangers* (25 women), Philip Van Doren Stern's *Secret Missions of the Civil War* (3 women), and James Horan's *Confederate Agent* (11 women) all contain no mention of the 120 women who were convicted by Union military courts.[3]

Margaret Leech's *Reveille in Washington* describes seven women confined in Washington D.C.'s Old Capitol Prison; again, none of them appear in these pages as well, although Leech does describe secret tribunals conducted by Secretary of State William H. Seward and Secretary of War Edwin M. Stanton, asserting that 13,000 political offenders were arrested by the War Department. (No source is given for this figure.) Finally, Richard Brownlee's *Gray Ghosts of the Confederacy* discusses thirteen women, one of whom—Anna Fickle—also appears in this book, in a far more detailed form.[4] In brief, three of the women under consideration here have also been described elsewhere, though with little detail and, in the case of Fickle, apparent inaccuracy.

Turning to repositories of primary sources, the National Archives main facility at Washington, D.C., has four major collections that document women who were the object of concern by Union authorities. The first, already mentioned, is Record Group 153, which contains all the Union general courts-martial, military commissions, and courts of inquiry. The 80,000 names therein can be searched in the handwritten War Department index or by using this author's computerized index. The second source is the Union Provost Marshal's File of Papers Relating to Individual Citizens, (File M345, consisting of 299 rolls of 16-millimeter microfilm), which contains photographic reproductions of odd-sized, handwritten documents, arranged alphabetically. If the diligent searcher is able to find his or her quarry (and the quarry's code number) in M345, he or she can then turn to the third source, the 94 rolls of 35-millimeter film that form M416, Union Provost Marshal's File of Two or More Name Papers Relating to Citizens, to read further.

The fourth source is the Turner-Baker Index. Major Levi C. Turner was appointed associate judge advocate for the Army in August 1862, with jurisdiction over the District of Columbia and northern Virginia; he was charged with finding and arresting disloyal citizens, draft dodgers, and army deserters. Lafayette C. Baker, who was at various times a spy, a secret agent, and a special provost marshal, also served as colonel of the First District of Columbia Cavalry, a unit used to enforce Union rule in the nation's capital. Baker's files included investigations of crooked contractors, slave stealers, smugglers, conspirators, defrauders, vandals, and traitors. Altogether, Turner and Baker investigated over eight thousand cases. Their files were combined and indexed between 1869 and 1873. The index is semi-alphabetical. All those whose last names begin with the same letter are grouped together, but within that group the cases are chronological.

To further complicate matters, in the first year of the war, the investigation of disloyal persons fell under the aegis of the U.S. State Department, and many interrogations were conducted under the direction of Secretary Seward. It would appear from some sources that many of these interrogations were conducted in secret, and the records themselves were kept sequestered.

To illuminate the subject of how one might search for the records of pro-Confederate women, let us take the Scott sisters, who should be easy to trace, since their case occupied the front page of one of the country's most widely read newspapers, *Harper's Weekly*, on August 3, 1861, complete with a woodcut illustration showing the two offenders being escorted into Union lines by armed soldiers. The Scott family lived near Falls Church, Virginia, and had assisted Confederate forces in the capture of a Connecticut captain. The article referred to the women as "the Misses Scott," giving no first names. With this data, the search began.

The author's computerized database of Record Group 153, with its thousands of military commissions, was examined first and did not contain the Scotts. M345, the so-called "One Name Index," contained hundreds of Scotts, but with no first names. It was thus not surprising that an hour's effort yielded nothing.

Without a code number, a search of M416, the "Two Name Index," would have been close to hopeless. The fourth possible source, the Turner-

Baker File, also seemed hopeless, since these files were begun five months after the arrest of the Misses Scott. However, the sisters might have been held for five months, and it seemed wise not to overlook any possible avenue. However, fifteen minutes invested in reading all the "S's" in the Turner-Baker index proved fruitless.

Perhaps a secondary source would shed light on the Misses Scott. A search of all the books mentioned above yielded a few Scotts, but none were the Misses Scott. A return visit to the National Archives and a seance with one of the Old Army consultants left the women still lost in the mists of time. All the usual approaches to this search, which at first had seemed so straightforward, had yielded nothing. It was now time to impose upon the talents and remarkable memory of the National Archives' legendary Michael P. Musick (now retired).

Musick's initial search was no more fruitful than the author's, in itself an unusual turn of events. He did, however, have two suggestions: contact the archivist for State Department records, housed at College Park, Maryland, and review the early records from the Two Name Index, since that index is chronological. Musick also thought that a search of the Connecticut regiments might yield a captain captured in midsummer 1861.

*The Army Register of the Volunteer Force,* an eight-volume reference work, seemed to offer an easy avenue for continuing this search, since it lists all commissioned officers, state by state, with their fates. However, no Connecticut officer was listed as "captured." Frederick H. Dyer's *Compendium of the War of the Rebellion* states that the First, Second, and Third Connecticut Volunteer Infantry regiments were at Falls Church on picket duty in June and July 1861. However, this left dozens of captains who might have been the one to suffer at the hands of the Misses Scott. Luckily, the Connecticut adjutant general's list of Civil War soldiers soon provided a captured captain—forty-eight-year-old Abram Kellogg. His compiled service records revealed that he had been "taken prisoner at Falls Church, Va. June 21, 1861." (He was sent to Raleigh, where he was exchanged for a Confederate navy officer, a Lieutenant Butt.) Surely, this was the Union officer named in the *Harper's Weekly* article. But the errant Scott sisters remained unidentified.[5]

Returning to the Two Name Index, a review of every July and August entry for 1861 revealed no Scotts of any gender or locale. The last hope for success seemed to be the State Department records. These compose Record Group 59, within which there are nine series of records that, in the words of archivist Dr. Michael Hussey, "look promising." These series have titles such as "Records of Arrests for Treason, 1861–1862" and "Records of Arrests for Disloyalty, 1861–1862." The author leaves this search to others.

A chance remark by the author's eye doctor led the search to a published history of Falls Church, one that added the sisters' full names—Artemisia Scott and America Virginia Scott—but no further information about any legal proceedings.[6]

What is the point of this digression upon the two Scotts? Simply this: there are probably hundreds, maybe thousands, of arrested women not in Record Group 153, the group that contains military commissions. To find such women in the other record collections just described would be a valuable task, one to be done by future researchers. The author's only partially successful experience with the Scotts, who were on the front page of a prominent newspaper, suggests that finding less publicized women might be even more difficult.

In a step toward estimating the numbers of pro-Confederate women, the author went through the 8,930 entries in the Turner-Baker Index and found 163 names that appeared to be female. Thus approximately 1.8 percent of those recorded in the index were female. Extrapolating this percentage to the unsourced 13,000 political arrests claimed by Leech in *Reveille in Washington*, the Federal records may contain 234 women arrested by the Union authorities in and around Washington, D.C.

Without such a search of all the records that might contain information about women arrested by Union authorities, it is impossible to state an exact number of women caught up in the Union search for disloyal, suspicious, or treasonable activities. The last word has not yet been said about the Civil War. There is still much to be learned about every aspect of that enormous conflict and, in particular, the women who played an active part in it.

# APPENDIX

British military justice, based on the Army Regulations and the Articles of War, had been in place for centuries before the American Revolution. George Washington borrowed these guidelines almost word for word in governing the Continental armies. These same rules were essentially unchanged as the Civil War opened, and they were used by both the Union and the Confederacy.

Three different types of proceedings were governed by these rules: military commissions, courts-martial, and courts of inquiry. The first was intended for civilians in areas under martial law. Courts-martial were for uniformed servicemen accused of offenses. The third type of proceeding was to answer questions such as, "Is there sufficient reason to court-martial this person?" In the Union army, during the Civil War, there were 5,456 military commissions, 70,310 courts-martial, and 193 courts of inquiry. All three types of trials are filed together in Record Group 153 in the National Archives.

Courts-martial usually had thirteen officers serving as members, but fewer might serve if not enough officers were available. Article 39 of the Articles of War gives a general outline of courts-martial. The president of the court was always the highest-ranking officer. The authority convening the court—the general commanding that region or department—designated its location and the members composing it; only he could dissolve the court. The president's job was to keep order and conduct the business of the trial. The necessity of and procedures for swearing-in were rigidly prescribed. The court record was to be clearly written, with numbered pages. The final document was to be "stitched together" and sent first to the convening authority and then to the judge advocate general in Washington, D.C., who had the authority to present it to the president of the United States.[1]

Each court also had a judge advocate. A handbook for judge advocates published shortly after the Civil War gives considerable further detail on their role: "A judge advocate appears at a court-martial in three distinct characters: first, as an officer of the court, for the purpose of recording its proceedings and administering the requisite oaths to the members; second, as the adviser to the court in matters of form and law; and, third, as public prosecutor." Persons appointed as judge advocates were to be skilled and experienced both in military and legal matters, "not only because it is of importance to have sensible and well-settled rules of procedure, even under ordinary conditions, but likewise, that dangers and embarrassments may be guarded against during emergencies of martial government when the courts of civil judicature are closed and silent."[2]

"The following principles should be observed upon all trials by military tribunals. First, that justice is the object for which a military tribunal is convened and the judge advocate appointed. Second, that the great principle of a military tribunal is honor—a conscientious adherence to substantial justice. Third, that the business of a military tribunal is not to discuss points of law, but to get at the truth by all the means in their power."[3]

These general observations hint at the complexity of military law. A further discussion of its history and its application in the Civil War may be found in other works by this author.[4]

# NOTES

## PREFACE

1. Quoted in John Chester Miller, *The Wolf by the Ears: Thomas Jefferson and Slavery* (New York: Free Press, 1976), 181.

2. John M. Coski, *Capital Navy: The Men, Ships, and Operations of the James River Squadron* (Campbell, Calif.: Savas Woodbury, 1996), 82–83; Ladies' Gunboat Society broadside, in author's possession.

## INTRODUCTION

1. Case of Sarah Jane Smith, Records of the Judge Advocate General's Office (Army), Record Group 153, entry 15, file LL2742, National Archives, Washington, D.C. Hereafter, trial records will be cited as RG 153, entry 15, followed by the file folder number.

2. William J. Seymour Papers, Schoff Collection, Clements Library, University of Michigan.

3. Robert E. Lee, review of Cyrus Drum's trial sentence, October 1, 1863, Orders and Circulars Issued by the Army of the Potomac and the Army and Department of Northern Virginia, CSA, 1861–1865, RG 109, microfilm M921, frame 958, National Archives.

4. Records of General Courts-Martial and Courts of Inquiry of the Navy Department, 1799–1867 (National Archives Microfilm Publication M272), RG 125, case 3492, Feb. 1, 1864, Records of the Judge Advocate General (Navy).

5. Quoted in Robert E. Denney, *The Distaff Civil War* (Victoria, B.C.: Trafford, 2002), 12.

6. Margaret Leech, *Reveille in Washington, 1861–1865* (New York: Carroll & Graf, 1941); Bell I. Wiley, *The Life of Johnny Reb: The Common Soldier of the Confederacy* (Indianapolis: Bobbs-Merrill, 1943) and *The Life of Billy Yank: The Common Soldier of the Union* (Indianapolis: Bobbs-Merrill, 1952); Katharine M. Jones, *Heroines of Dixie: Confederate Women Tell Their Story of the War* (Indianapolis: Bobbs-Merrill, 1955).

7. Mary Elizabeth Massey, *Bonnet Brigades* (New York: Knopf, 1966).

8. Richard Hall, *Patriots in Disguise: Women Warriors of the Civil War* (New York: Paragon, 1993); Juanita Leisch, *Who Wore What? Women's Wear, 1861–1865* (Gettysburg, Pa.: Thomas,

1995); Drew Gilpin Faust, *Mothers of Invention: Women of the Slaveholding South in the American Civil War* (Chapel Hill: University of North Carolina Press, 1996); Anne S. LeClercq, *An Antebellum Plantation Household, including the South Carolina Low Country Receipts and Remedies of Emily Wharton Sinkler* (Columbia: University of South Carolina Press, 1996); Nancy S. Garrison, *With Courage and Delicacy: Civil War on the Peninsula: Women and the U.S. Sanitary Commission* (Mason City, Ia.: Savas, 1999); Elizabeth D. Leonard, *All the Daring of the Soldier: Women of the Civil War Armies* (New York: W. W. Norton, 2000); Laura F. Edwards, *Scarlett Doesn't Live Here Anymore: Southern Women in the Civil War Era* (Urbana: University of Illinois Press, 2000); Jacquelin Tobin and Raymond G. Dobard, *Hidden in Plain View: The Secret Story of Quilts and the Underground Railroad* (New York: Doubleday, 1999); Louise Barnett, *Ungentlemanly Acts: The Army's Notorious Incest Trial* (New York: Hill and Wang, 2000); Denney, *Distaff Civil War*; Michelle Krowl, "Dixie's Other Daughters: African-American Women in Virginia, 1861–1868" (Ph.D. dissertation, University of California, Berkeley, 1998); DeAnne Blanton and Lauren Cook, *They Fought Like Demons: Women Soldiers in the American Civil War* (Baton Rouge: Louisiana State University Press, 2002); Rita Mae Brown, *High Hearts* (New York: Bantam, 1986).

## 1. MISSOURI

1. James M. McPherson, *Battle Cry of Freedom: The Civil War Era* (New York: Oxford University Press, 1988), 292–93.

2. For one account of Missouri's misery, see the inflammatory autobiography of Union guerrilla William Monks, *History of Southern Missouri and Northern Arkansas*, ed. John Bradbury and Lou Wehmer (1907; reprint, Fayetteville: University of Arkansas Press, 2003). See also Albert Castel, "Order No. 11 and the Civil War on the Border," *Missouri Historical Review* 57, no. 4 (July 1963): 357–68.

3. RG 153, entry 15, file LL2742.

4. Ibid. In this and all other cases, direct quotes are drawn from the trial record under consideration unless otherwise noted.

5. Ibid. This may be the same Dr. George Rex who was court-martialed in November 1862. For his trial, see ibid., file KK328.

6. Ibid., file LL2742; Alton Military Prison Register, RG 109, NA. Alton Prison and its dreaded annex, Smallpox Island, were noted for epidemics of fatal diseases. The prison opened for business in January 1862; in September 1864 it still lacked an adequate water supply, and even the guards' quarters were described as "disgracefully filthy." U.S. War Department, *War of the Rebellion: A Compilation of the Official Records of the Union and Confederate Armies*, ser. 2, vol. 1, p. 162, and ser. 1, vol. 41, pt. 3, p. 65. Hereafter cited as *OR*.

7. Reminiscences of Salem H. Ford, unpublished typescript, State Historical Society of Missouri, Columbia.

8. *OR*, ser. 2, vol. 5, pp. 319–21.

9. RG 153, entry 15, file LL2097.

10. Ibid., file LL2533.

11. Mark J. Crawford, *Confederate Courage on Other Fields: Four Lesser Known Accounts of the War between the States* (Jefferson, N.C.: McFarland, 2000), 95, 114–16.

12. Ibid., 115. The reported killing of civilians at Pulliam Spring is still hotly debated by historians, and primary sources are scarce. A series of increasingly inflammatory letters to the editor in the *Poplar Bluff (Mo.) Daily American Republic* (April 8 and 28, May 17, 2002) shows that the subject of the massacre is still passionately debated.

13. RG 153, entry 15, file NN3520, folder 2.

14. OR, ser. 2, vol. 7, p. 1119; Roy P. Basler, ed., *The Collected Works of Abraham Lincoln* (New Brunswick, N.J.: Rutgers University Press, 1953), 8:223.

15. RG 153, entry 15, file LL2643. Ben Roach, a wealthy Vicksburg planter is mentioned twice in the OR: ser. 1, vol. 17, p. 793, and ser. 1, vol. 24, pt. 3, p. 595. Douthitt's dislike of him, or another Roach, remains a mystery.

16. RG 153, entry 15, file NN2145.

17. Ibid., entry 18, "Numbered Court-Martials #73."

18. Ibid., entry 15, file LL1985, folder 1.

19. Ibid.

20. Ibid.

21. Ibid., file LL2959. This may be the Lingo family described in *History of Laclede, Camden, Dallas, Webster, Wright, Texas, Pulaski, Phelps, and Dent Counties, Missouri* (1889; reprint, Greenville, S.C.: Southern Historical Press, 1974). Tilley may be the man murdered for his buried treasure; the recent discovery of the hoard is described in James B. King Jr.'s *The Tilley Treasure* (Point Lookout, Mo.: School of the Ozarks Press, 1984). The Weaver trial is also described on p. 147 of King's book.

22. Mary Pittman's astonishing story can be found in RG 110, Box 4, M-RI, entry 36, NA.

23. RG 153, entry 15, file LL1229.

24. Ibid., file LL2592.

25. Ibid., file LL548. "Al Grimes" may the man described in *Absalom Grimes: Confederate Mail Runner*, ed. M. M. Quaife (New Haven: Yale University Press, 1926). A Mr. Bagwell was arrested as a spy on August 3, 1861, at Washington, Missouri (M416, roll, 2, frame 0414, NA).

26. RG 153, entry 15, file LL548.

27. Ibid., file NN3355.

28. Ibid., file NN2827.

29. Ibid., file NN2141.

30. Ibid., file NN2143.

31. Ibid., file NN2733.

32. Ibid., file NN2987.

33. Ibid., file OO227.

34. Ibid., file NN3437.

35. Ibid., file NN50.

36. Ibid., file OO1085.

## 2. MARYLAND

1. McPherson, *Battle Cry of Freedom*, 285.

2. Timothy Ackinclose, *Sabers and Pistols: The Civil War Career of Colonel Harry Gilmor, C.S.A.* (Gettysburg, Pa.: Stan Clark Books, 1997), 12.

3. Ibid., 67.

4. Ibid., 85. Duffield's Station, on the Baltimore and Ohio rail line between Harpers Ferry and Martinsburg, West Virginia, is now the MARC commuter station near Shenandoah Junction, West Virginia.

5. RG 153, entry 15, file MM1973.

6. Ibid., NN3028.

7. Doris Kirkpatrick, *The City and the River* (Fitchburg, Mass.: Fitchburg Historical Society, 1971), 1:286.

8. RG 153, entry 15, file NN3080, folder 2, and file NN3129. For Foley, see ibid., file NN3081.

9. Ibid., MM1466. For a general discussion of wartime Baltimore, see Kathryn W. Lerch, "Prosecuting Citizens, Rebels, and Spies: The 8th New York Heavy Artillery in Maryland, 1862–1864," *Maryland Historical Magazine* 94, no. 2 (Summer 1999): 132–71.

10. RG 153, entry 15, file MM1356.

11. Ibid. Commodore Robert F. Stockton was the designer of the USS *Princeton* and an opponent of flogging. The city of Stockton, California, bears his name.

12. RG 153, entry 15, file LL1968; Bakeless, *Spies of the Confederacy*, 352.

13. King was president of what is now Columbia University.

14. RG 153, entry 15, file LL2797.

15. Ibid., file MM1498.

16. Ibid., file NN1918.

17. Ibid., file NN3080, folder 1.

18. Ibid., file OO297.

19. Ibid., file NN2166.

## 3. TENNESSEE

1. Noel Fisher, "Feelin' Mighty Southern: Recent Scholarship on Southern Appalachia in the Civil War," *Civil War History* 47, no. 4 (December 2001): 334; Noel Fisher, *War at Every Door: Partisan Politics and Guerrilla Violence in East Tennessee, 1860–1869* (Chapel Hill: University of North Carolina Press, 1997); John C. Inscoe, *Mountain Masters, Slavery, and the Sectional Crisis in Western North Carolina* (Knoxville: University of Tennessee Press, 1989). Inscoe (p. 129) asserts that class conflict was a minor factor.

2. McPherson, *Battle Cry of Freedom*, 304.

3. RG 153, entry 15, file NN2041.

4. Ibid., NN1673. Julian Gap (now called Dead Man Gap) is in White Oak Mountain, just east of Ooltewah, and provides a route for the East Tennessee and Georgia Railroad

(courtesy of James Ogden III). Hayward McKeehan is not found in the Confederate roster or the OR.

5. Bakeless, *Spies of the Confederacy*, 182.

6. Ibid., 210, 217.

7. RG 153, entry 15, file NN1215.

8. Ibid., LL2953.

9. Ibid., "Numbered Court-Martials #18."

10. Ibid., entry 15, file OO1235.

11. Ibid., MM2887.

12. Thomas P. Lowry, *The Story the Soldiers Wouldn't Tell: Sex in the Civil War* (Mechanicsburg, Pa.: Stackpole, 1994), 76–87.

13. RG 153, entry 15, file NN1040, folder 2. For the treatment of venereal disease, see Lowry, *Story the Soldiers Wouldn't Tell*, 99–109.

14. The Guernsey letter is courtesy of John M. Coski, Guernsey's great-great-grandson.

15. RG 153, entry 15, file LL715.

16. Ibid.

17. Ibid.

18. Ibid., file MM618.

19. Ibid., file LL621.

20. Ibid.

21. Ibid.

22. Ibid., file LL1315.

23. Ibid., file LL1341.

24. Ibid., file LL2881.

25. Ibid., file LL2587. Before the Civil War, the South imported all its cotton cards from the North. In *Mothers of Invention* (p. 48), Drew Gilpin Faust discusses the myths of "homespun," although she may be in error when she says the cards were used to remove cotton seeds. In January 1864, the Confederacy had 112,000 pairs of cotton cards at Bermuda, awaiting shipment through the blockade. OR, ser. 4 , vol. 3, no. 129, Confederate Correspondence.

26. RG 153, entry 15, file LL2669. Jamison has no service record in the 154th, but he surely must have belonged to that unusually numbered Tennessee regiment at some point. J. P. Jamison/Jameson appears in the 1st and 13th Tennessee regiments. Courtesy of Robert K. Krick and Dorothy Kelly.

27. Ibid., file LL2667.

28. Ibid., file LL3214.

29. Ibid., file OO477.

30. Ibid., file OO1161.

31. Ibid., file LL2598.

32. Richard L. Fuchs, *An Unerring Fire: The Massacre at Fort Pillow* (Mechanicsburg, Pa.: Stackpole, 2002).

33. Denney, *Distaff Civil War*, 304.

34. RG 153, entry 15, file LL2598. For a general discussion of these issues, see Jeffrey N. Lash, "'The Federal Tyrant at Memphis': General Stephen A. Hurlbut and the Union Occupation of West Tennessee, 1862–64," *Tennessee Historical Quarterly* 48 (Spring 1989): 15–28.

## 4. SOUTH OF THE LINE

1. RG 153, entry 15, file MM3184.

2. Ibid., file LL2628, folder 2. The Museum of the Confederacy has an extensive file on Mary Hill. Her obituary appeared in the *Confederate Veteran* 10 (1902): 124.

3. RG 153, entry 15, file MM2049. Confederate general Francis R. T. Nicholls, an 1855 graduate of West Point, lost his left arm and right foot in combat during the Civil War and later served two terms as governor of Louisiana. The other bundles were addressed to less well-known Confederate officers.

4. Ibid., file OO952.

5. Ibid., file LL2756.

6. Ibid., file LL3064 (printed General Orders only).

7. Ibid., file LL3117, folder 1.

8. Ibid., file NN2592.

9. Ibid., file OO966; William Osler, *Principles and Practice of Medicine* (New York: D. Appleton, 1893).

10. RG 153, entry 15, file LL3117, folder 3.

11. Ibid., file LL2699.

12. Ibid., file LL3117, folder 3.

13. Ibid., file LL634.

14. Ibid., file MM2198.

15. Ibid., file LL3005.

16. Ibid., file MM3161.

17. Ibid., file MM2827.

18. Ibid., file MM2968.

19. Ibid., file MM3616.

20. Ibid., file OO216.

## 5. NORTH OF THE LINE

1. RG 153, entry 15, file NN3097. Champ Ferguson's trial is in ibid., file MM2977. The brandy julep is cited in Jack Welsh, *Medical Histories of Union Generals* (Kent, Ohio: Kent State University Press, 1996).

2. RG 153, entry 15, file NN1076, folder 1. For quinine dosage see *The Merck Manual*, 17th ed. (White House Station, N.J.: Merck Research Laboratories, 2001). The use of opium for diarrhea is seen in Babylonian times, nearly four thousand years ago. www.encyclopedia.com.

3. RG 153, entry 15, file MM1102.

4. Ibid., file NN3418.

5. Ibid., file LL391.

6. Ibid.

7. Ibid., file NN2429.

8. Ibid., files NN2340 and NN2341.

9. Ibid., file NN2514.

10. Ibid., file NN2848. Private Sheehan's regiment could be either Cowan's First New York Independent Battery of Light Artillery or the First Regiment of New York Light Artillery. The First New York Battalion (not regiment) of Heavy Artillery was reorganized into three batteries of light artillery in March 1863. Courtesy of Benedict Maryniak.

11. RG 153, entry 15, file NN2846.

12. The use of showers as punishment is well documented. See ibid., files KK414, MM2817, NN2645, OO1245, and OO1382. Also ibid., NN2453.

13. Ibid., file NN2652. "Captain Potts" is almost certainly John Potts, chief clerk of the War Department, who ran the confidential Secret Service account. See Fischel, *Secret War for the Union*, 595.

14. RG 153, entry 15, file OO773.

## 6. IT TAKES A VILLAGE

1. RG 153, entry 15, file MM2302.

2. Ibid. The Confederate government issued two important general orders governing partisan troops. The first, dated April 21, 1863, stated that captured horses would be turned over to the Confederate quartermaster and the partisan would be paid the animals' full cash value. There was no provision for distinguishing Union horses from privately owned horses; thus the partisans would be paid for any stolen horse. General Orders No. 82, issued two months later, stated that partisan rangers would be subject to the same regulations and discipline as other soldiers, but that "such partizan corps as are serving within enemy lines are for the present exempt from this order." It would seem that in regard to McCue's case, Holt was correct. McCue—deep within enemy lines, wearing nothing distinguishable as a Confederate uniform, far away from a superior officer, possessing no order instructing to him to rob convenience stores, and having the self-confessed goal of being a robber—was a freelancer, not a soldier under any formal military orders or discipline.

3. RG 153, entry 15, file MM2302.

4. Ibid., file MM2802.

## EPILOGUE: WHERE ARE THE OTHERS?

1. Mark E. Neely Jr., *Southern Rights: Political Prisoners and the Myth of Confederate Constitutionalism* (Charlottesville: University Press of Virginia, 1999).

2. Lowry, *Story the Soldiers Wouldn't Tell*, 76–85.

3. Bakeless, *Spies of the Confederacy*; Louis A. Sigaud, *Belle Boyd, Confederate Spy* (Richmond, Va.: Dietz Press, 1944); Jeffry D. Wert, *Mosby's Rangers* (New York: Touchstone Books, 1990); Philip Van Doren Stern, *Secret Missions of the Civil War* (New York: Wings Books, a division of Random House, 1959); James D. Horan, *Confederate Agent: A Discovery in History* (New York: Crown, 1954).

4. Leech, *Reveille in Washington*; Richard S. Brownlee, *Gray Ghosts of the Confederacy: Guerrilla Warfare in the West* (Baton Rouge: Louisiana State University Press, 1986), 199, 203.

5. *Official Army Register of the Volunteer Force of the United States Army* (1865; reprint, Gaithersburg, Md.: Olde Soldier Books, 1987), 1:260–65; Frederick H. Dyer, *A Compendium of the War of the Rebellion, Compiled and Arranged from Official Records of the Federal and Confederate Armies, Reports of the Adjutant Generals of the Several States, the Army Registers, and Other Reliable Documents* (1905; reprint, Dayton, Ohio: Morningside Press, 1994), 2:1008–10.

6. Bradley E. Gernand and Nan Netherton, *Falls Church: A Virginia Village Revisited* (Virginia Beach, Va.: Donning, 2000), 48.

## APPENDIX

1. *Revised Regulations for the Army of the United States* (1861; reprint, Harrisburg, Pa.: National Historical Society, 1980), 125.

2. James Regan, *The Judge Advocate and Recorder's Guide* (Washington, D.C.: Beresford, 1877), 11.

3. Ibid., 14.

4. Thomas P. Lowry, *Don't Shoot That Boy! Abraham Lincoln and Military Justice* (Mason City, Ia.: Savas, 1999), 9–22; Lowry, *Tarnished Eagles: The Courts-Martial of Fifty Union Colonels* (Mechanicsburg, Pa.: Stackpole, 1997), 2–8.

# BIBLIOGRAPHY

Ackinclose, Timothy. *Sabers and Pistols: The Civil War Career of Colonel Harry Gilmor, C.S.A.* Gettysburg, Pa.: Stan Clark, 1997.

Bakeless, John. *Spies of the Confederacy.* 1970. Mineola, N.Y.: Dover, 1997.

Barnett, Louise. *Ungentlemanly Acts: The Army's Notorious Incest Trial.* New York: Hill and Wang, 2000.

Basler, Roy P., ed. *The Collected Works of Abraham Lincoln.* 9 vols. New Brunswick, N.J.: Rutgers University Press, 1953–55.

Blanton, DeAnne, and Lauren M. Cook. *They Fought Like Demons: Women Soldiers in the American Civil War.* Baton Rouge: Louisiana State University Press, 2002.

Brown, Rita Mae. *High Hearts.* New York: Bantam, 1986.

Brownlee, Richard S. *Gray Ghosts of the Confederacy: Guerrilla Warfare in the West, 1861–1865.* Baton Rouge: Louisiana State University Press, 1984.

Castel, Albert. "Order No. 11 and the Civil War on the Border." *Missouri Historical Review* 57 (1963): 357–68.

Coski, John M. *Capital Navy: The Men, Ships, and Operations of the James River Squadron.* Campbell, Calif.: Savas Woodbury, 1996.

Crawford, Mark J. *Confederate Courage on Other Fields: Four Lesser-Known Accounts of the War between the States.* Jefferson, N.C.: McFarland, 2000.

Denney, Robert E. *The Distaff Civil War.* Vancouver, B.C.: Trafford, 2002.

Dyer, Frederick H. *A Compendium of the War of the Rebellion, Compiled and Arranged from Official Records of the Federal and Confederate Armies, Reports of the Adjutant Generals of the Several States, the Army Registers, and Other Reliable Documents.* 1905. Reprint, Dayton, Ohio: Morningside Press, 1994.

Edwards, Laura F. *Scarlett Doesn't Live Here Anymore: Southern Women in the Civil War Era.* Urbana: University of Illinois Press, 2000.

Faust, Drew Gilpin. *Mothers of Invention: Women of the Slaveholding South in the American Civil War.* Chapel Hill: University of North Carolina Press, 1996.

Fishel, Edwin C. *The Secret War for the Union: The Untold Story of Military Intelligence in the Civil War.* Boston: Mariner, 1996.

Fisher, Noel C. "Feelin' Mighty Southern: Recent Scholarship on Southern Appalachia in the Civil War." *Civil War History* 47, no. 4 (December 2001): 334–46.

———. *War at Every Door: Partisan Politics and Guerrilla Violence in East Tennessee, 1860–1869.* Chapel Hill: University of North Carolina Press, 1997.

Ford, Salem H. "Reminiscences." Unpublished typescript. State Historical Society of Missouri, Columbia.

Fuchs, Richard L. *An Unerring Fire: The Massacre at Fort Pillow.* Mechanicsburg, Pa.: Stackpole, 2002.

Garrison, Nancy S. *With Courage and Delicacy: Civil War on the Peninsula. Women and the U.S. Sanitary Commission.* Mason City, Ia.: Savas, 1999.

Gernand, Bradley E., and Nan Netherton. *Falls Church: A Virginia Village Revisited.* Virginia Beach, Va.: Donning, 2000.

Hall, James O. *On the Way to Garrett's Barn: John Wilkes Booth and David E. Herold in the Northern Neck of Virginia, April 22–26, 1865.* Clinton, Md.: Surratt Society, 2001.

Hall, Richard. *Patriots in Disguise: Women Warriors of the Civil War.* New York: Paragon, 1993.

Horan, James D. *Confederate Agent: A Discovery in History.* New York: Crown, 1954.

Inscoe, John C. *Mountain Masters, Slavery, and the Sectional Crisis in Western North Carolina.* Knoxville: University of Tennessee Press, 1989.

Jones, Katharine M. *Heroines of Dixie: Confederate Women Tell Their Story of the War.* Indianapolis: Bobbs-Merrill, 1955.

King, James B., Jr. *The Tilley Treasure.* Point Lookout, Mo.: School of the Ozarks Press, 1984.

Kirkpatrick, Doris. *The City and the River.* Vol. 1. Fitchburg, Mass.: Fitchburg Historical Society, 1971.

Krowl, Michelle. "Dixie's Other Daughters: African-American Women in Virginia, 1861–1868." Ph.D. diss., University of California at Berkeley, 2002.

Lash, Jeffrey. "'The Federal Tyrant at Memphis': General Stephen A. Hurlbut and the Union Occupation of West Tennessee, 1862–1864." *Tennessee Historical Quarterly* 48 (Spring 1989): 15–28.

LeClercq, Anne S. *An Antebellum Plantation Household, including the South Carolina Low Country Receipts and Remedies of Emily Wharton Sinkler.* Columbia: University of South Carolina Press, 1996.

Leech, Margaret. *Reveille in Washington, 1860–1865*. New York: Carroll and Graf, 1941.

Leisch, Juanita. *Who Wore What? Women's Wear, 1861–1865*. Gettysburg, Pa.: Thomas, 1995.

Leonard, Elizabeth D. *All the Daring of the Soldier: Women of the Civil War Armies*. New York: W. W. Norton, 1999.

Lerch, Kathryn W. "Prosecuting Citizens, Rebels, and Spies: The 8th New York Heavy Artillery in Maryland, 1862–1864." *Maryland Historical Magazine* 94 (Summer 1999): 132–71.

Lowry, Thomas P. *Don't Shoot That Boy! Abraham Lincoln and Military Justice*. Mason City, Ia.: Savas, 1999.

———. *The Story the Soldiers Wouldn't Tell: Sex in the Civil War*. Mechanicsburg, Pa.: Stackpole, 1994.

———. *Tarnished Eagles: The Courts-Martial of Fifty Union Colonels*. Mechanicsburg, Pa.: Stackpole, 1997.

Massey, Mary Elizabeth. *Bonnet Brigades*. New York: Knopf, 1966.

McPherson, James M. *Battle Cry of Freedom: The Civil War Era*. New York: Oxford University Press, 1988.

Miller, John Chester. *The Wolf by the Ears: Thomas Jefferson and Slavery*. New York: Free Press, 1976.

Monks, William. *History of Southern Missouri and Northern Arkansas, Being an Account of the Early Settlements, the Civil War, the Ku-Klux, and Times of Peace*. Ed. John F. Bradbury Jr. and Lou Wehmer. Fayetteville: University of Arkansas Press, 2003.

Neely, Mark E., Jr. *Southern Rights: Political Prisoners and the Myth of Confederate Constitutionalism*. Charlottesville: University Press of Virginia, 1999.

*Official Army Register of the Volunteer Force of the United States Army*. 8 vols. 1865. Reprint, Gaithersburg, Md.: Olde Soldier Books, 1987.

Osler, William. *Principles and Practice of Medicine*. New York: D. Appleton, 1893.

Quaife, M. M., ed. *Absalom Grimes: Confederate Mail Runner*. New Haven, Conn.: Yale University Press, 1926.

Records of the Judge Advocate General's Office (Army), Record Group 153, National Archives, Washington, D.C.

Regan, James: *The Judge Advocate and Recorder's Guide*. Washington, D.C.: Beresford, 1877.

Sigaud, Louis A. *Belle Boyd, Confederate Spy*. Richmond, Va.: Dietz Press, 1944.

Stern, Philip Van Doren. *Secret Missions of the Civil War*. New York: Wings Books, a division of Random House, 1959.

Tidwell, William A., with James O. Hall and David W. Gaddy. *Come Retribution: The Confederate Secret Service and the Assassination of Lincoln.* Jackson: University Press of Mississippi, 1988.

Tobin, Jacqueline L., and Raymond G. Dobard. *Hidden in Plain View: The Secret Story of Quilts and the Underground Railroad.* New York: Doubleday, 1999.

Welsh, Jack D. *Medical Histories of Union Generals.* Kent, Ohio: Kent State University Press, 1996.

Wert, Jeffry D. *Mosby's Rangers.* New York: Touchstone Books, 1990.

Wiley, Bell I. *The Life of Billy Yank: The Common Soldier of the Union.* Indianapolis: Bobbs-Merrill, 1952.

―――. *The Life of Johnny Reb: The Common Soldier of the Confederacy.* Indianapolis: Bobbs-Merrill, 1943.

# INDEX